# THE VIEW FROM CHURCHILL

Travels in the Footsteps
of Britain's Last Lion

MATTHEW MILLS STEVENSON was born in New York City and grew up on Long Island, attending Buckley Country Day School and Friends Academy. His university degrees are from Bucknell and Columbia universities, and he spent a year abroad with the Institute  of European Studies in London and Vienna. He moved to Geneva, Switzerland, in 1991. He is a contributing editor to *Harper's Magazine* and has worked professionally in finance and investing. His essays and reporting have been published in many magazines, including, most recently, in *CounterPunch*. He is the author of many books, including *Reading the Rails, Appalachia Spring, The Revolution as a Dinner Party* (about China throughout its turbulent twentieth century), and *Biking with Bismarck*, about the Franco-Prussian wars and the Treaty of Versailles. His recent books include *Our Man in Iran*, an account of travels across the Islamic Republic, and *Donald Trump's Circus Maximus & Joe Biden's Excellent Adventure*.

His email address is matthewstevenson@sunrise.ch

www.matthewmstevenson.com

# THE VIEW FROM CHURCHILL

Travels in the Footsteps
of Britain's Last Lion

MATTHEW MILLS STEVENSON

Marble Hill London

First published in 2024 by Marble Hill Publishers
Flat 58 Macready House
75 Crawford Street
London W1H 5LP
www.marblehillpublishers.co.uk

© Matthew Mills Stevenson 2024


Matthew Mills Stevenson has asserted his right to be identified as the author of this work in accordance with the Copyright, Designs and Patents Act 1988.

All rights reserved.

No part of this book may be reproduced or transmitted in any form or by any means, electronic, mechanical, recording or otherwise, without prior written permission of the copyright owners.

A CIP catalogue record for this book is available from the British Library.

ISBN: 978-1-7392657-9-3

Typeset in Adobe Caslon and LDN Cable Street
Printed and bound by IngramSpark
Text and cover design by Paul Harpin

# CONTENTS

| | |
|---|---:|
| *Introduction* | 1 |
| 1. A Tale of Two Blenheims | 11 |
| 2. The Playing Fields of Harrow and Sandhurst | 14 |
| 3. Arrested in South Africa | 20 |
| 4. Escape From a Pretoria Prison | 26 |
| 5. Failure at the Dardanelles | 32 |
| 6. Another Look at Gallipoli | 37 |
| 7. An Ottoman Endgame | 40 |
| 8. In the Trenches at Plugstreet | 44 |
| 9. Churchill Returns to Westminster | 52 |
| 10. Winston of Arabia | 57 |
| 11. Return to Mesopotamia | 62 |
| 12. Weekends in the Country; Countries in a Weekend | 66 |
| 13. The Storm Gathers Over Europe | 71 |
| 14. Neville Chamberlain Stumbles Towards War | 77 |
| 15. Hitler Chews the Carpets in Munich | 80 |
| 16. Poland and Czechoslovakia: What-if History | 84 |
| 17. Underground in the War Cabinet Rooms | 86 |
| 18. Italian Stalemates at Monte Cassino and Anzio | 90 |
| 19. From Roosevelt's Hyde Park to Yalta | 96 |
| 20. The Terms of Yalta | 102 |
| 21. Churchill — On the Road Again | 106 |
| 22. The Great Success of Failure | 112 |
| *Places and Books* | 118 |
| *Acknowledgements* | 124 |
| *Copyright Permissions* | 127 |
| *The Cycling Historian* | 128 |
| *About the Bicycle* | 130 |

This book is dedicated with love
to my British family,
Helen and Liam,
and now to Laura

# INTRODUCTION

I HAD NOT thought I was stalking the legacy of Winston Churchill until I realised, reading one of his biographies, that I had visited many of the places important in his life.

The revelation came as a surprise, as I have rarely undertaken a trip specifically in search of Churchill. In the last forty years, however, I have visited his birthplace at Blenheim Palace (not to mention the battlefield in Germany for which it is named) and Chartwell, his weekend house in Kent; the veld where he was captured on the battlefields of the Boer War in South Africa and his prison in Pretoria; the dusty hillsides at Gallipoli in Turkey where his political career fell into ruins; and his national creations around the Middle East (the borders of Syria, Israel, Iraq, Lebanon, and Palestine all bear his trademarks). I have also sensed his historical presence in Iran, India, Russia, and throughout the Far East, for example in Singapore, which he left undefended to a Japanese invasion, with the big guns pointed seaward, in the opposite direction from which the attack was launched. From Morocco to Malaysia, if you check into a fancy hotel, invariably you will discover a plaque indicating when and in which room Churchill stayed. (Of London he liked to say, "I don't stay in a hotel. I stay in Brown's.")

Despite such devotion to the times and places of Churchill, I rarely think of myself as a man on pilgrimage. I don't have pictures of Churchill hanging in my office, and I cannot say that I stand in awe of his political career, despite admiring his leadership during World War II. (A lesser man might have surrendered England.) For whatever reason, when I think of Churchill I often reflect less on his successes than on his failures: the botched attacks on the Dardanelles in 1915, his tone-deafness over India, and the 1919 intervention in the Russian civil war, his legacy in the Middle East (we're still paying for his poor judgment in Iraq), and his deadly adventures in places such as Trondheim and Dieppe. At the same time, I often enjoy having Churchill as a plumb line in my travels, as his peripatetic life (from 1874 to 1965) and his obsession with being the man on the spot no matter what the crisis make him an eyewitness to many events in 20th century history that interest me.

I cannot say that I am a serious Churchill scholar. In every school I attended, there were collections of Churchilliana in the libraries, including his multi-volume histories of World Wars I and II, but growing up I read only a handful of these books. I remember buying the first volume of Churchill's account of the Duke of Marlborough when I was in high school. I was led to it not so much by a thirst to grasp the tactics that, in 1704, allowed the English, German, Dutch, and Danish coalition to defeat the French, as by the circumstance that Churchill's work had appeared on a list of books that had influenced the young John F. Kennedy. That connection had piqued my interest. I never got past page twenty-five, and I remained sketchy about the life and times of the first Duke of Marlborough, John Churchill, until the summer of 2009 when I took my children camping in Germany and we biked around the battlefield of Blenheim.

Even now, I have read relatively few of the many Churchill biographies (literally hundreds have been published.) I have read neither the multi-volume official biography by Martin Gilbert, nor the more celebrated life, in one volume, by Roy Jenkins.

# INTRODUCTION

Nor have I read more than a few volumes in Churchill's own autobiographical works, which begin with *My Early Life* (1874–1904). I did like and admire Richard Holmes's *In Churchill's Footsteps*, an appreciation of his life and time. In recent years I have also read William Manchester's three-volume biography of Churchill, *The Last Lion*, which for a long time ended in the early days of World War II. (After Manchester died, his friend, journalist Paul Reid, wrote the third volume from the surviving materials.) I do admire Violet Asquith Bonham-Carter's *Winston Churchill: As I Knew Him*, an account into the 1920s of their personal friendship. Much of her book dwells on his impatience, although in a way that makes him more human and substantial. From David Reynolds's *In Command of History: Churchill Fighting and Writing the Second World War*, I realized that rather than composing his books as a lonely author, Churchill presided over his memoirs as the chairman of the composition committee.

Mostly, however, my extended reading about Churchill has come from the military and diplomatic histories I have squeezed into my suitcases to make sense of places I was visiting. For example, on a 1985 trip to the Anzio beachhead near Naples, I read several books about that ill-fated campaign, including Raleigh Trevelyan's excellent *Rome '44: The Battle for the Eternal City*, in which Churchill makes cameo appearances from London. At Gallipoli, I used for a guide several books about the battle, including one by Robert Rhodes James, who also published a critical biography of Churchill with the subtitle: *A Study in Failure, 1900–1939* (the period when many things Churchill touched turned to mud). In Australia in the 1980s, I read Christopher Thorne's excellent *Allies of a Kind: The United States, Britain, and the War Against Japan, 1941–1945*, which is about the differing war aims of Churchill and Roosevelt. Not long ago, in South Africa, I read Candice Millard's *Hero of the Empire: The Boer War, a Daring Escape, and the*

*Making of Winston Churchill*, an account of his detention at Ladysmith and flight from a jail in Pretoria.

Living in Europe for the past thirty years (I grew up in New York and was in grammar school when Churchill died), I have often gone in search of the battle lines from World Wars I and II, and Churchill was a participant and keen observer in both of those conflicts. For example, in London (in the War Cabinet Rooms beneath Whitehall), Belgium (he served as a battalion officer in the lines at Ploegsteert), Italy (in both wars, Churchill was in endless search of Germany's soft underbelly), and Turkey (notably the Dardanelles but also in Iskenderun, formally Alexandretta), I often find the Churchill story to be more instructive than the guide at hand, which explains why many of the books I have taken with me in my travels have a Churchill component.

Here's an example: I once spent a very happy café hour in the old city of Damascus, where I had gone (before the civil war) with my son Charles, then fourteen. He had gone in search of souvenirs, notably a travel-sized backgammon set, and I settled into a rooftop café that overlooked the Grand Mosque (and also the souk below, so I could watch Charles make his way around the souvenir stalls). There, over Turkish coffee, I spent a very pleasant hour reading David Fromkin's *A Peace to End All Peace: The Fall of the Ottoman Empire and the Creation of the Modern Middle East*, which makes the point that the world is still living with the borders that Churchill (among others) drew in the sand.

As an American student doing a junior year abroad in 1974–75, I first came across Churchill's footprints when, together with some others in my program, I visited Blenheim Palace, about nine miles from Oxford. In subsequent years, I found myself at Gallipoli (in Turkey); on the Boer War battlefields in South Africa; in India and Pakistan where he served as an officer; at Cassino and Anzio in Italy; and at Ploegsteert, Belgium—all

# INTRODUCTION

No perk of power ever gave Churchill more pleasure than the yacht *Enchantress*, which was available to the First Lord of the Admiralty, and thus to Churchill between the years 1911 and 1915. Whether this picture shows Churchill aboard *Enchantress* or another naval vessel isn't known, but it captures the engagement that Winston felt when at sea, especially in the Mediterranean, where he could indulge his interests in military and classical history while calling at such outposts of the British Empire as Malta and Gibraltar. During his time at the Admiralty, he spent some eight months aboard *Enchantress*, and what he learned at sea about Europe and the Middle East paid dividends during the subsequent two world wars.

places on Churchill's compass. At nearly every stop, I was reminded that Churchill was an odd mixture of personal fortitude and some of the worst political judgment in the 20th century. He often said that he had "not become the King's First Minister in order to preside over the liquidation of the British Empire"—which he served bravely from the Northwest Frontier Territory to the Normandy beaches. At the same time, during the course of his lifetime and after, imperial Great Britain shrank from an empire on which the sun never set to something that now feels like London and some surrounding suburbs.

Churchill badgered and blustered his way in the world while writing forty-five books, finishing hundreds of paintings, and serving in numerous British governments. (The others in power, in both parties, may not have liked him, but they didn't think they could get on without him.) On many political questions—from Turkey to Ireland and India—Churchill was often dead wrong, for all his bravado. At the same time, I enjoy following his footprints around the world, if only because—for me anyway—they reduce complex issues of war, peace, imperialism, and colonisation to concrete images I can understand. (If you ever want to understand the complexities of the Middle East, drive out from Cairo and have lunch along the banks of the Suez Canal, where England, France, Israel, and Egypt have fought savage wars of peace.) Churchill didn't manage to save the empire but he did leave his stamp on many worlds, and in my wanderings I have been a beneficiary.

What was Churchill like as a man? Obviously, I never met him, so it's difficult to say from the distance of time and place, but let me try. By all accounts, Churchill spent his entire life as a young man in a hurry. He knew what he wanted in life—fame and power—and he didn't mind ruffling feathers or breaking china to get them. I am sure many in his path found him overbearing, and obnoxious, with too much entitlement and too little humility. He was persistent and persuasive in the heat of an argument, and many ended up agreeing with him just so he would leave them in peace. I suspect he was given to obsession, at least on the subject of himself. His friend T. E. Lawrence (of Arabia) said in admiration and frustration that "if Winston's interests were not concerned in a question, he would not be interested." I don't think he was a bully—more a self-assured public-school man. At the same time, he did not mind cutting corners to get where he was headed. One of his political opponents once said of him: "His *forte* is to be a disturber of the peace, whether at home or abroad. He is a political adventurer, with a genius for acts of mischievous irresponsibility. He is militant to his finger-tips."

It could be said that his devotion to self-interest was in the larger cause of British self-interest, but since he so often conflated Great Churchill with Great Britain it would be wrong to give him a pass on the many political decisions he got wrong in his life. (One newspaper editorial described him this way: "Mr. Churchill is still his own Party, and the chief of the partisans. He still sees himself as the only digit in the sum of things, all other men as mere cyphers, whose function it is to follow after and multiply his personal value a million-fold.") That said, what's clear from reading about his life and visiting the places where he had an impact is that Churchill's greatest personal quality was his ability to inspire action in others. And he had physical and (often, but not always) moral courage. He showed that courage when leading the men of his battalion at Ploegsteert in 1916, and again as prime minister from 1940–45, when his great gift to western civilization was to persuade Franklin Roosevelt to fight on the side of the Allies. (Churchill once gushed about FDR: "If anything happened to that man, I couldn't stand it. He is the truest friend; he has the farthest vision; he is the greatest man I have ever known.")

Churchill could be a stalwart friend, but it came at a cost.

Early in Churchill's political career, when he stood for Parliament in Oldham, outside Manchester, he emulated the speech patterns and opinions of his late father, Randolph Churchill, who by all rights should have been a British prime minster. Instead Randolph—although he became Chancellor of the Exchequer in 1886—had an erratic relationship with the Conservative Party leadership in the late 19th century, and died tragically in 1895, when Winston was 20. Like his father, Winston would write out and memorize all his speeches before delivering them, and his pursuit of high office often saw him move between the Conservative and Liberal parties, leading some to question his loyalties.

# INTRODUCTION

Lady Asquith wrote, "He demanded partisanship from a friend, or, at the worst, acquiescence." His Chartwell neighbour and government collaborator Major Desmond Morton, who liked Churchill, said, "The full truth, I believe, is that Winston's 'friends' must be… persons who were of use to him. The idea of having a friend who was of no practical use to him, but being a friend because he liked him, had no place…." That said, he was a faithful (if trying) companion to his wife, Clementine, during their fifty-six years of marriage, although she might have smiled at the description Lord Beaverbrook (an on-again, off-again Churchill friend and admirer) gave of her husband: "He is strictly honest and truthful to other people, down to the smallest detail of his life. Yet he frequently deceives himself." Winston was a devoted father, if at times overbearing, which affected some of his children more than others. He was a demanding, inconsiderate boss, wanting everything to be done yesterday, but most of his staff loved him.

Would I have liked Churchill if I had met him? That's hard to say. I would have shared his passion for history, places, politics, travel, art, and books, but think I would have grown tired of the brandy, cigar smoke, egocentrism, and temper tantrums. I can think of no better travel companion than Churchill on his World War II Boeing 314 Clipper, heading off in the night to places such as Casablanca or Tehran, but I cringe at the thought of going to a meeting with Churchill and listening to him bluff and bluster through a subject about which he knew very little (such as the gold standard or the Polish partitions). I would have loved to "walk off" the battlefield of Blenheim with him, but don't think the after-dinner Churchill—droning on about "Mr. Gandhi" or Bolshevism—would have been much fun. To me Churchill would have been most engaging somewhat early in the day, before the whiskey or champagne had soaked in, when he was alone in his writing studio, hunting among his books for a quotation about Marlborough or Disraeli. Then, I suspect, he would have been at his best—curious, engaged, reflective, witty, and generous with his many thoughts and experiences—and perhaps that's the Churchill I went looking for in this book.

# 1
# A TALE OF TWO BLENHEIMS

MY FIRST BRUSH with the life of Winston S. Churchill came in 1974, when I went to England in early September as part of a junior year abroad at the Institute of European Studies. I was enrolled in a politics program affiliated with the London School of Economics, which had begun classes only in late September. Before then, the program director, Edward Mowatt, arranged for several weeks of European orientation, which began in Oxford. After a charter flight left our duffle bags and ourselves at Gatwick Airport, we took a bus to Oxford and were assigned rooms at St. Hilda's College, at the far end of the High Street beside the banks of the River Cherwell.

Oxford, in early September, had cool crisp mornings and warm afternoons. We spent our days in a variety of lectures (along the lines of "Whither the Common Market," as it was then called) and trying to finish several books from an assigned reading list, including: *The New Europeans* by Anthony Sampson, and Alan Bullock's biography of Adolf Hitler, *A Study in Tyranny*. These were also carefree student days. I would get up early and walk along Iffley Road to buy several English newspapers. As American students, we were introduced to tepid English beer and its more extended cousin, the pub crawl. We rode double-decker buses and climbed the towers of many Oxford colleges. One day, a few new friends and I rented bicycles and pedaled beyond the spires of Oxford to visit Blenheim Palace, where Winston Churchill was born in 1874.

Recalled forty years later, Blenheim stills looms larger than life. Somewhere inside the main gates, we leaned our bicycles against a fence and, once inside the front door, joined a tour group inspecting a portrait of the Duke of Marlborough on horseback in the battle of Blenheim. My impression of Blenheim was of splendid isolation. Even in September sunshine, the front courtyard was forlorn, as out of scale and devoid of humanity as are some East European squares commemorating a revolution.

I don't remember much about the interior, save for the hush in which we inspected canopied beds and gilded chairs. Blenheim is more a monument to John Churchill, the first Duke of Marlborough, than it is a springboard for the life and times of Winston Churchill, who grew up more in London and at boarding schools than he did on these ancestral lands. When I later read accounts of Winston's largely isolated, unhappy childhood, I always had in mind the image of a small boy lost for companions while "playing" in the empty vastness of the castle's grounds. To me, it is little wonder that later in life he should have pursued such solitary occupations as painting and writing.

As for the battlefield of Blenheim, I only made it there in the summer of 2008, when I took my two sons on a camping and cycling trip in Germany. We spent our first night at the campground in Landsberg, where Hitler was imprisoned in 1925 and where he wrote the first volume of *Mein Kampf*. (Hitler treated his imprisonment as if it were a scholarship to a writer's retreat.) From Landsberg we moved on to a lake in the Munich suburbs, where we pitched our camp and from which, each day, we explored Germany's tortured history in places such as Nuremberg and Dachau.

On one of the excursions I stopped the car in what is now Blindheim (formerly Blenheim), and in a drizzle the boys and I rode our bikes along the contours of the battlefield on which the army of the Duke of Marlborough (a.k.a. John Churchill), in coalition with the Austrians, defeated a combined French and Bavarian force, helping to decide the favorable outcome of the War of the Spanish Succession. Much like the World Wars of the 20th century, it was fought to maintain a European balance of power, at the expense of dynastic inheritance lines.

Neither the boys nor I had a firm grasp of the battle's tactics or of the larger sweep of the war (in this battle, Marlborough cut off the French before they could capture Vienna). We did have a map I had copied from one of Churchill's books that guided us on various small agricultural roads along the north bank of the River Danube. (In effect, Marlborough pushed the French into the river and its surrounding swampland.) Closer to the hamlet of Unterglau (a church and a few houses), we got off the bikes and had a picnic at what had been the centre of Marlborough's lines—knowing that Winston Churchill would have approved. But John Churchill chose Blenheim (it's just several miles down the road) as the name for the castle that the grateful English people bestowed on him for saving Britain and her allies from French continental dominance. (After he won World War II, all Winston got was to be voted out of office.)

One reason, among many, that Winston devoted so much time and energy to his multi-volume biography of Marlborough is that the battle of Blenheim reconfirmed the established precedent that Great Britain could militarily intervene on the European continent were the balance of the great powers ever threatened—something that Churchill believed to be the case when, 230 years later, Nazi Germany devoured Austria, the Rhineland, Czechoslovakia, and Poland.

# 2
# THE PLAYING FIELDS OF HARROW AND SANDHURST

CHURCHILL GREW UP not just in the shadows of Blenheim Castle and his parents' dysfunctional household, but also in the twilight of the British Empire. He is given credit as one of its saviors, although during World War II it expired during the rescue. In the first volume of William Manchester's *The Last Lion*, entitled *Visions of Glory*, which covers the years between 1874 and 1932, there are numerous accounts of Churchill's upper-class childhood. He went to Harrow and the Royal Military Academy Sandhurst, although the only subject that interested the young Winston was empire. Of that era it was said, "The British soldier was given a small island for his birthplace and the whole world as his grave."

Winston first went away to boarding school at the age of seven. Both of Churchill's parents ignored him at school, in part because their marriage was so dysfunctional. Manchester writes of his early leave-taking to school at Ascot: "Jennie rode with him to Paddington Station in Randolph's private hansom, but on the train platform they parted; she gave him three half crowns and sent him on alone." His father, then a rising political figure, once had a meeting across the street from Churchill's school in Brighton but did not bother to look in on his young son. Nor did either parent ever write him more than prodding or scolding letters. His mother was a particular friend to the Prince of Wales, later Edward VII, although that hardly rose to the level of scandal. Speaking of the relationship, Manchester quotes a familiar phrase of the time: "It doesn't matter what you do in the bedroom, as long as you don't do it in the street and frighten the horses."

Gratifying to anyone who has struggled through elementary Latin, Winston Churchill was a terrible student and was occasionally threatened with expulsion from various schools. He recalled, "Where my reason, imagination or interest were not engaged, I would not or I could not learn." (I know the feeling.) Unbeknownst to his parents and tutors, he had numerous passions, among them horses, writing, collecting stamps, painting, family history, and political oratory. Manchester writes, "He would always be a dud in the classroom and a failure in examinations, but in his own time, on his own terms, he would become one of the most learned statesmen of the coming century." His sentimental education in the grand myths of empire, however, left him ill-prepared to articulate political views that were at odds with the White Man's Burden.

I went once to the Royal Military Academy Sandhurst, in August, 1983, to see the school and visit a family friend, the historian John Keegan, and his family. I had gotten to know Keegan several years before, when I was working in New York as magazine editor. That summer, when I passed through London after spending two months in Asia, he encouraged me to come out their house for lunch, which I did by taking a suburban train from London to the small town of Camberley. Keegan had not yet written his excellent short biography of Churchill (it came out only in 2002), but he walked me around the grounds of the military academy, which feels less like West Point or a barracks and more like a small college where, by chance, most students go to class in uniform.

After graduation, Churchill held what might be called a joint commission in the military and journalism: he held rank

# THE VIEW FROM CHURCHILL

Churchill (top left on the stairs) and some his classmates at Harrow School, which is about thirteen miles northwest of London, beyond Wembley Stadium. Churchill boarded there from 1888 – 1892. Overall, he did well only in the subjects that interested him, such as history and geography. He made friends, but also cultivated, at times, a solitary air. After Harrow, he attended the Royal Military College, Sandhurst, and served as a subaltern in the army. It was while he was stationed in India, with time on his hands, that Winston read deeply in classical literature and began to write in a way that probably would have astonished his old masters at Harrow.

in both establishments for his entire life. When he served as a cavalry officer, there were long waits between engagements. Churchill filled his idle hours observing and writing about wars in Cuba, the Northwest Frontier Territory, and along the Nile. During some of these engagements, he would throw down his scribe's attire and join the fray as a moonlighting cavalry officer with what might be called a field commission.

During the summer of 1983 (which I spent, partly, in India) I didn't think all that much about Churchill, as he had been posted in Bangalore (in the south) and I traveled by trains from Calcutta to Bombay and up north to Delhi and Amritsar, where I crossed into Pakistan. Later, in reading about Churchill's early military service in India (I think a lot of it bored him), I discovered that while he was in Bangalore he devoured the classics that he had missed (or ignored) in his early schooling. He read Edward Gibbon's *Decline and Fall of the Roman Empire*, Adam Smith's *The Wealth of Nations*, and a number of books about Greek philosophy.

In effect, second lieutenant Churchill got his bachelor's degree in politics from the barracks of Bangalore. And it was from there, as a war correspondent, that he followed British troops to the Malakand Pass (now in Pakistan) and Swat Valley to write about the 1887 siege of Malakand and the ceaseless Afghan wars. (He wrote, "I pass with relief from the tossing sea of Cause and Theory to the firm ground of Result and Fact.")

The nearest I got to Malakand in my subcontinental travels that summer was Peshawar, about an hour to the south. But in driving across northwestern Pakistan at the time of the Russian intervention in Afghanistan, I thought a lot about the looming cold (and hot) war between the West and Islam, about which Churchill said this: "Indeed it is evident that Christianity, however degraded and distorted by cruelty and intolerance, must always exert a modifying influence on men's passions, and protect them from the more violent forms of fanatical fever, as we are protected from smallpox by vaccinations. But the Mohammaden religion increases, instead of lessening, the fury of intolerance. It was originally propagated by the sword, and ever since its votaries have been subject, above all the peoples of all other creeds, to this form of madness."

The irony is that Churchill's time in Malakand, in form and substance, varied little from the American presence in Afghanistan and Pakistan that began in 2001, if not after the Soviet intervention in 1979. As Churchill wrote of the wars in the 19th century, "We proceeded systematically, village by village, and we destroyed the houses, filled up the wells, blew down the towers, cut down the shady trees, burned the crops and broke the reservoirs in punitive devastation." At one point in the fighting Churchill personally intervened to assist a wounded soldier, although his hope to be awarded a medal was never realized.

In any number of colonial encounters, Churchill showed physical bravery, be it charging enemy entrenchments or covering a rearguard action. He cabled these front-line impressions to Fleet Street, where he became a celebrated correspondent. My guess is that among military officers, Churchill thought himself a journalist; among writers, he considered himself a front-line officer.

In his preface to *Churchill's Generals*, a collection of essays, John Keegan writes, "It was not, however, as a soldier that his brother officers thought of him. He had been a minister and sat in the cabinet. He remained a member of Parliament. Above all, he had been a war correspondent, a trade he had begun while still a subaltern. It caused resentment at the time…" In William Manchester's book, Churchill is described as someone "jaywalking through life," and as a man incapable of "party loyalty." More likely, Churchill, no matter where he was, always felt out of place, as he had in school, despite his long family pedigree.

And it was as a correspondent, not as a cavalry officer, that he attended the Boer War, which established his reputation as a swashbuckling author.

# 3
# ARRESTED IN SOUTH AFRICA

IN SEPTEMBER 1984, a few weeks after our marriage, my wife and I spent several days of our honeymoon "walking off" the battlefields of the Boer War, and the scenes of Churchill's early greatness. Although it does not sound very romantic, we went to South Africa during the era of apartheid to meet Alan Paton, the author of *Cry, the Beloved Country*, and to explore the contours of the Boer War.

At the time, Paton and his wife Anne lived in Hillcrest, outside Durban. To get there we rented a car in Johannesburg to make the two-day drive to the Indian Ocean. At the time, neither my wife nor I knew many of the details of the Boer War or even its exact topography. We had seen and admired an early 1980s film, *Breaker Morant*, which tells a story of British wartime atrocities against the Boers. And I had read some accounts of early 20th century warfare that touched on the fighting. But for both of us, the war came to light only when, four hours from Johannesburg, on an early spring day, we parked the rental car and scrambled among the scrub hills of Colenso and Ladysmith, where the British first met the Boers in combat and where Winston Churchill was taken prisoner of war.

For those behind in their school reading, the Second Boer War (1899–1902) was yet another savage war of peace, undertaken to protect English commercial interests (notably diamonds and some coaling stations) along the Horn of Africa and the sea lanes to the Orient. The British also had it in mind to extend their colonial footprint across much of southern Africa. The Boers (Afrikaners, descended from Dutch settlers) fought in loose formations, called commandos, and the British retaliated by burning some 30,000 Boer farms in the Transvaal and Orange Free State, and by rounding up thousands of Boer families (mostly women and children, as their men were away in battle) and herding them into concentration camps (these were not a Nazi invention). In that archipelago of camps, in which conditions were inhumane, some twenty-six thousand Boers (mostly children) died in British captivity.

Several months before hostilities broke out between the British and the Boers, Churchill had stood in Oldham during a by-election (the filling of a vacant seat in between normal parliamentary elections). He lost. Oldham was a textile town outside Manchester, and a Liberal defeated him. (Candidates for British parliamentary seats in those days need not live in their districts or even know much about them. Carpet-bagging is the rule in Britain.) Denied the chance to sit in Parliament and no longer a serving military officer (he had graduated from Sandhurst), Churchill heard with glee the news of a crisis in South Africa. Finally, he would have his chance to show his mettle under fire, although his ticket to the front lines was as a war correspondent for London's *Morning Post* newspaper. (His influential and doting mother had helped secure the assignment.)

Churchill had often, in his early career, blurred the lines between combatant and correspondent, even before he resigned his military commission. If he could not get to the front as an infantry or cavalry officer, he would switch hats and go as a newspaper man. He had seen action in the Northwest Frontier Territory and in Cuba, but most notably in a cavalry charge in Sudan during the battle of Omdurman (it's outside Khartoum), resulting in his best-selling book, *The River War: An Historical Account of the Reconquest of the Soudan (1899)*. But warrior fame had so far eluded him.[1]

Heading to South Africa—Winston traveled with a servant and a full wine cellar—Churchill's great fear was that the war would be over before he got his chance for a dance with lady fame. No sooner had his troopship docked in Cape Town than he was on his way to Durban, where he connected with a train heading north toward Ladysmith and the front lines.

The Boers carried small knapsacks and long rifles, and little else. They slept in the wild and lived off the land, which they considered their own. By contrast, a British cavalry officer might ride to the front weighing 400 pounds, when you added in all of his kit (and perhaps a bottle of champagne). Tactically, the British Army had advanced little from those skirmish lines deployed at Waterloo. Troops marched and shot their rifles in tight formations, which to Boers hidden behind boulders turned the thin red line into sitting ducks. In the early months of the fighting around Ladysmith, the British experienced heavy losses, and eventually the town was surrounded and besieged, as happened in Mafeking.

With their technological superiority—not unlike the Americans in Vietnam fighting the Vietcong—the British hoped to relieve the Ladysmith siege by sending an armor-plated train, full of troops, up the line toward the city. Think of it as an early tank, but one on rails, and with steam flowing from the engine, which made it easy for the Boers to spot and track its slow progress up the line.

Most British troops in that theater of operation thought of duty on the armored train as little more than orders for suicide,

---

[1] I have thought about a visit to Omdurman, which is outside Khartoum, but the closest that I ever got was Aswan, in southern Egypt, where at the Old Cataract Hotel there is a Winston Churchill Suite. It costs about $400 a night. Instead, my family and I hired a *falouca* and drifted down the Nile for several days.

# ARRESTED IN SOUTH AFRICA

Ever keen to experience military conflict, Churchill often straddled the worlds of the army and journalism. As a junior officer in India in 1897 he wrote about the wars on the Northwest Frontier Territory in Malakand, and, as a journalist, he covered the Boer War (1899-1902) for the London *Morning Post*, although later in the war he joined the South African Light Horse. At Ladysmith in South Africa, while a war correspondent, Churchill was captured after he tried to rally British soldiers under fire, in clear breach of war norms for a journalist. He was imprisoned in Pretoria, but managed to escape on a goods train to what is now Mozambique, and he came back to London as both a war hero and a celebrated author.

such were the casualties inflicted on the men huddled inside the reinforced-hopper cars. (They had gun holes punched through the sides, and thus it resembled a medieval serpent steaming toward destruction.) In a letter, Churchill wrote, "An armoured train! The very name sounds strange. A locomotive disguised as a knight-errant; the agent of civilisation in the habiliments of chivalry."

So impatient was Churchill to get to the front lines in Ladysmith, both to scoop his newspaper rivals and to engage in some glory hunting, that he agreed to join an operation on the armored train. Part way up the line, in the hamlet of Frere, the Boers cut off Churchill's train, killed a number of men, and knocked several cars off the rails.

Under the terms of warfare in 1899, a war correspondent should never carry a firearm. Nor should he, in any way, participate in the fighting. The punishment for breaking this code of conduct, if the correspondent was captured by the other side, was often summary execution.

With his train under attack and some of the officers wounded, Churchill responded bravely to the challenge. He helped to clear the line, he directed fire against the Boers, and he loaded wounded men onto the engine and sent it off in the direction of the British lines, thus saving the lives of many.

Churchill compromised his journalistic credentials when he took up arms alongside the waylaid train. And then he was captured. The Boers did not know what to make of a Lord's son with military rank and a spent pistol who claimed to be a newspaperman. Not a few Boers wanted to kill him, but instead they put him in a Pretoria prison, from which he escaped. Ironically, the wanted poster for this escaped convict contained one of the most succinct portraits of the future prime minister.

# ARRESTED IN SOUTH AFRICA

One the formative events in the life and legend of Winston Churchill was that he was captured near Ladysmith in 1899 during the Boer War. At the time, however, he was serving as a war correspondent for a British newspaper. After his capture, he was marched to Pretoria, where he was imprisoned in a school. By climbing over a wall and dropping to the sidewalk, he managed to escape captivity. As he was dressed in civilian clothes and had some money, he was able to elude capture and head toward what is now Mozambique by foot and rail. The Boer authorities posted a notice of his escape and described him in these terms:

> Englishman 25 years old, about 5 ft 8 in height, medium build, stooping gait, fair complexion, reddish brown hair, almost invisible mustache, speaks through his nose, cannot give full expression to the letter 's', and does not know a word of Dutch. Wore a suit of brown clothes, but not uniform – an ordinary suit of clothes.

Churchill made good his escape and on a steamer from the Indian Ocean port of Lourenço Marques returned to the British lines in South Africa. He wrote about the harrowing experience in the press and various memoirs, and the account's widespread distribution made Churchill a national hero.

# 4
# ESCAPE FROM A PRETORIA PRISON

THE CHURCHILL PART of our honeymoon ended with his capture near Ladysmith, so I always wondered how he managed his escape from prison in Pretoria. I had a hard time imagining it until I returned to South Africa in 2017, as part of an overland trip that took me from Kenya to Johannesburg largely by rail. (To be sure, I needed planes and a few buses to bridge the gaps in the line that connects Cairo to Cape Town.)

To enter South Africa on this occasion, I came through the border town of Mafeking (the spelling of the town has changed over the years, and now it's called Mahikeng or Mafikeng). Besieged by the Boers in the Second Boer War for 217 days, Mafeking was a key junction in the great power politics of the region that included the endless struggle in southern African between English colonists (Cecil Rhodes is the best known) and the instruments of German power, which controlled land on both African coasts in southern Africa. German South West Africa was to the west of Mafeking, and German East Africa, later Tanzania, was to the east. Hence the siege lines around the railroad town.

In Mafeking, I ate lunch and poked around a Boer War history museum. (A soldier went with me around the exhibits, to make sure that I did not take any pictures.) The siege was lifted in May 1900, a month before British troops—Churchill among them—took Pretoria, ending the phase of conventional warfare in the conflict, which continued for almost two more years as a guerrilla struggle. Then I flew to Johannesburg, having tired of African trains and buses. (One of them, the train from Dar es Salaam to Kapiri Mposhi, arrived two days late.)

From the Johannesburg airport I rented a car and drove to Pretoria, in part to see if I could find the prison from which Churchill had escaped. To guide me around the capital, I had a copy of Candice Millard's gripping history *Hero of the Empire: The Making of Winston Churchill*.

Millard's book doesn't unearth a lot of new information about Churchill, his weird parents, his many ambitions, or the route of his prison escape to Mozambique. She quotes from Churchill's own letters and books on the subject. But her story is briskly told, so it is both a riveting account of Churchill's capture and escape, and a clear summary of the Second Anglo-Boer War. Millard's take on Churchill's interest in South Africa and the coming Boer War is that it could offer him the chance for glory, which he believed was the missing ingredient on his resumé for election to Parliament.

According to Millard, after Churchill was surrounded and captured at Ladysmith, many in England feared that the Boers might execute him for having press credentials and for wielding a gun in battle. What probably saved him was that he was the son of an English Lord, and perhaps useful as a bargaining chip. Already by then, Churchill's accounts of the fighting at Ladysmith had won him the reputation for gallantry that he had desperately been seeking.

From Ladysmith, the British prisoners—officers and their men along with the correspondent (Churchill)—were marched off to prison in Pretoria's Staats Model School. When I got to Pretoria, I tracked down its location at the corner of Lilian Ngoyi and Nana Sita (my GPS made a hash of the pronunciations). The school is one of a handful of Dutch buildings from the Boer era that is still standing and it feels like a gymnasium you might come across in The Hague.

Millard writes that from the moment Churchill entered the prison, he devoted most of his waking hours to planning his escape. As you might expect from someone who loved strategic brainstorming, his schemes grew grander and grander until, in one plan, he would not simply break out of jail and flee to the border, but would kidnap President Paul Kruger and hold him hostage until the Boers surrendered and the war was over. (Churchill never thought small.)

In the end, the rash Churchill bolted over a back fence of the prison but without waiting for two of his fellow prisoners, who were to have gone with him (one spoke both Afrikaans and the Zulu language, which would have helped out on the road). Hence Winston was on his own. At least he was dressed in local clothing, albeit that brown suit described in the wanted poster.

After striding through the town like a burgher going for a walk, Churchill hopped a freight train that took him forty miles from the capital, where he ran out of schemes and ideas. He had no food, little water, and the countryside was crawling with Boer police on the lookout for the son of Lord Randolph Churchill, who had written a number of articles belittling the Boers.

Churchill had no chance of walking several hundred miles to the Mozambique border through such terrain, so he knocked on a random door, hoping to bribe his way to freedom (he might have been a prisoner but he was flush with cash). By remarkable good fortune, Churchill knocked on the door of a transplanted Englishman who managed a prosperous coal mine in the Transvaal and who undertook to orchestrate Winston's escape.

Churchill was given food, whiskey, and cigars, and stashed down a mine shaft until he could be hidden on a goods train taking wool to the docks of Lourenço Marques. An English sympathizer went with him to bribe away nosy custom inspectors and the like, and in a few days Churchill made it to freedom in what is now Mozambique. Millard writes:

> He didn't have a weapon, a map, a compass, or, aside from a few bars of chocolate in his pocket, any food. He didn't speak the language, either that of the Boers or that of the Africans. Beyond the vaguest of outlines, he didn't even have a plan—just the unshakable conviction that he was headed for greatness.

BACK IN DURBAN on a coastal steamer by the end of December, 1899, Churchill was given a hero's welcome, and for the rest of his life he would remain a household name in Britain. Millard writes, "He had reminded the world what it meant to be a Briton—resilient, resourceful and, even in the face of extreme danger, utterly unruffled." One of the men who saved Churchill turned out to be from Oldham, which at the next election sent him to Parliament, where he would serve various constituencies until 1964 (he died the next year).

The Boer War was Great Britain's Vietnam or Algeria, a colonial war that could only be fought, unsuccessfully at that, with violence against the citizenry, and from which British colonialism never recovered.

Churchill never questioned British righteousness in taking on the Boers, who had South African roots dating to the 17th century. He did question the strategic competence of the theater commander, General Sir Redvers Buller. As Manchester writes, "The general struck him as the kind of man who plodded 'on from blunder to blunder and from one disaster to another.'" But nothing in his South African adventures weaned Churchill

# THE VIEW FROM CHURCHILL

Lost in Churchill mythology, which attributes his vacillating party alliances to ambition for power, is the extent to which the younger Winston was a champion of social reform, especially for workers in the north of England and in Scotland. Politically, Churchill is most associated with his defence of the British Empire, if not imperialism, but a review of his campaign speeches in the early 20th century show that he took progressive stands on such issues as workers' unemployment compensation and tariff reform. He also formed close bonds with local leaders in his constituencies, which ranged from Manchester and Dundee, Scotland, to Epping, and he warmed to politics for the friendships that he made in his campaigns.

from English mercantilism. In summing up the effort, he wrote, "I hope that in considering the lessons of the South African war we shall not be drawn from our true policy, which is to preserve the command of markets and the seas."

Rudyard Kipling said famously that the Boer War had taught England "no end of a lesson." But Churchill no more took to those classes than he did to those intoned at Harrow. Even to honeymooners picnicking at Spion Kop (a particularly bloody encounter where the British failed again to relieve the besieged Ladysmith) or to a tourist in Mafeking, the Boer War speaks of the limits of colonialism and the inability of imperial powers, in the 20th century, to impose their wills along distant ramparts.

In the timeline of history, the Boer War is in the continuum with the Irish uprising, Indian independence, Vietnam, and, most recently, the war in Iraq. (The British fought the Boers as did the Americans taking on the Iraqi insurgency, with a blend of counterterrorism and internment camps.) Before the Boer War, England had muddled through on Queen Victoria's policy of "splendid isolation." For the next five decades, during the height of Churchill's political power, however, it would find itself fighting around the world, although perhaps for reasons more complicated than those he raised in the context of the Boer War. As Churchill wrote in his twenties, "…then shall we continue to pursue that course marked out for us by an all-wise hand and carry out our mission of bearing peace, civilization, and good government to the uttermost ends of the earth."

# 5
# FAILURE AT THE DARDANELLES

CHURCHILL ENTERED World War I in the service of the Admiralty, as First Lord. Nothing enhances Churchill's reputation more than the Royal Navy's readiness for war in August, 1914, and its ability to bottle up the German fleet, through much of the war, in North Sea ports. Despite the presence of U-boats in British home waters and the casualties suffered in encounters such as that at Jutland, Churchill succeeded in keeping the British navy as a "fleet in being," to use Admiral Mahan's phrase for un-sunk ships.

Churchill's Admiralty service in World War I, however, is most often linked to the disaster at Gallipoli, where the Allies suffered several hundred thousand casualties. (One critic said later: "His dominant qualities are imagination, courage, and loyalty; his dominant defect, impatience.") Had I never been to that battlefield along the Dardanelles, I might concur with Churchill's critics that the Ottoman adventure was inept and harebrained. Now I sometimes believe (it depends on my mood) that it could have been a good idea, but one that was poorly resourced and executed—a flanking operation that walked the thin red line between failure and success.

I have read a number of accounts of Churchill and the Dardanelles, and three times have visited the narrow straits (at the site of ancient Troy) that divide Europe from Asia. On my first visit, I was on a family vacation in the summer of 1976, and we took a Russian steamer from Athens to Istanbul—the only boat that made the sea passage between Greece and Turkey, who were then often locked in conflict. I set my alarm for 5:30 a.m. and got up in time to be on deck when the steamship *Adjara* (it was carrying tourists and a large number of Russian diplomats who were escaping the civil war in Lebanon) transited the Hellespont, as the Dardanelles were called in the time of classical Greece and the *Iliad*.

At dawn in the summer of 1976, Gallipoli struck me as rocky, hilly terrain that loomed over the straits as if a medieval escarpment. I could imagine the Turkish defenders of the high ground fighting with daggers and lances, as they did often during the nine-month battle that ended with more than 500,000 Allied and Ottoman soldiers wounded or dead.

From the deck of the *Adjara* I could see, to my right, the outlines of Troy, where Achilles killed Hector and dragged his body around the city walls. To my left, I could see Cape Helles, where Allied troops landed in the spring of 1915 to begin what was to be a disastrous campaign to dislodge Turkish troops from the hills overlooking the narrow channel. It was in the Dardanelles strait that Churchill's hopes for a quick end to World War I were, literally, torpedoed.

By the winter of 1915, the trenches of World War I stretched from the English Channel to the Swiss border, some 466 miles. At the war's end, after 51 months of fighting, an average day along the Western front saw 2,533 men killed, 9,121 wounded, and 1,164 go missing. In wartime, the non-conformist Churchill sought solutions at variance with school solutions (here the school masters were army generals).

For the Dardanelles operation—at least the naval portion—Churchill was the inspirational godfather, and he conceived of a flying column of British and French ships forcing open the narrow straits and steaming into the Bosphorus Sea, from whence they could shell the tottering Ottoman government into submission. It was a bold plan to break the stalemate in the trenches on the Western Front, and, as First Lord of the Admiralty, Churchill was its spokesman in the war cabinet of Prime Minister Herbert Asquith. Not long after the war started in August 1914, the prime minister had said of his dashing, younger colleague: "I can't help but be fond of him. He is so resourceful and undismayed, two of the qualities I like best."

In the Bosporus, the sea around Constantinople, Churchill hoped to send a nimble but heavily armed fleet to capture the Sublime Porte and take Turkey out of the war. By so doing, he sought to relieve pressure on the Russian front in the Caucasus and open a third European front in the Balkans from which the Allies could attack Austria-Hungary on its exposed flank. All that stood in his way were the mines laid across the Dardanelles, some long guns hidden in the surrounding hills, and Ottoman cruisers that no one believed would be a match for the Royal Navy and the French navy.

On March 18, 1915, a combined fleet of British and French ships attempted to force the straits. Ahead of the imperial cruisers and destroyers, however, was a weak link in the attacking formation: a makeshift deployment of mine sweepers. Some were converted North Sea fishing trawlers, and they failed sufficiently to clear the mines. When the capital ships then proceeded toward the narrows between Chanak and the Gallipoli peninsula, they were hit both with battery fire and the subsurface mines, some of which the Turks had cut loose to drift with the current into the Allied fleet.

Of the eighteen battleships that were attempting to force the narrows, three were sunk on the morning of March 18, and several others were badly damaged. On the Turkish side, the hillside batteries had run out of ammunition, and the only mines available were those already deployed in the Dardanelles. More effective mine sweeping or simply another run at the Chanak narrows would have broken the Turkish resistance, and then nothing would have stopped the fleet from taking Constantinople and realizing Churchill's dream of knocking Turkey out of the war. But for a few minesweepers his hopes were dashed, as subsequently was his political career.

After the failure of the initial assault, British and French admirals conferred and decided it was best to withdraw from the Dardanelles and await an Allied landing force that could come ashore on the Gallipoli peninsula to silence the batteries. At that moment, there were few if any Turkish forces at Gallipoli, and a rapidly deployed regiment might have done the work later attempted with several armies. A few days later, Churchill drafted orders to resume the naval attacks at once. But by that time the war cabinet had gotten wind of the March 18 naval losses and the recommendation of the military brass to await land reinforcements before renewing any naval attacks. Not until April 25, 1915, were Allied soldiers put ashore on the far side of the Gallipoli peninsula.

In the meantime, mustered by the commanding German General Otto Liman von Sanders, the Turks had deployed stopgap forces across the Gallipoli peninsula, and disastrous Allied landings put the invasion forces ashore either against steep cliff sides (Anzac Cove) or in the gun sights of awaiting Turkish forces (Cape Helles). One survivor wrote, "The plain, for all its openness, was a prison, which became a tomb." The political history of the British Empire, as regards the perceptions of the Australians and New Zealanders, was rewritten in the scrub brush hillsides above Anzac Cove, where one of the Allied commanders was heard to mutter, "Casualties? What do I care about casualties?"

As far as the British public was concerned, Churchill himself might have spoken these words. That autumn of 1915 he left the

## THE VIEW FROM CHURCHILL

war cabinet in disgrace. Against him was arrayed the contempt of the British government and people. Richard Holmes recalls words written by Churchill's wife, Clementine: "I thought he would never get over the Dardanelles. I thought he would die of grief." Even his patron, Prime Minister Herbert Asquith, turned against him, saying (as quoted by Robert Rhodes James) that Churchill "will never get to the top in English politics, with all his wonderful gifts; to speak with the tongue of men and angels, and to spend laborious days and nights in administration, is no good if a man does not inspire trust."

Nevertheless, as I looked at Gallipoli from the deck of my Russian steamer in the summer of 1976, I found myself in sympathy with the historian Liddell Hart who said that Gallipoli was a "sound and far-sighted conception, marred by a chain of errors in execution almost unrivalled even in British history." Another historian, Philip Guedalla, writes that Churchill was "sacrificed" for being "far too enterprising about the Dardanelles."[2]

---

[2] Churchill's friend Sir Alan Herbert said many years later: "For more than twenty years I had adored (that is the right word, I fear) Mr. Churchill.... I did not think, as so many thought in those days, that he was brilliant, resourceful, brave, but nearly always wrong. I thought he was nearly always right—right for example, about the Dardanelles, right about Antwerp, in both of which affairs our Division (the Royal Naval Division) was involved. But I did think that he rather enjoyed a war: and, after three years in the infantry, in Gallipoli and France, I did not."

# 6
# ANOTHER LOOK AT GALLIPOLI

TWENTY-FIVE YEARS after first glimpsing Gallipoli from the deck of a Russian steamer, I had gone back to the Dardanelles and spent several days touring the remains of the battlefields, which cover a vast area from Cape Helles in the south to the more northerly Anzac Cove, where the Australians and New Zealanders landed. The Peter Weir film *Gallipoli* is set in the dry pine hills above Anzac Cove, and it ends with a slaughter.

This time, I went to Gallipoli after several days of business in Istanbul. It's a four-hour drive along the Sea of Marmara coastline. I went with a driver, and we crossed the Dardanelles on a small ferry from the insignificant town of Geliboulu (Gallipoli), from which Allied cartographers named the peninsula and the battle (the Turks named the encounter for the town across the water, Çanakkale, rendered in English as Chanak). By then I had read several histories of the battle, including Alan Moorehead's *Gallipoli* and Robert Rhodes James's history, also entitled *Gallipoli*, as well as several Churchill biographies. I was open to the revisionist hypothesis that Churchill's strategy (at least the naval portion) could well have worked.

What made me more sympathetic to Churchill this time was reading an account of the naval battles in the waters off Çanakkale on March 18, 1915, in which the French and English lost several capital ships to drifting Turkish mines. Apparently, the British especially went into the straits with everything at hand except for sufficient mine sweepers. The few they had were not enough to clear the Dardanelles, and the Turks were lucky in that the strong current propelled several drifting mines into Allied warships. By the afternoon, the Allies had lost three battleships and 700 sailors, and they retreated to Cairo, where it was decided that ground troops were needed to seize the high ground adjoining the straits so that no further mines could upset the imperial progress of the fleet toward Constantinople.

Had sufficient mine sweepers been deployed, it is possible that the fleet could have taken the straits and knocked the Ottoman Empire from the war on the Eastern Front. At least it would have taken control of the straits, Constantinople, and opened up the sea lanes to Russia. (Turkey might well have continued the fight from Anatolia.) Churchill wrote later, "Not to persevere—that was the crime." It matched the sentiments of the Turkish war minister at the time, who said, "If the English had only had the courage to rush more ships through the Dardanelles they could have got to Constantinople."

Instead, Gallipoli turned into one of the costliest battles of the war—in a war made up of disasters—and by November 13, 1915, as the Allies were withdrawing from the peninsula, Churchill had resigned from the cabinet. As Peter Apps writes in *Churchill in Trenches*:

> Churchill always maintained he did nothing wrong, that the strategy was a reasonable risk undermined by colleagues who gave it inadequate resourcing. But he felt destroyed. "I am finished," he told his friends.

Nor did Churchill have command of the landing forces or have any influence in their tactics. But he had been a guiding star in shaping Britain's policies in the Middle East, not just at Gallipoli, and their lack of coherence and general rashness could well explain the confusion that has guided Britain in the Middle East ever since.

# 7
# AN OTTOMAN ENDGAME

I CAME TO a third and more nuanced view of Churchill's confusions in the Middle East only after another trip to Gallipoli, when in the winter of 2019—just before the great pandemic shut down the world—I traveled overland from Albania to Turkey and ended my travels in Gallipoli. This time I came away believing that even if the combined British and French fleets had taken the Dardanelles, it probably would not have shortened the course of the war.

On my way across the southern Balkans, I carried on my Kindle a number of histories, including Sean McMeekin's *The Ottoman Endgame*, in which he blames Churchill (by canceling two warships that would have been delivered to Turkey in 1914) for tilting Turkey into alliance with the Central powers (Germany and Austria). He also assigns Churchill some of the blame (although there were other willing partners in government) in the transition of policies that made the destruction of the Ottoman Empire a core war aim of the British in 1914.

For most of the previous century (notably during the Crimean War and at the 1878 Congress of Berlin) Britain had worked hard to maintain the Ottoman Empire as a buffer state in southeast Europe against Russian and Austrian imperial ambitions. Turkey's weakness was an asset, allowing the British to control Egypt and the Suez Canal and protecting the lifeline to imperial India.

# AN OTTOMAN ENDGAME

At the outbreak of war in 1914, Britain—led in large part by the energetic Churchill—decided that its interests (against Germany in the short term and the Middle East in the longer term) would be best served if the Ottoman Empire were no more. Hence the seizure of the paid-for Ottoman warships and the sea and land attacks at Gallipoli the following year.

On this trip to Gallipoli, I also read George H. Cassar's *The French and the Dardanelles: A study of the failure in the conduct of war*, which was published in 1971. I gave it to my father for Christmas in 1974, before our family trip to Greece and Turkey, and was happy to discover that the book had come down to my library. Cassar is an excellent writer, and the book is a scholarly analysis of French politics and diplomacy that explains why France went along with the Gallipoli offensive (mostly to protect its colonial interests in Syria). But the book also has long sections describing how Churchill implored the French to go along with his plan to rush the straits with warships. ("Remarking later, [Minister of Marine Victor] Augagneur listed two reasons why he acquiesced in Churchill's proposals. First, Churchill's assurance that this was only an experimental attack, losses would be limited, and ships could be withdrawn at any time.... Second, Augagneur was under the impression that Churchill had the unanimous backing of naval and civil authorities in England.")

Cassar comes to the conclusion that the campaign, both on land and at sea, was based on Churchillian folly and that even if the Dardanelles had been breached (a big if), the Allies did not have resources at hand to open a front between Constantinople and Germany. The French went along with the Churchill scheme because they had very little skin in the game—some old warships—and Russia played along without committing any forces, because it would inherit Constantinople. Cassar writes:

## THE VIEW FROM CHURCHILL

> A strategic plan must be evaluated on the
> strength of its achievement or merit and
> not on speculative consequences. The naval
> operation was designed as a short cut to
> victory and on this alone it must be judged.
> In this sense it was an utter failure. To quote
> Sir Gerald Ellison, 'the underlying idea of the
> whole plan was Utopian in the extreme'....

From this welter of confusion and illusion one thing emerges quite clearly. The Allies were trying to gain the advantage of a victory without finding the means to win that victory. Regardless of the direction from which the naval operation is viewed, it was not likely to have succeeded on any of the terms actually available.

Whether Churchill should have been the only scapegoat in the failed enterprise is another question. As he showed at Dieppe and at Anzio in Italy during World War II, he spent much of his adult life endlessly searching for an open back door to the German heartland, and he thought he had found one through the Dardanelles—one that might have delivered to the British the carcass of the Ottoman Empire.

Cassar presents evidence that Lord Kitchener, among others in the British high command, was enthusiastic about such end runs, including this one at Gallipoli. He writes:

> The imperialist-minded Kitchener had
> his sights fixed on Alexandretta [a port in
> southeastern Turkey] which he hoped to link
> with the Persian Gulf and with the Euphrates
> after the Indian army had conquered
> Mesopotamia. He was convinced that if
> Russia moved into Constantinople, France
> into Syria and Italy into Rhodes, Britain's

>   position in Egypt would be untenable without Alexandretta.

In Cassar's telling, Gallipoli was a game of three-dimensional colonial chess in which knights and rooks were moved around the board as if part of some latter-day crusade. Of Winston, he writes, "But Churchill, who was captivated by the mirage of success, persisted in ignoring every difficulty."

Before it was over, it was Churchill himself who was exchanged for a few pawns, and he was turfed out of the cabinet and government. Not even his wife's pleading letter to the prime minister, whom she knew well, could save him. (She wrote: "Winston may in your eyes and those with whom he has to work have faults, but he has the supreme quality which I venture to say very few of your present or future Cabinet possess—the power, the imagination, the deadliness to fight Germany…") By then, however, her husband was preparing himself for the front lines, which meant getting outfitted with several new uniforms and putting together another portable wine cellar that could make the Channel crossing to the front lines in Belgium.

# 8
# IN THE TRENCHES AT PLUGSTREET

AS PENANCE FOR the debacle at Gallipoli, Churchill left the cabinet, although, again to his credit, he retreated in the direction of the Western front, where he volunteered for service as an infantry officer. Richard Holmes writes, "Winston spent five months in command and, despite his inauspicious start, was an unqualified success as CO." He commanded the 6$^{th}$ Scots Fusiliers from the beginning of 1916, in the line between Ypres, Belgium, and Lille, France, at Ploegsteert, known to the troops as "Plugstreet."

Not only did I foolishly go to Plugstreet in the month of January, but I got there on my bicycle, as part of an off-season visit to the Western Front. At the time I was doing research on the British writers Siegfried Sassoon (*Memoirs of an Infantry Officer*) and Robert Graves (*Good-Bye to All That*). As I was heading for the French town of Laventie, where the two memoirists first met, I decided to detour toward Ploegsteert and see if I could make sense of where and how Churchill had spent his five months in the trenches. At the very least, having Plugstreet as my starting point would allow me to focus on yet another corner of a foreign field that will be "forever England," as during the war years Ploegsteert Wood had trench lines with such names as Hyde Park Corner, Charing Cross, the Strand, Oxford Circus, Regent Street, Piccadilly Circus, and Hampshire Lane.

To reach Ploegsteert, I took a succession of trains from Geneva to Paris, Arras, and Lille before alighting (as the English like to say) in Armentières, a French town on the Belgian border. Unfortunately, as it was the dead of winter, much of the train journey took place in fog and darkness. The sun did not rise until well after 8 a.m., and the ground was often obscured in a dreary mist.

Even though I was traveling with several Michelin and World War I battlefield maps, I got lost riding from the station to the Belgian border. I had thought that I could follow, in a northerly direction, the arrow on the bicycle compass I had bought on eBay. I guess paying $1.95 wasn't sufficient to acquire a working compass, and that meant having to stop often in the back streets of Armentières to check the more accurate compass on my iPhone. After that, for more precise directions to Ploegsteert, I had to flag down a passing postman who set me on the right road.

Modern Ploegsteert is a line of shops and houses, plus some small businesses, on either side of a main street, but in the misty rain I was not able to figure out the exact spot where Churchill had served in the trenches. I had with me Peter Apps's excellent history, *Churchill In the Trenches*, in which he writes, "The battalion HQ—including Churchill—settled into some convent buildings in the center of the village. Several nuns were still in residence and were soon co-opted—"seduced," in Churchill's words—into providing cooked food for the occupants. The other companies, meanwhile, bedded down in outlying farms."

If the convent buildings are still there, I could not find them. Nor could I find the exact location of Churchill's trenches, although I found their general vicinity. I did see the famous plaque on the wall of the town hall that shows an older Churchill—with a bowler, walking stick, and cigar, and dressed in a business suit—surveying the ruins of the town and trenches, as if about to give a campaign speech during a by-election. It is a mixture of many metaphors, but not particularly accurate, as the Churchill who was in Ploegsteert on-and-off from January to May 1916 was not an old man surveying the embers of war, but someone who was in them.

Initially, Sir John French, the British commander on the Continent, had thought of making Churchill a general and giving him command of a brigade (about 4,000 men), but such were the concerns in the army about showing political favoritism that Churchill was taken on as a major and later, as a lieutenant-colonel, was given command of a battalion (about 800 men) in the lines at Plugstreet.

Churchill took up his existing commission in the Queen's Own Oxfordshire Hussars (literally a family regiment in the territorial reserve, made up of footmen and others from around Blenheim, the Churchill family manor) and then for better training moved to the Grenadier Guards, in which his friend Raymond Asquith was serving. Churchill, however, went into combat with only the Royal Scots Fusiliers, who were fed into the line at Ploegsteert, at the time considered one of the quieter sectors of the front line. Still, it was a trench line facing hostile Germans, and Churchill's battalion was assigned a sector just east of the main street in town to defend, which meant enduring numerous shellings and nightly patrols into no-man's land. He never did "go over the top" in a frontal assault.

Although Churchill had graduated from the Royal Military Academy Sandhurst, and had seen fighting in Cuba, the Northwest Frontier Territory, South Africa, and at Omdurman in Sudan, most of the combat he had endured came while he was covering colonial wars for a newspaper. By the time he arrived at Ploegsteert with his men, he was a forty-year-old major who for the previous seventeen years had served in Parliament and

# IN THE TRENCHES AT PLUGSTREET

After his resignation from the Asquith cabinet in autumn 1915, when it was clear that the campaign in Gallipoli was failing, Churchill had his commission in the army restored, and eventually he commanded a battalion of the Royal Scots Fusiliers in the trenches near the Belgian town of Ploegsteert. Luckily, the sector was relatively quiet in winter 1916, but Churchill fulfilled his duties admirably, visiting his men along the front lines three times a day and sharing with them the privations that came with trench warfare. He was a fearless officer and liked to encourage those under his command: "Laugh a little, and teach your men to laugh—great good humour under fire. War is a game that is played with a smile. If you can't smile, grin. If you can't grin, stay out of the way till you can." While in the trenches, he kept his seat in parliament and bombarded his colleagues back in Westminster with advice on how best to win the war. He asked his wife to send a typewriter to the trenches.

written a number of best-selling books about military adventures (mostly his own).

His reason for being in the trenches wasn't so much to bring the fight "to the Hun" but to rewrite the narrative arc of his political career to blot out the stain of the Dardanelles. At Ploegsteert, Churchill was in search of political redemption. He thought the best way to find it was to patrol no-man's land with satchel bombs.

Churchill was not a typical battalion commander of the Great War. Often, while he was serving in the trenches or at rest behind the front lines, he would entertain visiting cabinet officers, newspapermen, publishers, and parliamentarians who were out on fact-finding missions. At other times in his front-line service, Churchill would slip away from the action to return to London, where he remained a member of Parliament. During his time in the lines, Churchill kept up a vast correspondence with friends and colleagues in London, such that, in one letter home to his wife Clementine, he asked her to send him out a typewriter so his official correspondence would be more presentable.

For all that Churchill had the look of a stuntman at the front—there to show British voters that even cabinet officers were doing their bit in the front lines—he turned out to be an excellent battalion commander, one his men grew to admire and respect. To be sure, he got off to a rough start with the Royal Scots Fusiliers when he told his sixth battalion that he would "break" anyone who challenged him. And I am sure more than a few of his fellow officers wondered about any commanding officer who came to the lines with a bathtub and hampers from Fortnum & Mason. But Churchill was generous in sharing his perquisites with his men, and he was ceaseless in visiting all the men of the battalion three times daily, no matter how much artillery was in the air. According to Peter Apps, his routine was this:

> Their initial spell in the front line had been only forty-eight hours. Thereafter, the Fusiliers would spend six days in and six out. It was a broadly typical pattern—the average British soldier would spend perhaps 100 days a year in the trenches, the rest in training or reserve. The reserve positions at "Plugstreet," however, were so close to the front that they too would be under near perpetual shellfire.

Not only was Churchill personally brave in commanding his men and in sharing their discomforts, but he also grew to understand, better than many front-line officers, the qualities of leadership that were needed for the British Army to win the war. In particular, he believed that officers needed to show their men that the misery of the war would not get the best of them, and that they could carry on, despite the rats, high water, and dead bodies that filled up the trenches and no-man's land.

Churchill liked to say to his subordinates: "Laugh a little, and teach your men to laugh—great good humour under fire. War is a game that is played with a smile. If you can't smile, grin. If you can't grin, stay out of the way till you can." In turn, they came to respect him as someone who was undaunted by artillery attacks or nighttime patrols. Peter Apps quotes one officer in this way:

> One night, under a heavy barrage, Gibb recalled Churchill looking over the parapet and asking, "in a dreamy voice: 'Do you like War?' The only thing to do was to pretend not to hear him," wrote Gibb. "At that moment I profoundly hated War. But at that and every

moment, I believe Winston Churchill revelled in it. There was no such thing as fear in him."

Another quality that served Churchill well in the trenches, and later when he was back in government, was that he thought about the war as if he were the commander-in-chief. On nights when he was away from the line, he wrote letters to colleagues in London, suggesting strategies that might shorten the war or improve conditions for the army as a whole, not just himself. He was a proponent of the weapon that became the tank—a truck on caterpillar tracks that could breach the opposing wire—and he thought that only conscription could bolster the depleted Regular Army.

The image of Churchill in his Ploegsteert convent directing the entire war effort (at least in his mind) matches entirely a description left to us by Harold Macmillan, then a Conservative MP. Macmillan remembered Churchill at home in Kent in April, 1939, trying to make sense of the Italian invasion of Albania: "It was a scene that gave me my first picture of Churchill at work. Maps were brought out; secretaries were marshalled; telephones began to ring. 'Where is the British Fleet?' That was the most urgent question.... I shall always have a picture of that spring day and the sense of power and energy, the great flow of action, which came from Churchill, although he held no public office. He alone seemed to be in command, when everyone else was dazed and hesitating."

In the Belgian trenches, Churchill concluded that wars in the future would be won only with mechanized armies, not dashing men with bayonets. He learned the bitter lesson that modern wars required professional armies. (Richard Holmes describes the sacrifice of the regular British Army in 1914 at Mons: "Once war was joined it meant Haldane's regulars, regular reservists and the part-time Territorials, who together might have provided the cadres for a greatly expanded fighting force, were sacrificed to buy time while an army of millions was extemporized.")

From his trenches or crumbling convent farmhouse, Churchill was endlessly banging the drum for the better use of submarines, air power, and amphibious assaults behind German lines. He hated the stalemate of trench warfare, and in his letters or when speaking to visiting politicians he was forever suggesting ways to get around the wires in front of him, much as, in World War II, he would think up second fronts in such places such as Norway, North Africa, and Anzio. During World War I he even suggested another landing in Asia Minor, this time at Alexandretta (current day Iskenderun, in Turkey), but by that point no one was listening to him—although if you ask me, the idea had some merit, just as did Gallipoli, at least in its early stage.

# 9
# CHURCHILL RETURNS TO WESTMINSTER

AS AN AMBITIOUS politician, albeit one in uniform on the Western Front, Churchill also spent much of his time in Belgium plotting the best way to return to London and Parliament. He needed to serve long enough on the front lines to look like any other officer doing his time at the front. But he did not want to be gone so long from London that he would be forgotten in Parliament or not considered for an available job at cabinet level.

Churchill also needed to position himself in the public eye so that it would overlook his earlier enthusiasm for Gallipoli and replace that blunder with more appreciative sentiments about his time in the trenches fighting "the Boche." He wondered if the issue of general conscription might put him in a more favorable London light. Apps writes, "As a front-line battalion commander, Churchill was all too aware that the volunteer army was exhausted. As a politician, he wondered whether the dispute [about conscription] might speed him back to power."

After several months on the line in Ploegsteert, he wrote to Clementine to say that he thought now was the right time for him to come home. She discouraged him, saying he needed to spend more time "out there". Otherwise, she said, he might be viewed as yet another opportunist who was getting his "ticket punched" in the war zone and then heading back to London. (During the Vietnam War, the word "chairborne" was a popular expression.)

# CHURCHILL RETURNS TO WESTMINSTER

Churchill married Clementine Ogilvy Hozier in September 1908 after a brief courtship, and they were married for 56 years, until his death in 1965. He called her "Clemmie". He was ten years her senior, but otherwise they were equals in a never-dull marriage that produced five children (one died as an infant) and endured two world wars and innumerable political battles. Clementine often campaigned for Winston when he was standing for parliament, and she attended hundreds of his political dinners. As supportive as she was of her husband and his many passions, she had an active life beyond his shadow and the lives her children, who suffered from growing up in the spotlight of such a prominent and peripatetic family.

# THE VIEW FROM CHURCHILL

The exchange prompted a heartfelt letter from Clementine to Winston, in which she tries to balance concerns for his safety with those for his political career. Apps has this passage, quoting from her letter, which balances the emotions of wanting to see him soon and those of wanting his career to continue:

> "Dear Winston I am so torn and lacerated over you," she wrote on April 6. "If I say 'stay where you are' a wicked bullet may find you where you might but for me escape." To be truly great, she told him, his actions must be understandable "by simple people." [Hence maybe he should stay out there a little longer?]

He was home for good in May, 1916, became a government minister in charge of munitions—a job well suited to his search for technology (including development of the tank) that would shorten the fighting—and only in 1919 rejoined the cabinet as Secretary of State for War.

It was also after he came back from the trenches that he befriended the poet and essayist Siegfried Sassoon, who in 1917 would publicly denounce the barbarity of the war. Sassoon went public with his opposition, writing in a statement that was widely circulated in the newspapers, "I have seen and endured the sufferings of the troops and I can no longer be a party to prolonging those sufferings for ends which I believe to be evil and unjust. I am not protesting against the military conduct of the war, but against the political errors and insincerities for which the fighting men are being sacrificed."

Today, opposition from serving troops in a war is somewhat commonplace, but in 1917 it was a flagrant dereliction of duty. Churchill, however, intervened to spare Sassoon from a firing squad. One wonders if Churchill would have been as lenient with Sassoon if he himself had not done duty on the front lines. Churchill might well have empathized with the sentiments expressed in Sassoon's famous poem, "Suicide in the Trenches," which reads:

> *I knew a simple soldier boy*
> *Who grinned at life in empty joy,*
> *Slept soundly through the lonesome dark,*
> *And whistled early with the lark.*
>
> *In winter trenches, cowed and glum,*
> *With crumps and lice and lack of rum,*
> *He put a bullet through his brain.*
> *No one spoke of him again.*
>
> *You smug-faced crowds with kindling eye*
> *Who cheer when soldier lads march by,*
> *Sneak home and pray you'll never know*
> *The hell where youth and laughter go.*

Years later Churchill wrote, "Before the war it had seemed incredible that such terrors and slaughters, even if they began, could last more than a few months. After the first two years it was difficult to believe that they would ever end."

After serving in the trenches, Churchill acquired the scepticism that is the trademark of many returning war veterans. For example, he said of the War Office that it "kept three sets of figures—one to mislead the public, another to mislead the Cabinet, and the third to mislead itself." As I am sure Sassoon did, Churchill distinguished between what he called the "trench and non-trench population." He wrote, "The hopes of decisive victory grew with every step away from the front line," reaching "absolute conviction in the Intelligence Department." Having served in a sector that lost 22,316 junior officers in one offensive, he could write at war's end: "Scarcely anything which I was taught to believe had lasted.... And everything I was taught to believe impossible had happened."

# 10
# WINSTON OF ARABIA

PART OF THE world that vanished in the Great War was the Ottoman Empire, although it did not happen as quickly as Churchill would have liked. Allied forces entered Constantinople in 1918. That occupation became untenable, however, in the early 1920s when the Greeks were forced out of Asia Minor and Turkey reclaimed the city it called Istanbul. Again, it was something of a humiliation for Churchill to give back the city that he had broken his reputation to capture.

Before the fall of occupied Constantinople in 1922, Churchill tried to rally the Allies to renew their war effort against the Ottoman Turks, if only to keep the straits in Western possession. None of his cabinet colleagues were in the mood for another Asian adventure or war, but still the Chanak crisis, as it was called, contributed to Lloyd George's fall from power—due partly to Churchill's impetuous enthusiasm for another conflict. Robert Rhodes James writes in *Churchill: A Study in Failure, 1900–1939*:

> The Chanak crisis was an excellent demonstration of the irrationality that so frequently comes to dominate such episodes. The necessity of concerting action with the French and Italians—who also were guarantors of the Treaty of Sèvres—was

> ignored; the arguments of the Foreign Secretary (Curzon) went largely unheeded; and, by the end, the advice of the senior British officer, General Sir Charles Harrington, was being misinterpreted and to a large extent overlooked. All the essential elements for a rational solution of the crisis were at hand, and all were set aside.

Much of this was Churchill's handiwork.

In the postwar British government, Churchill was a Liberal member of the coalition government (having jaywalked away from the Conservative party in 1904, he would return to it in 1924) and a cabinet member, first at the War Office and later as the Colonial Secretary. In neither post did he cover himself with glory. (When he returned to the Tory party, it was as Chancellor of the Exchequer, the post that his father had once held.)

As the Secretary of War, Churchill ran afoul of the party leadership (Lloyd George in particular), if not of British public opinion, for promoting (without always consulting others) military intervention not just at Chanak but also in the Russian civil war. James writes, "The downfall of Bolshevism was universally desired in the Cabinet. Ministers hoped that this could be achieved with British material assistance but without the need to intervene militarily. It was rather reminiscent of the prelude to the Dardanelles campaign: a leaderless Cabinet desiring a substantial victory without too much danger attached, and Churchill assuring them that this could be accomplished."

Labour leader Ramsay MacDonald said, "Churchill pursues his mad adventure as though he were Emperor of these Isles, pacifying us with a pledge, and delighting the militarists and capitalists with a campaign." As in the Dardanelles, the troops that Churchill deployed in Russia were insufficient to turn the red tide. A British general then noted, "So ends in practical disaster another of Winston's military attempts—Antwerp, Dardanelles, Deniken [the White Russian military leader in the Caucasus, supported by British troops]."

In February 1921, Churchill became responsible for colonial territories, notably those in the Middle East. Toward the goal of partitioning the Ottoman Empire, he convened the Cairo Conference of 1921, which sealed the fate of the modern Middle East, with many artificial borders drawn around numerous Arab tribes. As a traveler, Churchill was well acquainted with the Near East, although to judge by his paintings he spent his most relaxing moments in North Africa, particularly Morocco and Tunisia. Nevertheless, after World War I, when he was Colonial Secretary, Churchill gathered the likes of T.E. Lawrence, the author Gertrude Bell, and Britain's air marshal, Sir Hugh Trenchard, and together they made a grand tour of Cairo, the Nile, Gaza, and Jerusalem. (Greeted by rioters in Gaza, Churchill misinterpreted their rude gestures and waved back, oblivious to the fact that they were denouncing Britain.)[3]

In my trips around the Middle East, I am often reminded of Churchill. His life and times had a *Ragtime* quality, in that he was seemingly everywhere: in Cairo, Jerusalem, Iraq, or Pakistan. Numerous books describe these periods of his life. Perhaps the most thorough and anecdotal is David Fromkin's *The Peace to End All Peace*, which I read, in part, at that café above the souk in Damascus. My personal favorite, at least about Churchill's role in Mesopotamia, is *Winston's Folly: Imperialism and the Creation of Modern Iraq* by Christopher Catherwood, a professor

---

[3] The Cairo Conference was held on the banks of the Nile at the elegant Semiramis Hotel, where now Intercontinental has put up a more modern edition of the classical hotel. The original sweeping lobby has been replaced by a driveway for Ubers and scanners to x-ray arriving guests. Later on, Churchill switched his allegiance to the Mena House Hotel in Giza, which overlooks the Pyramids. Between the two hotel locations, Churchill presided over the restoration of the British Empire in Palestine, Mesopotamia, and Egypt, dooming the region to a hundred years' war.

both in England and Virginia, who wrote a diplomatic history entitled *Why Nations Rage*.

Because the subject interested him, Churchill did his homework on the Middle East, although his effort to placate both the Arabs and the Jews, as well as to maintain Britain's spheres of influence, proved too ambitious an assignment. Churchill had been in government at the time of Balfour's declaration that pledged a Jewish homeland. ("Personally, my heart is full of sympathy for Zionism," he said often.) It later became uncomfortable for Churchill to balance his commitment to the Jewish state with protecting Britain's mercantile interests—securing commercial passage from England to India and developing the nascent oil fields of Arabia. Although in some cases it took more than fifty years to recognize the effects of imperial gerrymandering, the postwar deconstruction of the Ottoman Empire into colonial spheres of influence, some of them British, left later incarnations of the Near East vulnerable to sectarian violence.

I credit Churchill with prescience for his thinking that the Turkish port of Alexandretta held many keys to the geopolitics of the Middle East. Even after the failure at Gallipoli, he was banging the tables in power, urging the Allies to seize the port city, which lies at the extreme northeast corner of the Mediterranean where Turkey and Syria now meet. After the casualties at Gallipoli, no one in the British high command wanted to hear about another amphibious landing in Turkey, although in terms of the war it made a lot of sense.

On our train trip to Aleppo and Damascus in 2010 (just before the Syrian civil wars), my son and I made an unexpected stop in Iskenderun, after we discovered in Adana, Turkey, that the train service to Aleppo, Syria, was suspended. (We should not have been surprised.) Instead of spending the night in Adana, a commercial Turkish city, we hired a taxi and drove ninety minutes down the coast to Iskenderun, where we found a center-city hotel room with a balcony overlooking the expansive port. Arriving about 10 p.m., we were hungry and keyed up from the long days of traveling. Seeking a light supper and distraction, we walked to a waterfront café where we ordered dinner and where our backgammon game attracted a group of friendly kibitzers, all of whom wanted to ensure that my son beat his father in the games. (He would have won anyway.)

As I sat with my cold beer and losing strategies, I looked at the sweeping harbour of what was once Alexandretta and came to the Churchillian view that he (and Kitchener) were right in thinking that it is one of keys to the Middle East board games.[4] Had the Allies landed here in World War I instead of at the Dardanelles, and had they pushed inland to Aleppo, much of the Ottoman Empire would have been cut in two and withered on the dry and dusty vines of the Middle East, shortening the fighting on that front and perhaps allowing for a more peaceful dissolution of the empire (and, who knows, possibly a more peaceful Middle East).

---

4 In another context Kitchener once said to Churchill: "Unfortunately we had to make war as we must, and not as we should like to." It echoes a notice that used to hang in a French barracks in Hanoi in the 1950s: "Remember—the enemy is not fighting this war as per French Army regulations."

# 11
# RETURN TO MESOPOTAMIA

CHURCHILL CAME TO the Middle East with something of a crusader mentality. He liked the idea of Christian nations capturing Jerusalem and Constantinople during the war, and afterward, left to his own devices, he would have preferred to reduce Turkey to a small Anatolian country, with Orthodox Greece in control of the straits, and the combined empires of Britain and France astride the desolate lands of Palestine and the Hejaz.

I cannot gauge if Churchill's commitment to a Jewish state was moral or geopolitical, but it was firm. Nevertheless, he alienated both Arabs and Jews with his national divisions. For example, he was associated with the secret Sykes-Picot Agreement, which divided the Middle East into British and French zones of influence, infuriating Arabs when it became public. They had joined the Allied cause against the Ottomans on pan-Arabian promises made by Lawrence, who, by the time he mounted camels with Churchill and Gertrude Bell in Cairo in 1921, knew that his country had sold out the Arabs, scattering them among League of Nations mandates. Robert Rhodes James writes, "Henry Wilson's scathing description of Churchill's Middle East policies as 'hot air, airplanes, and Arabs' was perhaps too severe, but it contained a strong element of the truth."

Hoping that he had pacified Arabs and Jews and secured

long-term petroleum supplies for Britain, Churchill, instead, left a confused legacy as Colonial Secretary with a number of discontents. Both the French and Arabs felt cheated over their rival claims to a greater Syria; governed by Damascus, the rump state of Lebanon—a patchwork of Christian, Sunni, and Shiite communities—became a civil war waiting to happen; Jews in the Mandate, who felt that their colonial masters (the British) were wavering on enforcement of the Balfour declaration, waged a guerrilla war to seek independence; and in Mesopotamia, the British were perceived as wanting to fill their oil tanks, not Arab aspirations, which led directly to colonial control over Basra and later an artificial construct called Iraq, in which minority Sunnis from the north and west ruled the majority Shiites in the South. When the League of Nations' mandates were ended after World War II, and countries emerged around the lines Churchill (among others) had drawn in the sand, it left Israel, Lebanon, Syria, Jordan, and Iraq with artificial borders and unhappy minority and majority populations.

Nowhere did Churchill struggle harder and get fewer results than in Mesopotamia, later renamed Iraq. At the Paris Peace Conference, President Woodrow Wilson thought that Basra, Baghdad, and Mosul should be "regarded as a single unit for administrative purposes." In his book, Catherwood observes, "Iraq was created out of three Ottoman *vilayets* that had previously been quite separate. The Kurds are Sunni, like the Arabs in the middle of the country, but ethnically they are Indo-European, like the Iranians. The Shiite majority in the south might be Arabs, but religiously they are the same branch of Islam as Iran—Shiite—and therefore have loyalties that are distinct from those of the rest of Iraq's people."

As minister for colonial affairs in the early 1920s, Churchill had to oversee the direct occupation around Basra along with managing general Arab unhappiness over the British subdivision of the Arabian Peninsula. "In Africa," he observed, "the population is docile and the country is fruitful; in Mesopotamia the country is arid and the population ferocious. A little money goes a long way in Africa and a lot of money goes a very little way in Arabia."

Churchill tried to solve several problems with one prince. He appointed Faisal, son of the Sharif of Mecca, as king of Iraq while at the same time promoting the Sunnis as the local governing party. Catherwood brings the Churchillian past to the present when he writes about modern Iraq: "Democracy would bring Shia majority rule and the possibility of endless Sunni intransigence after having lost control of a state they had dominated for over eighty years." That is still the short story of Iraq.

Churchill had no more luck governing Iraq than did the presidential administration of George W. Bush. At least Churchill was realistic, confessing "It is an extraordinary thing that the British civil administration should have succeeded in such a short time in alienating the whole country to such an extent that the Arabs have laid aside the blood feuds that they have nursed for centuries...." He contemplated withdrawal, recognizing that "the cost of the military establishment in Mesopotamia appears to me to be out of all proportion to any advantage we can ever expect to reap from that country..." He did, however, fear that withdrawal might lead to domestic chaos. Catherwood explains: "Churchill and Lloyd George were wrestling with the same issues the U.S. administration [was] facing in 2004: how to have a genuinely democratic Iraq that did not at the same time deliver the nightmare scenario of a clericalist and theocratic Shiite regime on the Iranian model."

To please the auditors in London, Churchill wanted colonialism on the cheap. As William Manchester describes it, "Churchill decided to withdraw them [British ground troops], and, in a grand if absurd gesture, declared that the entire country—116,000 square miles—would be defended by the emaciated RAF, thereby saving the Exchequer £25,000,000 a year." (Saddam Hussein had the same idea when he gassed the Kurds in 1988.) On the annexation of troubled regions, Churchill might well have recalled his own words written earlier about the struggles for the Northwest Frontier Territory, in what is now Pakistan:

"Financially it is ruinous. Morally it is wicked. Militarily it is an open question, and politically it is a blunder."

# 12
# WEEKENDS IN THE COUNTRY; COUNTRIES IN A WEEKEND

IN CHURCHILL LORE, he spent the 1930s alone and out of political power, at Chartwell Manor, in the Weald of Kent, painting and building brick walls.[5] Only with the approach of World War II did the Britons throw out the appeasers—Stanley Baldwin and Neville Chamberlain—and embrace Churchill as the country's savior.

It is an appealing legend, one told in many books, such as the second volume of Manchester's biography *Alone*, and in movies, such as the TV docudrama *The Gathering Storm* (2002), which stars Albert Finney and Vanessa Redgrave as Winston and Clementine. On many rainy Friday nights when our children were growing up, we watched Churchill laying bricks and taking on the Germans.

In all these accounts of the lean years, Churchill is dogged in his vision of Adolf Hitler and the Nazis as the resurrection of evil on the continental mainland. Only after the failures at Munich, and the annexations of Austria and parts of Czecho-

---

[5] Robert Rhodes James concludes: "We may be somewhat sceptical of [Leo] Amery's judgment that Churchill's exclusion from office between 1931 and 1939 was 'one of the best things that ever happened to England. For they were the years in which the strong vintage of his personality matured; the years in which he wrote the story of his great ancestor, Marlborough, and so trained himself for the conduct of another Grand Alliance; the years in which he earned the right to leadership by his consistent warnings of the danger ahead.' The judgment may be challenged because it alleges a late development of political and personal character that is difficult to substantiate. It was Churchill's greatest deficiency in the 1930s that he was unchanged; it was to be his greatest strength in the ordeal that began on September 3, 1939."

slovakia, is Churchill recalled to the cabinet. Baldwin had toyed with his appointment earlier but confessed, "If I pick Winston [to co-ordinate defence policy], Hitler will be cross." Meanwhile, Churchill brooded in Kent. Manchester writes, "Central to the appeaser's creed was the assumption that no one wanted war. They did not know, or refused to believe, that the German chancellor was an exception."[6]

My own visit to Chartwell came in the spring of 2006. I had several days of meetings in London. One afternoon my schedule became free, and I decided to make a run for Chartwell, south of London. At Victoria Station I caught a suburban train for Sevenoaks and found a taxi that would take me to the house. Chartwell is only twenty-five miles from the city, and I got there in less than hour, feeling like I had been summoned for a meeting.

The weekend Churchill is on display at Chartwell. The house, while large and at the center of enormous gardens, retains a sense of modesty. Because it passed directly from the Churchills to the National Trust, nearly everything inside the house is authentic. Rather than schedule tours, the administrators station guides in each room. Visitors feel more like weekend guests than tourists, and they go at their own pace through the house, stopping here and there for explanations from the docents. As I stepped through the front door, one of them showed me the daybook, opened to the year 1956, when "Montgomery of Alamein," made several visits. In the bedroom of Churchill's wife, Clementine, the guide showed me the view of the estate's many brick walls, noting in a whispered aside, "Well, I think Mr. Churchill had a hand in their construction, but not a big one."

---

6 In *Churchill: A Study in Failure*, 1900–1939, James writes: "Much of his contempt for MacDonald, Baldwin, and Neville Chamberlain was based upon his disgust at what he deemed to be their betrayal of England's grandeur and destiny."

In his biography of Churchill, James writes:

> During these years Churchill spent as much time as possible at Chartwell, which he had bought in 1922 when it had been long uninhabited and was, as one of his daughters has written, "wildly overgrown and untidy, and contained all the mystery of houses that had not been lived in for many years." Although Mrs. Churchill was responsible for most of the alterations and the running of the house, its personality was very much that of Churchill, and it was, as one who knew it well has remarked, "an astonishing combination of private home, Grand Hotel, and a Government Department."

On the tour is Churchill's bedroom, where he would stay in bed until noon, dictating chapters of his books and sipping on a weak whisky-and-soda. I spent a long time in his study, trying to figure out how someone so busy during his political days managed to write forty-five books (the answer: be good at dictation, as he was, and have three secretaries to do the typing and proofing). I inspected his art studio, a cottage on the grounds where many of his paintings are on exhibit. The good ones, done in a post-impressionist, almost pointillist style, are excellent, evoking North African villages or Mediterranean sunsets. As for the lesser works, he once wrote to his aunt, Leonie Leslie: "They're too bad to sell and too dear for me to give." But now at auction, Churchill's paintings can fetch thousands, if not millions, of pounds.

Churchill liked to say that he painted to keep the "black dog" (depression) from nipping at his heels, not for commercial

Churchill bought the rambling mansion of Chartwell in 1922, and used it as a country house until he died in 1965 (although after 1946, it belonged to the National Trust, having been purchased by a circle of Churchill admirers, who wanted to be sure he could remain there). He probably loved it more than did his wife or their children (with the exception of Mary, who grew up there). Chartwell embodied all the things that Winston loved about England—its landscape (in the Weald of Kent), sweeping history, and isolation in a dangerous world. He used some of his idle moments there to become a bricklayer on the grounds and to carry on with his many writing projects. He wrote to a friend in September 1928: "I have had a delightful month building a cottage and dictating a book: 200 bricks and 2000 words a day." It was at Chartwell in the 1930s that Churchill brooded on the menace of Hitler and fascism, and began to articulate in newspaper columns and parliamentary speeches the policies that would drag England away from its strategy of isolation and appeasement.

success or artistic praise. He reflected, "Happy are painters for they shall not be lonely. Light and colour, peace and hope, will keep them company to the end, or almost to the end, of the day." Of book writing he said in a similar vein, "Writing a long and substantial book is like having a friend and companion at your side, to whom you can always turn for comfort and amusement, and whose society becomes more attractive as a new and widening field of interest is lighted in the mind." Both sound like the sentiments of a Blenheim childhood, spent in gilded isolation.

From his bedroom, Churchill also issued orders for his gardens, which close to the house are English formal. Beyond the roses and the croquet lawn, however, the land gives way to rolling fields and few other houses or roads can be seen from its terraces. Even now, what is distinctive about Chartwell is its isolation from modern intrusions.

# 13
# THE STORM GATHERS OVER EUROPE

HOW DID AN often disgraced, out-of-work cabinet minister, dabbling with paint brushes and dictating slightly dense political histories about his ancestors, take the correct measure of Hitler's territorial ambitions and persuade a nation to follow him?

Churchill never met the German Chancellor. Their paths nearly crossed in Munich, in the 1930s, when Churchill went to Bavaria to see the battlefield at Blenheim.[7] (He says of primary research, "One has to visit the actual places…tread the terrain, as it were," words that I appreciate.) There's a poignant scene in *The Gathering Storm*, at a dinner party, when Churchill asks a German baron, Herr Schroeder, if he has ever met Hitler. The German says that he has, at a friend's dinner, and continues:

> What's he like? My first impression…
> insignificance. Utterly insignificant. A gray
> face, slate gray. Melancholy jet-black eyes,
> like raisins. A figure out of a ghost story. He
> talked on and on, endlessly. "Out of *Parsifal*,"
> he said, "I shall make a religion." His oily
> hair fell into his face when he ranted. Then…

---

[7] Biographer Robert Rhodes James writes: "His son Randolph accompanied Hitler on part of his 1932 campaign, and had sent Hitler a telegram of congratulation on the surprisingly impressive Nazi performance in the election. A meeting between his father and Hitler was arranged, but never took place."

> quite suddenly, he left. He bowed to me like
> a waiter...who has just received a fair tip.
> When he left...nobody moved...nobody
> spoke. We all sat in silence.

Had they met, they might have found that they had something in common. In World War I, Hitler and Churchill both served in the same sectors south of Ypres. (After I biked to see Churchill's trenches at Ploegsteert, it was a short ride to where Hitler served at Aubers Ridge.) Beyond those experiences the two men shared little, other than painting and the sense of oratory as a fulcrum in the modern political state. Hitler correctly sensed in Churchill someone who could not be browbeaten or charmed. But I think Hitler would have missed the fact that Churchill, who looked to all the world like the consummate Tory politician, was an outsider who felt most at home with his books and paintings in Kent. Manchester raises the image of an upper-class social outcast when he quotes one of Churchill's contemporaries, "How could you entertain a man who wouldn't laugh at anti-Semitic jokes?"

I do not think that, over tea in Munich, Churchill would necessarily have grasped the full extent of Hitler's madness. During the 1930s, as is described in Julia Boyd's *Travellers in the Third Reich*, many upper-class Englishmen came away from their visits to the continent impressed with German efficiency and order. Even Churchill's Liberal party mentor Lloyd George was enthusiastic, as Boyd writes:

> Back in England, Lloyd George's praise of
> Hitler verged on the ecstatic, as his notorious
> interview with the *Daily Express* makes clear.
> 'He is a born leader of men. A magnetic,
> dynamic personality with a single-minded

Churchill lost his position as First Lord of the Admiralty (although for a time he remained in the cabinet as Chancellor of the Duchy of Lancaster) as a result of the 1915 Gallipoli fiasco, and in the apparent denouement of his political career he took up painting, which helped him fend off what he called "the black dog," which otherwise might be called clinical depression.

He painted quickly and with relish, using colour more than detailed drawing, to produce some 550 paintings in his lifetime. In front of his easel and landscapes, Churchill was lost to the world, and he returned from his canvases refreshed to take on the latest struggles of his renewed political career (which lasted another forty years). Many of the paintings can be seen on a visit to Chartwell, and they are surprisingly good. They form a timeline of his travels, as even at summit meetings—for example, in Morocco in 1943—Churchill found time to paint.

> purpose, a resolute will and a dauntless
> heart ... He is the George Washington of
> Germany – the man who won for his country
> independence from all her oppressors.'

Although it does not make the final rushes of *The Gathering Storm*, which sticks to the theme of Churchill as a prophet in the wilderness, Churchill's judgment in the 1920s and 1930s—save for his opposition to Nazi Germany—was anything but prescient.

After World War I, Churchill made a hash of Ireland and the question of independence. (He alienated the Irish by throwing his lot in with the Unionists in the North.) As Chancellor of the Exchequer, he returned Britain to the gold standard, another act of folly. (James writes, "It was a step backwards into a dream world, in which Britannia rules the waves and the pound sterling commanded awe and respect throughout the world.") In the 1930s he bitterly opposed increased autonomy for India, saying, "I am quite satisfied with my views on India, and I don't want them disturbed by any bloody Indians." Churchill called Gandhi "a seditious Middle Temple lawyer, now posing as a fakir of a type well known in the east, striding half-naked up the steps of the viceregal palace, while he is still organizing and conducting a defiant campaign of civil disobedience, to parley on equal terms with the representative of the king-emperor..."

In the Far East, Churchill thought war with Japan impossible even to contemplate. (To the question of a submarine base in Hong Kong, he responded, "For what? A war with Japan! But why should there be a war with Japan? I do not believe there is the slightest chance of it in our lifetime.") He believed in air power and taught himself to fly, but before World War II he held to his belief that ships could defend themselves against aircraft. In the crisis over the abdication of Edward VIII, who wanted to marry the American divorcée, Wallis Simpson, Churchill stood longer than most for Edward, and must have felt a bit sheepish when the abdicated king, on his honeymoon in Germany, saluted some Nazis with his own variation of "Seig, Heil."

Initially Churchill had enthusiasm for Mussolini. He wrote in 1935 that he was "a really great man." And two years later he said, "It would be a dangerous folly for the British people to underrate the enduring position in world-history which Mussolini will hold; or the amazing qualities of courage, comprehension, self-control and perseverance which he exemplifies."

Even on the subject of Hitler, Churchill was prone to excess, exaggeration, and error. He wrote, for example, in 1935 and 1937, "Although no subsequent political action can condone wrong deeds or remove the guilt of blood, history is replete with examples of men who have risen to power by employing stern, grim, wicked, and even frightful methods, but who, nevertheless, when their life is revealed as a whole, have been regarded as great figures whose lives have enriched the story of mankind. So it may be with Hitler."

Beyond Germany, Churchill wasn't very prescient in his attitudes toward other international conflicts. James writes:

> From the moment that his attention had turned back to European affairs Churchill had been obsessed by German ambitions to the exclusion of all other perils. On virtually all the major international crises of the 1930s involving unilateral belligerence by other totalitarian regimes his position was somewhat equivocal. In effect he condoned Japanese aggression in Manchuria; his attitude to the Abyssinia question was something less than heroic; he supported

> the Franco regime in the Spanish Civil War. In taking such attitudes Churchill may well have been realistic, but his approach served to divorce him from those in Britain and elsewhere who were slowly beginning to see in the European and world situation a clash between fundamental ideologies. Churchill saw it in purely nationalistic terms, and when the question is posed as to why Churchill's efforts to awaken the nation to its peril so conspicuously failed, this factor requires emphasis.

What gave him clarity on the subject of Germany? I believe what saved Churchill from himself, and England from defeat, was his sense of history. From his research in the 1930s on his ancestor, the Duke of Marlborough, and the battle of Blenheim, he concluded, "For four hundred years the foreign policy of England has been to oppose the strongest, most aggressive, most dominating power on the Continent, and particularly to prevent the Low Countries [Belgium, Luxembourg, and Holland] falling into the hands of such a power." Applying this observation to Nazi Germany, Churchill wanted a "Grand Coalition" of European states, small and large, to encircle Hitler's designs. But while Churchill could read the German Chancellor—"Hitler never negotiated. He lied, he bluffed, he blackmailed, but serious negotiation was a skill he despised, a refuge of weaklings..."—he was kept out of the cabinet in the 1930s and in exile at Chartwell for the same reason he wasn't invited to many dinner parties: few of the British ruling class felt comfortable with him around.

# 14
# NEVILLE CHAMBERLAIN STUMBLES TOWARDS WAR

ONE THING THAT rescued Churchill from exile in Chartwell was the incompetence of Neville Chamberlain. As quoted in Manchester, Lloyd George said that "his vision was no greater than that of 'a provincial manufacturer of bedsteads.'" Even after the start of World War II, Chamberlain "disliked being disturbed, telephonically or otherwise, at weekends or after dinner at 10 Downing Street."

When Chamberlain succeeded Stanley Baldwin as prime minister in 1937, Churchill said in the House of Commons, "We seem to be moving, drifting, steadily, against our will—against the will of every race and every people and every class—towards some hideous catastrophe. Everybody wishes to stop it, but they do not know how." He said on another occasion, "There's no plan of any kind for anything. It is no good. They walk in a fog. Everything is very black, very black."

While Churchill was spending his weekends at Chartwell, brooding over the alliance and tactics that succeeded at Blenheim, Chamberlain was playing parlor games at Nancy Astor's Cliveden, a country retreat the prime minister loved. One guest wrote of the festivities, "…the P.M. won the after-dinner game of musical chairs every time. They always let him win. It meant so much to him." Manchester concludes, "To Churchill's exasperation, Britain's ruling class continued "to take its weekends in the country," as he put it, while "Hitler takes his countries in the weekends."[8]

Attractive as the parable of Churchill standing alone against the Germans may be, Richard Holmes raises the intriguing possibility that all three British prime ministers in the 1930s wanted Churchill as fully informed as they were on German rearmament, so that he could "beat a warning drum when they could not." In his biography, James picks up on this point at length, writing about how the Conservative government, while it didn't want Churchill in its cabinet, did want him speaking out on defense matters:

> [Philip] Cunliffe-Lister [Secretary of State for Air] was from the outset anxious to have Churchill's assistance, partly because he valued Churchill's advice and experience, but also because he wanted Churchill to be accurately informed of what was being done to improve the air defenses. He accepted that Churchill would remain a public critic of the Government, but believed that a properly informed critic was of considerably more national value than an uninformed one. Baldwin immediately agreed to the proposal, and secured the appointment in the teeth of considerable opposition in the Cabinet, led by Neville Chamberlain....
>
> From this point onward, Churchill's position was a curious one. On the one hand he

---

8 Future prime minister Harold Macmillan said of the Conservatives in those years: "A party dominated by second-class brewers and company promoters—a Casino capitalism—is not likely to represent anybody but itself."

remained a strong critic of the Government for its allegedly pusillanimous defence program, particularly in the air; but that same Government and Prime Minister had permitted him to see highly confidential papers of the Committee of Imperial Defence since 1932, and had appointed him to serve as a member of this potentially influential body concerned with air defense. Furthermore, Churchill's position as an opponent of the Government was no longer as clear as it had been.

Churchill was not right in thinking that Germany's greatest threat to Britain was from the air. Yes, in violation of the Treaty of Versailles, Germany built up a considerable air corps in the 1930s, but what Churchill missed was that the air force would be most lethal when attached to, and in support of, German ground troops in their blitzkriegs.[9]

---

9 James writes: "Furthermore, the reality of the danger was wrongly assessed—by Churchill as much as by any other observer. The expansion of the German air force between 1933 and 1939 was in numerical terms astounding, but its purpose remained that of support for the ground forces; the German army, with its mighty air arm, was the real danger. Even by the outbreak of war in 1939, the Luftwaffe did not possess the capability to inflict the damage on Britain that Churchill and others depicted so graphically."

# 15
# HITLER CHEWS THE CARPETS IN EUROPE

ON THE CAMPING trip to Germany with my children, we spent several days on bicycles in Munich, which was much more Hitler's home city than Berlin. It was where, in the beer halls, Hitler got his political start, and where he lived in a succession of bourgeois apartments, as if a successful lawyer. It was also where he chose to receive (and browbeat) British Prime Minister Neville Chamberlain during the September 1938 crisis over the German Sudetenland in Czechoslovakia.

The building where the Munich Agreement was signed, ceding the Sudetenland to Germany, is no longer standing, but a neighboring building of similar style remains. Not far from where the agreement was signed is the Marienplatz, a large city square where Hitler's 1923 Beer Hall Putsch was put down in a hail of gunfire. No doubt he, for one, appreciated the juxtaposition of the two surrenders.

Churchill himself was not present in any of the Munich negotiations; he was back in the House of Commons and at Chartwell, expressing private and public scepticism about Hitler being a person amenable to compromise. Chamberlain returned from his meetings with Hitler in Munich with these well-known words, "My good friends, this is the second time in our history that there has come back from Germany to Downing Street peace with honor. I believe it is peace for our time."[10]

[10] Hitler recalled the meeting: "He seemed such a nice old gentleman I thought I would give him my autograph as a souvenir."

## HITLER CHEWS THE CARPETS IN EUROPE

Less well known, then and now, is that Chamberlain travelled to Munich with only two bodyguards and two typists, plus three diplomats, two of whom were junior. Manchester writes, "Like their leader, none in the party spoke a word of German."

One of the best accounts of the debacle, at least for allies, appears in Robert Harris's fictional account of the negotiations, *Munich*, which was published in 2018. He describes the building where the agreement was signed:

> It was not a government building, or a Party headquarters. Rather, it was a kind of monarch's court, for the enlightenment and entertainment of the emperor's guests. The interior was clad entirely in marble—a dull plum colour for the floors and the two grand staircases, greyish-white for the walls and pillars, although on the upper level the effect of the lighting was to make the stone glow golden.

Harris also makes clear Hitler's contempt for Chamberlain, writing of one particular exchange:

> Hitler was not to be deflected: "Chamberlain! He was even worse than the Czechs would have been! What has he got to lose in Bohemia? What's it to do with him? He asked me if I liked to fish at weekends. I never have weekends—and I hate fishing!"

For his part, Chamberlain said of Hitler, "He looked like a lodger who always kept himself to himself, or a nightwatchman who disappeared in the morning as soon as the day shift arrived."

Nevertheless, to avoid another continental war, and millions of casualties, Chamberlain decided to give up Czechoslovakia, overlooking that he was signing a deal with the devil. The Czechs were not even invited to the meetings that dismembered their country. Harris writes of their getting the bad news:

> At first the Czechs seemed too stunned to speak. Then [Czech ambassador to the UK] Masarík burst out: "You have given the Germans everything they asked for!" "We have only agreed to the transfer of those areas where a majority of the population is German." "But with them go all our border fortifications—it renders our country indefensible."

The difficulty for Chamberlain can be glimpsed in a letter from the 1930s that the British diplomat and historian, Harold Nicholson, wrote to his wife, Vita Sackville-West, about one of the many diplomatic crises between Britain and Germany:

> ...if we send an ultimatum to Germany, she ought in all reason to climb down. But then she will not climb down and we shall have war. Naturally we shall win and enter Berlin. But what is the good of that? It would only mean communism in Germany and France, and that is why the French are so keen on it. Moreover, the people of this country absolutely refuse to have a war. We should be faced by a general strike if we even suggested such a thing. We shall therefore have to climb down ignominiously and Hitler will have scored...

# HITLER CHEWS THE CARPETS IN EUROPE

When I think of Munich, I think of our bike trip there in high summer, where over our lakeside dinners beside a campfire I would ask the boys, "Do you think the Allies had a choice?"

# 16
# POLAND AND CZECHOSLOVAKIA: WHAT-IF HISTORY

IT WAS ON another trip, to Poland and Czechoslovakia in the 1980s, that I thought about Churchill's lonely stand, after Munich, against both the Germans and the British establishment.

On bicycles and trains, my wife and I went from Gdansk (earlier the Free City of Danzig, where World War II began) to the Czech-German border. In between, we saw the Polish borders that proved indefensible against German Panzers, plus the Czech highlands, where the Allies could well have succeeded in making an early stand against Hitler's conquests. Churchill's observation was that Chamberlain "had a hidden mercurial streak; he blew hot and cold, destroying a defensible Czechoslovakia one year and now guaranteeing Poland—which would prove far less defensible—the next."

Any firm opposition to Hitler between 1936 and 1938—in the Rhineland or along the Czech border—might have pushed the German military to topple Hitler in a coup. One of Harris's characters in *Munich* says:

> I bring this information to you in good faith,
> and at grave risk to myself, because I wish to
> urge you—even at this eleventh hour—not
> to sign the [Munich] agreement tonight.
> It will make Hitler's position in Germany
> unassailable. Whereas, if Britain and France

> were to stand firm, I am certain the Army
> would move against him in order to prevent a
> disastrous war.

One of the great "what ifs" in history is to imagine Churchill in government from 1936 to 1939 as Hitler began to sweep the pieces from the European chessboard. Churchill wrote to a friend in 1938, "We seem to be very near the bleak choice between War and Shame. My feeling is that we shall choose Shame, and then have War thrown in a little later on even more adverse terms than at present." That proved correct, as the government of Neville Chamberlain chose to make its stand in Poland—in the plains of central Europe—as opposed to the mountain redoubts that the Czechs had previously manned.

Churchill thought it mad to give up a defendable ally. As Manchester conveys, "Meanwhile, the Czechs, trusting their formidable defenses and their two fellow democracies in the west, were ready for anything—anything, that is, except betrayal by those two." The Chamberlain government tied its future to Poland—an indefensible ally—but without contemplating attacking Germany on its vulnerable front west of the Rhine. Manchester describes, "Instead of planning to break through the Siegfried Line—a golden opportunity because Hitler, confident that the democracies' fear would restrain them, had left only ten divisions to defend it—both Paris and London expressed their readiness to negotiate if the Führer's troops withdrew from Poland."

Even after the Polish invasion, the Allies failed to grasp the picture of despair all too clear in Churchill's mind at Chartwell. The French, for example, in 1940, sold off 235 of their 500 R-35 tanks to the Balkans and to Turkey. In England, in response to the German conquest of Poland, someone suggested bombing the Black Forest, to which an air minister responded, "Oh, you can't do that; it's private property."

# 17
# UNDERGROUND IN THE CABINET WAR ROOMS

TO IMAGINE CHURCHILL during his wartime years as prime minister, I often visit the Cabinet War Rooms, which are opposite London's St. James Park and beneath Downing Street.

Beginning with the London Blitz, Churchill retreated there whenever it was unsafe to be above ground. (In the museum you come away with the impression that he spent long stretches underground, fighting the war from a windowless office, but, in fact, he spent only a few nights in the bunker, preferring to work in the Number 10 Annex.) Here's how Richard Holmes describes Churchill underground and the working conditions:

> He was even admired by the long-suffering staff required to match his impossibly bohemian working hours and demanding standards. When in London he lived at No. 10 Downing Street, sometimes sleeping in the nearby Cabinet War Rooms…It is a telling comment on Britain's lack of preparedness for war that the War Rooms had only been conceived of as late as 1936, with an initial funding of £500. By war's end they totaled over 150 rooms, with offices, operations rooms and sleeping quarters, where over 600 people worked.

Neither Churchill nor Roosevelt had much good to say about the leader of Free France, General Charles de Gaulle, who always seemed to worm his way into their meetings and strategic plans. Both of them found de Gaulle egotistical, boorish, snobbish, and pushy, and away from his presence they despaired at having to include him in their war plans. Churchill let de Gaulle land in Normandy a week after D-Day, but only after the prime minister himself had visited a patch of liberated France. On another occasion, Churchill answered a question: "If I regard de Gaulle as a great man? He is selfish, he is arrogant, he believes he is the center of the world. He . . . You are quite right. He is a great man." At Yalta, Churchill argued in favor of a French zone of occupation in Germany, and he believed in the Anglo-French alliance.

## THE VIEW FROM CHURCHILL

The War Rooms are now a London museum, which includes exhibits on Churchill's life. Preserved are his metal desk and bunk room accommodations. Many of the walls are covered with maps, and pins indicate the positions of Allied troops on various fronts. What is extraordinary about the War Rooms, seen in the age of gadgetry, is the extent to which the World War was waged and won with black rotary telephones and Morse code.

Evocative as the Cabinet War Rooms are of the London Blitz and Churchill's heroic stand against long odds between 1940–42, another way to judge his performance as an Allied commander is to visit a theater of his operations. In my case, I toured the southern Italian battlefields of Monte Cassino and Anzio Beach, which the Allies attacked in the winter of 1943–44. Rome finally fell on June 5, 1944. Despite its eventual success, the campaign along the spine of central Italy is as close as the Allies came to a rerun of Gallipoli. In summary, the Allies—mostly Americans—landed at Salerno in September, 1943, and together with Commonwealth troops began a push north toward Rome and Hitler's Fortress Europa. Anzio followed, in January, 1944, and was largely a British operation, intended to outflank the Germans dug in around the Cassino high ground. Cassino and Anzio were meat grinders that chewed up Allied soldiers. Churchill himself said of the landing at Anzio: "I had hoped we were hurling a wildcat onto the shore, but all we got was a stranded whale."

Initially the Americans had wanted little to do with a campaign along the Italian spine, thinking it a sideshow to a cross-Channel invasion of the German heartland. Churchill wanted action before D-day forces were assembled, and Italy was a compromise between an invasion further east—for example, through Yugoslavia—and the American wish to attack southern France. As at Gallipoli, once Allied soldiers got ashore in Italy they found themselves bogged down in trenches—notably in the Liri Valley, directly below the Abbey of Monte Cassino.

To relieve pressure on that front, Churchill pushed through an amphibious landing at Anzio, also south of Rome. Casualties along that narrow front were appalling. By the end of 1943, some 40,000 men of the 5th Army were dead or wounded; another 50,000 were too sick to fight. Rome did eventually fall in June 1944, but the Italian war ended with the Allies only slightly north of Florence. In the meantime, despite Churchill's best intentions, Hitler's armies escaped the trap set at Anzio.

# 18
# ITALIAN STALEMATES AT MONTE CASSINO AND ANZIO

TO GET TO the vast battlefield that surrounds the town of Cassino, my daughter Laura and I took a local train about an hour south of Rome. Wanting to get the most out of the day, I had arranged for a guide with a car to meet us at the station. At 9:30 a.m. we met Michele Di Lonardo in Roccasecca, briefly visited the birthplace of Cicero in Arpino, and then headed up the long switchbacks above Cassino to the abbey.

Cassino is a nondescript Italian town, with a clogged central square and little to recommend it except for the abbey, which dates to AD 529 and was the home of St. Benedict and his Benedictine followers. Had it been a fortress, and not a monastery, it might have adjusted to the periodic invasions that coursed through its halls. Its location, on what looks like the door hinge of southern Italy, insured that everyone from the Lombards to Napoleon had a crack at its thick walls.

As we climbed the rocky, open hillside, Michele chatted about the different veterans that came back to Cassino. He said Americans came only once, complained about the hotels and the store hours, and said of the battle only that it was "confusing." The Germans, he said, came repeatedly. The French came hardly at all, and when they did they refused even to speak about the atrocities committed by French colonial troops, who raped and pillaged their way up the Liri Valley. Michele had toured a group of NATO officers on leave from Afghanistan.

It says something about those battles that the senior command would send junior officers to inspect a mountainous stalemate.

We got to the abbey just ahead of pilgrims in tour buses. Although the walls of the monastery were destroyed in February 1944, the Nazis had saved many of the treasures and works of art before the bombing—something that gave them a propaganda victory, of sorts, after the Allied air raid.

The abbey has a tranquil courtyard, like one you would find at an English cloister, and an imposing church. Near the altar we met the monk who in 1944, immediately after the fighting had passed, began work on the church's restoration. He was a man in his eighties with a slight stoop and an engaging smile. We chatted for a few minutes. When he left, Michele whispered that just after the war, money was raised in the US to help rebuild the abbey, but the money never got to Cassino (although subsequently American veterans paid to rebuild the monastery windows). From the courtyard we could see the Polish cemetery nestled in a saddleback along the ridge line. Among the forces of the many nations that attacked the abbey, the Poles were the ones who finally made it to the top. What they captured felt as hollow as the ruins at Hiroshima.

An Allied officer in the 1944 assaults, Fred Majdalany, described the abbey as "a symbol of defiance, a great fortress in the sky…Monte Cassino has been likened to the Rock of Gibraltar, and there is a rough similarity in the way it commands the 'straits' at the entrance to the Liri Valley, forcing the road to Rome to make a wide detour around its base, and looming over that like a sentinel." He called it "…the most perfect natural defensive position in Europe; a clearly defined battleground consisting partly of mountain, partly of river and valley, with one admirably complementing the other." It was here that the Germans chose to construct their Gustav Line.

Norman Lewis, a British soldier in the expeditionary forces and later a best-selling author, writes how the initial landings at Salerno were a near-run thing: "Official history will in due time set to work to dress this part of the action at Salerno with what dignity it can. What we saw was ineptitude and cowardice spreading down from the command, and this resulted in chaos. What I shall never understand is what stopped the Germans from finishing us off."

Once the Allies were firmly ashore, the Germans chose to make their stand at Cassino, in part by flooding the Liri Valley below the abbey. Majdalany recalls, "The geography of Italy is such that even in dry weather power of manoeuvre is severely restricted, but between November and April it is non-existent." Hence, Cassino had almost medieval qualities of battle. First the attackers were forced to cross numerous low-lying and heavily fortified moats. Then they had to ascend the steep walls of a hillside castle. Little wonder that Majdalany would recall: "Even in peacetime, Monte Cassino overwhelms the least imaginative visitor gazing up at it from below. In the cold desolation of winter and the fatiguing travail of unresolved battle, the spell of its monstrous eminence was complete and haunting."

In the first phases of the nearly yearlong battle, the Allies tried to jump across some of the swollen streams that sluice through the Liri Valley. General Mark Clark, commanding the $5^{th}$ Army group, was a particularly hated figure among the survivors of the $36^{th}$ Division, which was ordered to send battalions from two of its regiments across the Rapido River, near the town of Sant'Angelo. Majdalany remembers the river: "It is only sixty feet wide…though narrow, it was nine feet deep: it had an eight miles an hour current…it had vertical banks two or three feet above water level…" When Laura and I stopped there, it looked like a transplanted mountain stream running through a gorge.

# ITALIAN STALEMATES AT MONTE CASSINO AND ANZIO

In Matthew Parker's history of the battle, *Monte Cassino: The Hardest Fought Battle of World War II*, one officer is quoted: "The crossing is dominated by heights on both sides of the valley where German artillery observers are ready to bring down heavy artillery on our men. The river is the principal obstacle of the German main line of resistance… So I am prepared for defeat." In just one engagement, in January 1944, the Americans lost 430 men in the crossing. Of those who made it across, 770 were captured. Another 900 were killed before they even got to the water.

Unable to break through the Liri Valley, the Allies then tried a series of assaults on the high grounds of the abbey, hoping eventually to site their guns on those hillsides. Despite numerous acts of individual courage in trying to scale the precipice ("The full story of these deadly night battles can never be known, because too many of its authors died writing it"), the abbey remained in German hands.

Eyewitness accounts during the battle and later research indicate that the Germans had not fortified the actual monastery or used it to store weapons. The battle had become such a crucible and Allied casualties were so great in the shadow of Monte Cassino ("a malign presence") that finally, in February 1944, General Clark ordered the abbey's destruction by bombs. Even reducing its ancient walls to rubble did not decide the fighting; not one German soldier was killed in the raid. One witness said, "So the bombing, when it happened, expended its fury in a vacuum, tragically and wastefully. It achieved nothing, it helped nobody." Then the ruins of the abbey became a sniper's dream location. Only in May did Polish troops succeed in capturing what was left of the monastery.

About the time Allies entered the monastery, other forces succeeded in breaking out of the Anzio beachhead. It had been

Churchill's dream, in putting men ashore behind enemy lines, to trap the 10th German Army around Cassino, southeast of Anzio. But inexplicably, General Clark turned his forces to the left to capture Rome, rather than to the right toward Cassino. General Lucien Truscott thought this "a crowning act of strategic folly," believing that "had General Clark held loyally to General Alexander's instructions…the strategic objective of Anzio would have been accomplished in full." It was suggested that the publicity-obsessed Clark wanted the prize of Rome before D-day pushed Italy off the front pages, and indeed he took it on June 5. Norman Lewis writes that Clark's "reading of Clausewitz's famous dictum was that war was the pursuit of publicity by other means."

In the end, Churchill did not get what he wanted in Italy. The Germans escaped the snare and fought rearguard actions all along the Italian spine. Of Anzio, Fred Majdalany wrote, "One of Mr. Churchill's idiosyncrasies is known to have been a temperamental allergy to orthodox military men. He became impatient when the generals pointed out the practical aspects of any scheme on which he had set his heart. He had a strong buccaneering streak in him, which tended to favor irregulars—commandos, special forces, and their like—and was quick to assume that more orthodox commanders were unnecessarily making difficulties." Charles McMoran Wilson, 1st Baron Moran and Churchill's physician, said of him, "But Winston is a gambler, and gamblers do not count the coins in their pockets."

Salerno, Cassino, Anzio, and the Italian campaign can be seen in the historical continuum from Gallipoli to the coast of Norway and Dieppe—sideshows gone wrong—although Churchill's greatness as a military commander was that he would try literally anything at any time to beat the Germans. Harold Macmillan said of the early war years: "He alone

# ITALIAN STALEMATES AT MONTE CASSINO AND ANZIO

seemed to be in command, when everyone else was dazed and hesitating." President Franklin Roosevelt said, "Winston has fifty ideas a day, and three or four are good." [11]

---

11 When I finally made it to the invasion beaches at Dieppe in northern France, where several thousand Allied troops, mostly Canadian, were slaughtered attacking German coastal defenses that were dug into cliffs and fortified with barbed wire, I came to the conclusion that Churchill had gone forward with the disastrous attack not because he thought it would work—he must have known the raiding division was doomed—but to show the Soviets in 1942 that the western Allies could die as senselessly as the Russians. Churchill and the Americans had postponed the cross-Channel landings that summer, and Stalin was resentful that he was bearing the largest burden against the Germans. Dieppe was the play of a diplomatic card, although the doomed Canadians who never got off the enfiladed beaches were the ones who got to cash in Churchill's chips.

# 19
# FROM ROOSEVELT'S HYDE PARK TO YALTA

PERHAPS CHURCHILL'S BEST idea of the war was to persuade the Americans to fight on the side of the British. He had briefly crossed paths with Franklin Roosevelt during World War I, when both were secretaries of their respective navies. The partnership between the Allied war leaders did not, however, begin until after Churchill was elected prime minister in 1940 and Roosevelt was searching quietly for ways to bolster the British side.

It was Churchill who saw personal friendship with Roosevelt as a way to achieve his war aim, and throughout the war years—as I learned on a visit to the Roosevelt home at Hyde Park, New York—Churchill spent weeks in Roosevelt's company, almost to the point of becoming the 'prime minister who came to dinner'.

I have my doubts that photographs in Hyde Park cabinets or in books can grasp the subtle complexities of any friendship, and in that between Churchill and Roosevelt there was the added level of political necessity. Churchill knew that Britain would survive only with an American military alliance, while Roosevelt shared with Churchill what might be called the Blenheim concept that it was prudent to oppose the domination of the European continent by any one power.

# FROM ROOSEVELT'S HYDE PARK TO YALTA

No political relationship was more important in Churchill's life than his friendship with Franklin Roosevelt, especially during the Second World War. They had met briefly in 1918 at a London dinner. (Later Churchill did not remember meeting his younger American colleague, who was then assistant secretary of the Navy.) Their relationship developed after Hitler went to war, first against Britain (1939) and later the United States (in 1941), and Churchill came to the conclusion that only an American alliance would save the British Empire. Toward that end he met Roosevelt at the Atlantic Conference, in Placentia Bay off Newfoundland, and in late 1941 and early 1942 Churchill practically moved into the White House to secure American aid for the Allied war effort. Roosevelt quipped, "Winston has a hundred ideas a day, of which at least four are good." Their transatlantic friendship saved Europe from fascism.

## THE VIEW FROM CHURCHILL

Some of the keys to the relationship are revealed in Jon Meacham's *Franklin and Winston: A Portrait of a Friendship*. The book strings together vignettes of their friendship, quotes from their correspondence, and otherwise pursues the notion that the consummate politician, Churchill, had met his match in befriending the enigmatic Roosevelt. Meacham quotes from Kenneth Pendar, a vice counsel in Marrakech, who was "struck by the fact that, though Churchill spoke much more amusingly than the President, it was Mr. Roosevelt who dominated any room they were in, not merely because he was president of the United States, but because he had more spiritual quality than Mr. Churchill, and, I could not help but feel, a more profound understanding of human beings." [12]

Meacham quotes Churchill's daughter, Lady Mary Soames: "Being with them was like sitting between two lions roaring at the same time." She is also Meacham's source for a glimpse of the powerful foursome: "Churchill could be demanding, Clementine difficult, Franklin deceptive, and Eleanor wearying, but what Mary Soames once called 'the golden thread of love' bound each couple together." At the same time, they spent relatively little time together as couples. As president, FDR never went to England, and he met Chur-

---

12 Perhaps the most successful summit during the war took place in Casablanca, where Churchill and FDR gathered in the winter of 1943, not long after American ground troops cleared Morocco of its Nazi garrisons and French collaborators. The meetings took place at the Anfa Hotel in a seaside Casablanca suburb, where in spring sunshine Churchill painted in the garden and, together with Roosevelt, mapped out future landings in Europe and the Pacific, knowing that the war was turning in favor of the Allies. When I went to Casablanca, I hired a guide and bicycle to find the location of the conference and spent more than an hour quizzing residents around upscale Anfa for the exact location of the hotel, which, if we found it, now lies in disrepair. In more prosperous times, the hotel is where Churchill and Roosevelt rolled their eyes collectively at having to deal with the French wartime leader, Charles de Gaulle. As Churchill said to FDR (as is quoted in Meredith Hindley's *Destination Casablanca: Exile, Espionage, and The Battle for North Africa in World War II*): "We house him. We feed him. We pay him. We pamper him, and as best we can, we put up with his truculence and insults, but he refuses to raise a finger in support of our war efforts."

chill, often without his wife, at summit meetings, the evening dinner table in the White House, or Hyde Park. [13]

In the end it was Joseph Stalin who brought strain to an otherwise beautiful friendship. Beginning in 1943–44, when American and Russian soldiers began dominating the major fronts, Churchill and Great Britain were not held to be the equals of the emerging superpowers. Churchill's perseverance had kept Britain from falling to the Germans between 1939–42, and his alliance with Roosevelt had, in part, brought the US to the Allied cause. Churchill and Roosevelt agreed more on the tactics of stopping Hitler than they shared postwar goals, despite the enumerated beliefs of the Atlantic charter that were signed in their first face-to-face summit meeting. Roosevelt was concerned that Churchill viewed the war effort as cover for the restoration of the British Empire. He might also have felt that Churchill was a combustible element that could ignite the looming postwar confrontation with Stalin and the Russians. (He knew about Churchill's anti-Bolshevik past.)

In many senses the turning point came at Yalta, in February 1945, which for all the participants, except for Stalin, involved days of travel. Churchill quipped, "We could not have found a worse place for a meeting if we had spent ten years on research.... It is good for typhus and deadly on lice which thrive in those parts." On another occasion he called it "The Riviera of Hades!" One of his generals said, "From a gastronomical point

---

[13] I developed an unpleasant aftertaste from Meacham's research when I got to the Acknowledgements in his book and found that for a diplomatic history of World War II he thought it necessary to consult and effusively thank the likes of Henry Kissinger ("diplomat, strategist, and historian"), Richard Holbrooke ("historian who has been in the arena"), Tom Brokaw, Tina Brown, Sally Bedell Smith, Harold Evans, Arthur Schlesinger Jr., Louis Auchincloss, Robert Coles, Donald Graham (his boss at *Newsweek*), and on and on through what reads like the A list at an East Hampton cocktail party. Interestingly, the one source that I would value in this exercise, Lady Soames, who often traveled with her father, disagreed with Meacham's conclusions that Churchill had chased FDR as if he were a jilted lover and that, by war's end, he had been cast aside for the arms of Joseph Stalin. She might also have shared her father's scepticism about historians on bended knee.

of view, it was enjoyable: from the social point of view, it was enjoyable: from the military point of view, unnecessary: and from the political point of view, depressing."

In 2014, I booked train tickets from St. Petersburg to Yalta, so that my son, Charles, and I could visit the site of the conference at Livadia. It would take several days to get there, and along the way we could visit the Napoleonic battlefield of Borodino outside Moscow. Between the purchase of the train tickets and the start of the trip, however, Russia invaded Crimea and annexed the territory from Ukraine, which took away any hope—for a while anyway—of my getting to Yalta. Not until the summer of 2021, during the worst of the pandemic (but after I'd had several booster shots), was I able to make it to Crimea and Yalta. But my journey there proved as roundabout as Churchill's.

Because Crimea was under Russian occupation, I had to fly first to Moscow, and from there take a series of night trains to the south. Along the way I stopped in Volgograd (once Stalingrad, and scene of the epic 1942–43 battle), Novocherkassk (capital of the Cossack nation), Sevastopol (anchorage throughout history of many Black Sea fleets), and finally Yalta which, when I arrived, was suffering from rain and associated mud slides from the surrounding hills. To get around Crimea, I had brought with me my folding bicycle, which I rode through muddy streets to the village of Livadia, where the conference palace was located. (Roosevelt stayed there while Churchill was down the road in the Vorontsov Palace.) I also used it to track down the battlefields of the 1854 Crimean War, not knowing that in less than a year, war would return to the peninsula.[14]

---

14  During the 1945 Yalta conference, the British army staff took a day off and toured the Crimean battle sites around Balaclava, notably where the Light Brigade made its fatal charge. Churchill wrote back to Clement Atlee about the excursion: "All the Chiefs of Staff have taken a holiday to-day to look at the battlefield of Balaclava. This is not being stressed in our conversations with our Russian friends…" That was because the 1854 war ended in a Russian defeat, a fact not lost on Vladimir Putin in 2022.

At one point during the conference, a visitor to Vorontsov Palace was looking at the water when the figure of a robed Churchill ambled toward the beach. At the water's edge he dropped his robe, revealing nothing on his person save for a lit cigar. Distracted for a moment with his back turned toward the sea, Churchill found himself dowsed by a large wave that ended whatever pleasure he was having from the cigar. According to the witness, Churchill turned to the water, made a rude gesture to the Black Sea, put his robe back on, and stomped back to the palace.

# 20
# THE TERMS OF YALTA

AT YALTA, ROOSEVELT'S ambition was to persuade the Soviet Union to enter the war against the Japanese. For his part, Stalin sought to establish buffer states in eastern Europe to protect Russia from ever being threatened by a resurgent Germany. And Churchill's goals were to ensure that when the war was over, the British Empire could pick up where it left off in 1939. (He didn't want buffer states so much as "spheres of influence," according to the historian Lloyd C. Gardner.)

None of the men got exactly what they wanted, although an American admiral at Yalta said of the Russian agreement to fight the Japanese: "We have just saved two million Americans." Stalin went to Yalta not only to codify his presence in Europe but also to feast on the carcass of Japan in the east. FDR went along with those spoils of war, provided he could have his United Nations, with the United States as the first among equals. (FDR, who spent a lot of time denouncing "secret treaties" was the spiritual heir of Woodrow Wilson and the League of Nations; Stalin was a descendant of Ivan the Terrible.)

In that mix, Churchill's claim at the table to restore the influences of the British Empire fell on deaf ears. At one point at Yalta, he had this outburst (as is quoted by Serhii Plokhii in his account of Yalta), when he thought that Roosevelt and Stalin might put the British Empire into bankruptcy administration at the United Nations:

> I will not have one scrap of British territory flung into that.... After we have done our best to fight in this war and have done no crime to anyone I will have no suggestion that the British Empire is to be put into the dock and examined by everybody to see whether it is up to their standard. No one will induce me as long as I am Prime Minister to let any representative of Great Britain go to a conference where we will be placed in the dock and asked to justify our right to live in a world we have tried to save.

At Yalta, however, only power politics were on the agenda. Churchill's physician, Lord Moran, wrote in his diary (as quoted by Plokhii): "Stalin can see no point in vague sentiments and misty aspirations for the freedom of certain small nations. He is only concerned with the borders of Poland, with reparations and with what he can pick up in the Far East. Roosevelt would like to prescribe for the world, Stalin is content to make clear what the Soviet Union will swallow."

FDR was fading at Yalta and could not help Churchill push back against Stalin. Moran said of FDR that "he intervened very little in the discussions, sitting with his mouth open. If he has sometimes been short of facts about the subject under discussion, his shrewdness has covered this up. Now, they say, the shrewdness has gone, and there is nothing left. I doubt from what I have seen if he is fit for the job here." FDR had won his main point from the conference, getting the Russians to commit to the war in the Far East three months after the Germans surrendered—the Russians kept their word—and he persuaded Stalin to support and join the nascent United Nations. After that he was content to express homilies about the enduring

# THE VIEW FROM CHURCHILL

It is doubtful that Churchill ever fully trusted the Soviet leader Joseph Stalin, but he dealt with him personally at various summit meetings, including those that took place in Moscow, Tehran, and Yalta—and after the European war in Potsdam. In their wartime meetings Churchill tried to impress upon the Russian leader that his only ambition was to defeat Nazi Germany. Churchill was, however, a lifelong opponent of Bolshevism, and as Secretary of State for War and Air in 1919 had supported British intervention in the Russian civil war—a fact not lost on the suspicious Stalin. Churchill believed Stalin had made a grave error in his deal with the devil (Hitler) after the Soviets agreed to the Ribbentrop-Molotov Non-Aggression Pact in 1939 that partitioned Poland and brought war to Europe. Yet from their wartime summits, Stalin came to respect Churchill's eloquence and determination, even though by the time of Yalta (1945), Stalin wanted more direct dealings with his superpower colleague, Franklin Roosevelt.

friendship between the Russians and the Americans. But Churchill got nowhere with western claims for democratic elections in Poland, Czechoslovakia, Hungary, Romania, and Bulgaria. (Lord Moran wrote, "...Stalin means to make Poland a Cossack outpost of Russia...") Nor, as it turned out, did the Allies need Russian assistance to defeat Japan, even though much of the Yalta conference was spent restoring Russian rights to the Chinese Eastern and South Manchuria railways, which it lost in the Russo-Japanese War of 1904–5.

Churchill felt abandoned as he found himself isolated from the growing familiarity between Roosevelt and Stalin. At the same time, Richard Holmes has described the paradoxical appreciation that Stalin had for the British leader and aristocrat. He said, in tribute to Churchill, "There have been few cases in history where the courage of one man has been so important to the future of the world." They spent some evenings talking, and at times Stalin almost preferred the company of Churchill and his brandy to that of Roosevelt, who by all accounts was tired and distracted. But it was Roosevelt who thought he could charm Stalin out of Eastern Europe and Churchill who took his correct measure. Meacham records, "After the president went to bed, Churchill struck a dark note. 'Stalin is an unnatural man,' he mused. 'There will be grave troubles.'" Less than two months later, Roosevelt was dead, and in less than six months, Churchill was out of power.

# 21
# CHURCHILL—ON THE ROAD AGAIN

IN MY VOYAGES around the worlds of Churchill, I have often wondered how he himself traveled. Clearly (except during the war years) he went only first class. I am a little surprised there is not a chain of five-star hotels known as The Churchill Collection, comprising all the famous hotels where he stayed. But he also had the soul of a traveling salesman, one who keeps a provisional packed bag under his desk, just in case. And as his nomadic wanderings from India and South Africa to Tehran and Yalta all involved substantial risk, I sense in Churchill someone for whom danger was one of the allures of the road.

At one of the Churchill museums along my way, I picked up a copy of Brian Lavery's *Churchill's Travels*, sensing that it could have been written with me in mind. It is an account of Churchill's trips during the Second World War. What initially grabbed my attention was Lavery's assertion that the prime minister usually went abroad with about thirty pieces of luggage. Nevertheless, Churchill was almost constantly in motion, thanks to the Americans having given him several planes on which he could travel, notably a Boeing 314 Clipper that became the prime minister's winged chariot to the far corners of the fighting world.

Churchill was the only wartime leader of the Big Three to travel near the front lines, although Roosevelt braved the North Atlantic and German U-boats on many occasions and risked

In the late 1910s and early 1920s, when he was Secretary of State for War and Air, Churchill taught himself to fly, believing that air power might well be a key element in any future war. He usually flew with a more experienced pilot, and he survived several near-misses in his short-lived aviation career. During his travels to the front in the Second World War, Churchill occasionally took a turn flying the aircraft. His embrace of air power matched his earlier advocacy during World War I of an armoured, trench-busting vehicle that grew into the tank. In his daily life, Churchill did not dress himself or draw his own bath water, but in his political-military incarnation he was an early adopter of many technologies.

all to get to places such as Tehran and Yalta, as did Churchill. Ironically, for someone so dedicated to the maintenance of the British Empire, few of Churchill's travels during the war took him to English colonies. When he did stop over in places such as Newfoundland or Bermuda, it was for fuel.

As a traveler and a diplomat, Churchill appears most in his element when flying east to meet with the Russians. He had a visceral dislike of the Bolsheviks and a suspicious view of Stalin. Nevertheless, East European travel engaged his political senses, and he did better, diplomatically, with Stalin when they met one-on-one rather than collectively in Roosevelt's company.

Churchill's first trip to Moscow, in 1942, might have been his most successful mission, in that he kept Stalin's alliance with the Allies intact, despite the lack of a second front opening that year in France. Lavery writes about the trip: "It was one of the most dangerous of Churchill's voyages, as well as the longest and least comfortable, but arguably it was one of the most profitable."

Because the Russians never trusted even Churchill's pilots with updated charts or navigational aids, just to penetrate Soviet airspace required feats of improvisation and courage. Often, those flying Churchill's plane resorted to what was called "Bradshawing," navigating from a guide book, if not a road map. One pilot commented, "To all intents and purposes, we had either to map-read or Bradshaw our way across tens of thousands of acres of flat, featureless landscape."

Sometimes on these long voyages across the steppe—to avoid German air space, they entered Russia from the south—Churchill would pass the time flying in the co-pilot's seat. From such a vantage point he took stock of the Middle East that, as colonial minister, he had played such a hand in subdividing (with disastrous results, even to this day). Lavery recounts, "Churchill occupied the co-pilot's seat for a time as usual and looked out over the Gaza Strip, the Dead Sea and an oil pipeline linking Haifa and Kirkuk." And it was as a co-pilot that Churchill arrived in Iran for the Big Three Conference in late 1943.

It was not until 2015 that I myself made it to Tehran. My trip came during a lull in the long simmering Cold War between the United States and Iran. For a while, I had hopes that I might ride the train from Istanbul to Tehran (you cross Lake Van on a ferry), but that dream faded after it was made clear to me that Americans visiting Iran need to be accompanied by a guide, and no guide that I could find wanted to meet me at the rail junction at Razi, on the Turkish border.

Instead, I flew to Tehran and spent two weeks riding other trains (yes, I had a guide) to various relics of the old Persian Empire, which on the rails is absent the stridency associated with headlines about Iran. My guide was an engaging history student who worked for a travel agency, and he graciously took me everywhere, including to Palmyra and the Holy City of Qom.

One day in Tehran—a sprawling city, but one that I enjoyed—I asked to see where the Big Three Conference took place in November–December, 1943. We drove in a taxi to a high-walled Russian compound in the center of the city. I had no illusions that either the Russians or the Iranians would let me inspect what remains of the conference room at the Russian embassy. So we walked around the outside walls, noting that they are crowned with barbed wire. As a conference, Tehran is significant as it's where Churchill first sensed that Stalin was unbalanced and that Uncle Joe was replacing Churchill in Roosevelt's affection. Hereafter the Big Three would be the Big Two. [15]

---

[15] Lavery writes: "That evening over dinner Stalin suggested that 50,000 German officers would have to be shot when the war was over. Churchill…was shocked and was not placated when Roosevelt tried to ease the tension by joking that only 49,000 needed to be shot."

Churchill's habits as a fearless traveller and his penchant for conducting diplomacy on the fly got him into trouble at Yalta, where he arrived at the critical postwar conference with his familiar entourage—loyal aids, typists, a general or two, and a doctor—but without anyone who could rebut Stalin's claims for a Europe that would be divided by an Iron Curtain. (He might well have been Chamberlain at Munich.) Lavery writes:

> [General Hastings] Ismay thought that the Yalta conference was unnecessary from a military point of view. When the vital issue of the boundaries of Poland was under discussion, no suitable maps could be found, for Pim's Map Room was concerned with military operations, not ethnic divisions. Churchill could have found experienced economists, geographers, ethnographers and historians who would have helped his arguments on the Polish question, but as always he liked travelling with people he knew, and he had settled into a routine with his usual party.

Not just at Yalta but elsewhere on his front-line rambles, Churchill comes across as the motivational CEO of the war effort—someone inspirational at saying that the English would "never, ever give up"—but short on the facts at the center of a diplomatic discussion. One of his frequent traveling companions was General Sir Alan Brooke (later a Viscount) who was often appalled at what Churchill was committing to at the meetings. Brooke says of Churchill's style:

> He knows no details, has only got half the

> picture in his mind, talks absurdities and
> makes my blood boil to listen to his non-
> sense. I find it hard to remain civil. And the
> wonderful thing is that 3/4 of the population
> of the world imagine that Winston Churchill
> is one of the Strategists of History, a second
> Marlborough, and the other 1/4 have no
> conception of what a public menace he is and
> has been throughout this war!

As with everything he did in his life, Churchill's success in his wartime travels was that his perseverance allowed him to show up, no matter the logistics or hardships involved in getting there. Getting away from Yalta involved transiting Sebastopol, which a captain on his staff said was "undoubtedly the most terrible sight I had ever seen. There was not a single building in the whole town with a roof and very few with glass in their windows. The majority of the inhabitants were living outside the town in huts."

Across the boundaries of the Second World War, Churchill, to his credit, was seemingly everywhere. Once, on family vacation to Egypt, we took a train to Alexandria and then hired a car to take us to the battlefield at El Alamein, only to discover that Churchill had gotten there first (in August 1942). His picture was all over the local museum.

Nor did Churchill ever—at least publicly—lose the optimism that became his trademark: Lavery writes that on "1 July [1942] Churchill entered the House of Commons to face a vote of confidence. The defeats at Singapore and Tobruk and the retreat in the desert war were beginning to tell against him, and Aneurin Bevan, the great Welsh Labour orator, declaimed, 'The Prime Minister wins debate after debate and loses battle after battle.'" But he kept to his roads.

# 22
# THE GREAT SUCCESS OF FAILURE

HAD CHURCHILL DIED before becoming prime minister in May 1940, it is doubtful that he would be remembered today except as the son of Randolph Churchill who pressed for the landings at Gallipoli and later tried to explain away this disaster in his memoirs. (James writes, "It could be said with justice that the whole of Churchill's career up to the end of 1936 had been a struggle for political survival. Throughout this period, and particularly since 1915, he had usually been out of total sympathy with the political party with which he was cohabiting, and his attitude to party had not greatly changed with the years.") Churchill still would have lived a rich and compelling life—with journalism taking him to the Northwest Frontier Territory, Cuba, the Upper Nile, and South Africa; and with military service in the Admiralty, the trenches of Flanders, India, and Antwerp. It is possible that he could have been remembered for military inventiveness: he was one of the early advocates of the tank, an early believer in air power, a pilot, a believer in a cross-Channel pipeline, an advocate of radar (and then the use of strips of tin foil to confuse the enemy's radar), and the architect of artificial so-called Mulberry harbors (later used, with great effect, off the Normandy beaches).

At the same time, Churchill might have been recalled as a failed politician who tried to impose Victorian values on the modern age and found himself on the wrong side of such issues as Irish home rule, Ottoman subdivision, Russian intervention, and Indian independence. (The London *Times* once wrote, "It is no new thing, after all, to discover that judgment is not the most conspicuous of Mr. Churchill's remarkable gifts.") He could well have been castigated as the Chancellor of the Exchequer who errantly tried to reattach Britain to the gold standard, or as the Colonial Secretary who made such a mess in partitioning the Middle East. But the fact remains that in the late 1930s, Churchill was one of the few among the English ruling aristocracy who knew it was necessary to confront the Nazi threat. He said of Chamberlain after Munich: "In the depths of that dusty soul there is nothing but abject surrender." In the Commons he said, "All is over. Silent, mournful, abandoned, broken, Czechoslovakia recedes into the darkness."

Because Churchill was recalled to His Majesty's service to serve as prime minister from May of 1940 to the summer of 1945, he is linked with Britain's finest hour and his earlier failures are seen as unfortunate preambles for later success. The painful lessons learned at Gallipoli, Dieppe, Trondheim, and Anzio can be read among the reasons why the Allies succeeded at Normandy, although before the landings Churchill dreaded that he might be throwing ashore another "beached whale."

The Allies may also have embraced the concept of the mobile front in part because of what Churchill learned personally while stuck in the trenches of WW I. Richard Holmes writes, "Winston was a gambler, the antithesis of a chess player. Indeed, his favorite games were roulette and backgammon, where a quick assessment of the odds allied to blind chance can lead to instant gratification." I am sure he is correct in his assessment. At the same time, Churchill succeeded militarily in the way that the plodding Ulysses S. Grant succeeded: he learned from his many mistakes and advanced broadly on many fronts. In 1863, Grant's tactics failed seven times to capture the Mississippi town of Vicksburg. Only on his eighth try did he succeed. Similarly, what brought Churchill success wasn't the roll of the dice in North Africa or Normandy, but his dogged determination to apply the lessons of failure and then to go forth again. Keegan writes in his introduction to *Churchill's Generals*, "The tension between his emotional, romantic vision of war as an escapade and his somber, realistic appreciation of the relentless material character it had assumed in the modern age was to dominate his direction of operations and later his strategic diplomacy throughout the Second World War."

The more difficult assessment of Churchill's life comes not over the question of whether he won the battles—because he did—but whether Britain won the wars of his lifetime. At the time of his birth, Britain ruled not just the waves but also much of the world. The map was largely colored British colonial red. When he died in 1965, Britain was a second-rate power, clinging to friendship with United States, unsure about partnerships in Europe, and otherwise stripped of its empire and importance.

Churchill said many times that he refused to preside over the dismemberment of the British Empire. But that is exactly what happened in his lifetime—no matter how hard he worked to reverse such an outcome. Holmes writes, "The great paradox of his public life is that in defense of freedom he presided over the greatest and most irrevocable shift of power from the citizen to the state in British history." More critically, he continues, "The paradox of Winston's public life is that while he valued freedom, he loved power more." While clinging to that power over almost sixty years, Britain sank beneath the post-imperial waves.

I disagree, however, that the only way to measure a country's glory is by the extent of its colonial possessions or the number of its dreadnoughts. Personally, I think the measure of Churchill's greatness is the extent to which his sense of history guided his democratic spirit. Alone among the World War II leaders, he was the only one to leave office voluntarily. One reason why, in 1945, he accepted the verdicts of the first postwar election—that he was to give up power and that Britain was to be divested of its empire—is that, despite such reversals of his political fortune, he could claim credit for having saved the country's democracy.

Britain lost 350,000 men and women in World War II, and shortly thereafter most of its colonies, notably India. The Magna Carta, however, was among the war's survivors, and after defeat in 1945, Churchill retreated to Chartwell and the back benches with grace and even some humor. (Clementine said she thought it might be a "blessing in disguise," to which Winston responded that it was "very well disguised.") He even wrote his own epitaph in a speech given in 1956, when he said, "Meanwhile, never flinch, never weary, never despair."

Ironically, after his ancestor the Duke of Marlborough won the battle of Blenheim, he was rewarded with a palace and baronial lands. Churchill, for victories far greater in 1945, was thrown out of office and had to return to freelance writing to pay the bills at Chartwell.

For his multi-volume history of World War II (which tested my attention span in high school) and his lifetime contributions (both written and spoken), Churchill was awarded the Nobel Prize in Literature in 1953. Anyone who has lingered in his writing room at Chartwell knows he often wrote (or edited) these books word by word, although in his *In Command of History: Churchill Fighting and Writing the Second World War*, David Reynolds makes clear that at times Churchill was prime minister of the drafting committee. But what might be lost to the casual visitor to Chartwell or Blenheim is the extent to which Churchill's writing might have saved not just Winston but Britain itself. As Robert Rhodes James writes:

# THE VIEW FROM CHURCHILL

Churchill published some 43 books in his lifetime, including multi-volume histories of the First and Second World Wars. Very often, especially during the midnight hours when he paced his home office, he dictated his prose to a nearby secretary, who typed up his words so that Winston could later proofread the drafts or galleys. He was awarded the Nobel Prize for Literature in 1953, more for his lifetime contributions to the world of letters than for any one book. His earlier books, such as *The Boer War,* have a freshness that his later, dictated volumes lack. Of the Great War histories, one of his detractors quipped, "Winston has written an enormous book all about himself and calls it *The World Crisis.*"

But if Marlborough fails both as biography and history, its results on Churchill himself went far beyond the writing of the book. It gave him an absorbing interest at a dark moment in his political fortunes and it also gave him a more acute realization of the problems and hazards of creating and retaining a grand alliance. Some of the best passages in the book deal with these complexities. In casting himself as Marlborough, grappling with the manifold problems of diplomacy, strategy, supply, terrain, and tactics, he was affording himself a kind of dress rehearsal for the problems of 1940–45. Leo Amery goes even further, and has said that "In his great ancestor, Marlborough, he discovered that fusion of political and military ideals, as well as the inspiration of family piety, for which he had all his life been groping."

One of Churchill's gifts to the democracy he helped to save was his use of its language, which he later turned into decisive action—as if his books and articles were early drafts to buck up his courage in difficult times. Manchester makes a similar point: "What distinguished Churchill was his remarkable mastery of the language. As he used it, the English tongue was a weapon and a benediction." It may not have been enough to reverse the course of empire, but it kept Britain's democracy alive. Early in his career, Churchill said simply: "What people really want to hear is the truth—it is an exciting thing—to speak the simple truth." That he never failed to do, no matter where he was in the world, which is reason enough to walk in his footsteps.

# PLACES AND BOOKS

For anyone starting on the life of Winston Churchill, here are a few recommendations of places to visit and books to read.

**London.** I would begin at the Churchill War Rooms in King Charles Street. In truth, Churchill did not spend as much time down there as the directors of the museum might wish you to believe, but, nevertheless, it's an ideal place to imagine the wartime Churchill, defiant in the face of many long odds. I very much like the books on sale in its gift shop (beside tea towels and mugs), and I often go there just to browse the Churchill books.

**Blenheim Palace.** A wonderful trip from Oxford, where it is easy to imagine the baronial presence of John Churchill (the first Duke of Marlborough) and his descendants. But other than Winston Churchill having being born there, and living there as a child, Blenheim is not the home that sheds light upon his daily life. For that, I would head south to his weekend house of Chartwell, in Kent.

**Chartwell.** It's a touch hard to get to and get away from, unless you have a car. Maybe the easiest way to get there is by taxi from the Sevenoaks train station. Give yourself a half-day. Snack in the tea room, inspect Churchill's paintings (they are surprisingly good) in one of the out-buildings, judge for yourself if he was much a of a brickmason, talk to the excellent staff, and buy some second-hand books in the shop. It's a perfect excursion from London, but take along a phone number for a local taxi company to get home.

**Ploegsteert.** I loved my bicycle ride to Ploegsteert (British soldiers called it Plugstreet). It is in Belgium, just across the border from Lille in France (where Eurostar calls often throughout the day). It's where, after the debacle of Gallipoli, Churchill served in the trenches of World War I. There's a not-very-good statue of Winston on the main street and some excellent local museums, and you can enjoy walking in the nearby woods, in which paths have names such as Hyde Park Corner, and to the field where in the impromptu Christmas truce in 1914 German and British soldiers played football.

Combine such a visit with a longer tour to the battle sites of the Western Front, which for English travellers are best seen around Albert and along the River Somme. Churchill was friends at the end of the war with the poet Siegfried Sassoon, and Sassoon's *Memoirs of an Infantry Officer* is the book you want to read on such a trip. About Ploegsteert, Peter Apps' *Churchill in the Trenches* is well done.

**Gallipoli.** Go, by all means, but it will take some planning. Turkey has many planes and buses connecting Istanbul with Çanakkale, which is the base town from which to explore the Gallipoli battlefields.

Give yourself two days in Çanakkale, because a one-day trip from Istanbul is exhausting and will be too rushed, and because the area around Gallipoli is beautiful and exciting, with ships plying the Straits and classical Troy nearby.

Take any one of the advertised battlefield tours. Most hotels can arrange one. Keep in mind that Churchill wasn't present at the battle, but it was a long shadow over his career. Most tours focus on the Anzac Cove where the Australians and New

Zealanders had such a struggle, but at Cape Helles you will get excellent views of the Dardanelles, and there you can make up your own mind about whether Churchill was correct in trying to breach the Straits.

While visiting Gallipoli, I loved George Cassar's *The French and the Dardanelles: A study of failure in the conduct of war*, but it's long out-of-print. Not all the newer books are as readable as the old ones. I would still favour carrying along Alan Moorehead's *Gallipoli*. And Churchill's excellent biographer, Robert Rhodes James, has his own book on the subject: *Gallipoli: The History of the Noble Blunder*, which has much, as well, about Churchill.

**Ladysmith in South Africa.** On our honeymoon in 1984 (it was romantic, even if it does not sound like it!), my wife and I rented a car in apartheid Johannesburg and drove to Durban so that we could hike some of the battles of the Boer War (about which we knew very little). We spent the night in Ladysmith, and the next morning we walked through the hills around the town where Churchill was captured, and where, in many ways, he began his journey toward celebrity and politics. He was taken to a prison (actually a school) in Pretoria, and from there he escaped and took freight trains to freedom in Mozambique. He came home to fame in England. His escape remains a thrilling story, which Churchill told in his book *The Boer War*, and which Candace Millard retells in *Hero of the Empire: The Boer War, a Daring Escape, and the Making of Winston Churchill*.

To be sure, Ladysmith is a long way to go to think about the young Churchill, but my wife and I have been married for almost forty years so perhaps in tramping around the battlefields of the Boer War we picked up some of Churchill's own devotion to married life. (Winston and Clementine were married for fifty-six years.)

**Casablanca.** Just before finishing this book, I made a stopover in Casablanca, Morocco, where in winter 1943 Churchill met with Roosevelt in the upscale district of Anfa. Both men and their staffs conferred on the course of the war, and during lulls in the meetings Churchill painted in the hotel garden.

To find the Anfa Hotel, I hired a bicycle and guide, and for more than an hour, out along the windswept Atlantic coastline and up a hill in suburban Anfa, we searched for the hotel without having any luck. Finally, I asked a woman in a chauffeur-driven car, and while she had no clue about the Anfa Hotel (or Churchill's presence there in 1943), her driver knew about it, and he led us to the conference location. (Think of two bicycles following a limousine up a hill.)

Sadly, the building was undergoing renovation, and there was no sense that an important World War II conference had taken place on the site. But peering into the disheveled garden, I found it easy to imagine Churchill seated there in front of his easel, puffing on a cigar and painting in between discussions on how to defeat the Third Reich. He had his limitations—both as a painter and as a military strategist—but there is much to admire in his endless determination, and in his devotion to democracy, and the places in his story bring both qualities to life.

**Places associated with Churchill I have not visited.** I have never made it to Omdurman (it's in Sudan, outside Khartoum), where Churchill acquitted himself well in a cavalry charge in 1898. And I would love to visit Arroyo Blanco in Cuba, where the young Churchill came under fire for the first time in his life at age twenty-one.

At the moment Cuba seems a more realistic place to visit than Sudan, and what would interest me most is an appreciation of Cuba's place in North American history—from the Spanish-American War to the Cuban Missile Crisis to the present day. If along the way I could use Churchill as a plumb line to judge a certain period of Cuba's history (he was there in 1895, when it was still a Spanish possession), it would fit the pattern of this book.

**Churchill biographies.** There's no shortage of them, obviously, but you may find that many of them, even some best-sellers, are too long and filled with too many details. Later on, if you carry on with Churchill studies, you might well want to read Martin Gilbert and Roy Jenkins, and you will be rewarded for your efforts. But to start by putting your toes into literary Churchill waters, begin with some of the shorter Churchill works, such as Violet Bonham Carter's *Winston Churchill: An Intimate Portrait*. They were friends, and her biography ends with Churchill still a relatively young man. She doesn't gloss over his obvious faults, but she writes well and with affection, and you will not get bogged down in it, as you might if you were to begin your Churchill reading, say, with the 1152 pages of Andrew Roberts' *Walking with Destiny*.

John Keegan has an excellent short biography *Winston Churchill: A Life*, in the Penguin Lives series, and Keegan's superb history of World War I touches often on Churchill in the larger context of the war.

Americans might find the multi-volume biography *The Last Lion* by (the American writer) William Manchester to be more accessible than some of the English biographies, but keep in mind that Manchester only wrote the first two books (*Visions of Glory, 1874-1932*, and *Alone, 1932-1940*) in the three-volume biography, and they are the ones that deserve your attention. (Paul Reid wrote the third.) Critics will say Manchester never let the facts get in the way of a good story, but the trilogy is vivid, and it remains accessible for readers at many levels.

**Churchill as a traveller.** He did a lot of it. There are several books about the peripatetic Churchill that are very readable, including Brian Lavery's *Churchill Goes to War: Winston's Wartime Journeys* and Richard Holmes's *In the Footsteps of Churchill*. Both are excellent, especially about Churchill during World War II, when more than any other wartime leader he made it a point to visit his armies in the field. (Fearing a coup, Stalin would not leave Russia, and for the most part never went anywhere near the front lines. Remarkably for someone paralysed from polio, Roosevelt travelled tirelessly across many oceans to wartime conferences, but it was impractical for him to wander into foxholes.) It helped that Winston had destroyers, planes, and trains standing by, waiting for his commands; but he supplied the willpower.

I often think that Churchill as the wartime traveller was at his best—away from the distractions of home, office, and parliament; surrounded by his books, maps, and paintings; and happy to be sharing (to a point) the privations of the front-line soldiers (keep in mind that he went to the Boer War with a case of champagne).

# ACKNOWLEDGEMENTS

ALL BOOKS ARE collaborations, and this one is no exception. I have visited the places in the life of Winston Churchill over many years, and I would be taking a risk to attempt to name all those people who assisted me on what has become a long road. Nor do I want to default into some Churchillian construction, and say that never "was so much owed by so few to so many."

At the same time I would be remiss if I did not acknowledge my gratitude to Tom Wallace, a friend of forty-five years, whose life has been devoted to books as a publisher and literary agent. It was Tom who introduced me in London to Christopher Sinclair-Stevenson, no relation, although we share the same last name and similar tastes in writing, books, and French wines. As with Tom, Christopher has worked for some sixty years as a publisher and an agent, and one of his many great qualities is his ability to inspire his writers with his enthusiasm for their projects.

Christopher put this book in the hands of Francis Bennett, who I only met last year but with whom I developed an instant rapport—as if I had known him as long as I have Tom and Christopher. Working with Francis has only been a pleasure, as he has endless keen insights into the book business that he communicates in language that is succinct, professional, thoughtful, and, very often, wry.

Both Francis and I are grateful for the guidance and direction that we have received from Allen Packwood, a Fellow of Churchill College, Cambridge, and the Director of the

## ACKNOWLEDGEMENTS

Churchill Archives Centre, and his team. I first met Allen on a winter morning, after cycling from the Cambridge railway station to the Churchill Centre. I had no formal introduction; I was just hunting for Winston Churchill photographs, but what I found in Allen is one of the great Churchill scholars, who very kindly has allowed Francis and me to draw on his vast knowledge of the subject and the Centre's equally impressive photographic archive. Had the Centre been my first stop on this journey, and not my last, this would be a much better book, but the library in Allen's Centre has inspired me to keep reading and travelling in Churchill's footsteps.

In Cambridge—on that cold winter's morning—I also was reminded of my first trip to England in September, 1974, when I began the fall semester of the Institute of European Studies, which had an affiliation with the London School of Economics. The program's director was Edward Mowatt. That September we were about twenty American students trying to make sense of English university life (none of us drank tea or sherry). Guiding us—practically and intellectually—was Edward, who convened the group in Oxford and on our first afternoon introduced us to Blackwell's bookstore with the words: "This may be the best friend you will make in Britain." Indeed, many of the Churchill biographies that I have toted home to New York and Switzerland have come from Blackwell's, and one way to read this book is as a long letter to Edward, who, after all, encouraged me to cycle out to Blenheim on a perfect September afternoon and, back in town, to read Alan Bullock's *Hitler: A Study in Tyranny*.

During that London semester, which began in Oxford and ended in Freiburg, Germany, for the "continental perspective", I also became friends with Diane and Martin Daly, who invited me (a homesick American student) to their house in Chiswick for dinner and who inspired me with their love of books, British history, politics, and the Pacific islands. I am sure

Diane will chide me for being too kind in my judgments about Sir Winston, but we will have more lively grist for one of our pleasurable three-hour dinners.

Finally, I want to thank my wife of thirty-nine years, Constance Fogler, who more than anyone has made it possible for me to wander around places such as Gallipoli or the Staats Model School in Pretoria, where Churchill was held as a prisoner in the Boer War. Connie and I have four children (who have fledged), a house outside Geneva that needs managing, and cats that demand feeding, and one might think that she would not always be thrilled when I announce that I am on my way to Yalta or Penang. But Connie's great gift to her family, and our marriage, is an unfailing generosity of spirit that has allowed me to indulge in places like Monte Cassino and Casablanca, and not feel that I was letting down the side.

# COPYRIGHT PERMISSIONS

FOR PERMISSION TO reproduce photographs and documents from the Papers of Clementine Ogilvy Spencer-Churchill, Baroness Spencer-Churchill of Chartwell, which appear in pages 5, 8, 25, 53, 73, 97 and 116, and the cover photograph, the author is grateful to the Master, Fellows and Scholars of Churchill College Cambridge.

He also wishes to thank the team of the Churchill Archives Centre, Churchill College, Cambridge, for all their help.

For the photographs that appear on pages16, 23, 25, 30, 47,69, 87, 104 and 107, the author is grateful to Alamy Ltd (UK) for their permission.

The poem "Suicide in the Trenches" by Siegfried Sassoon is reprinted by kind permission of the Estate of George Sassoon.

The photograph on the front cover shows Winston Churchill watching the departure of the President Franklin Roosevelt from Placentia Bay, Newfoundland, at the conclusion of their 1941 Atlantic Conference.

# THE CYCLING HISTORIAN

*"I USUALLY GO in search of history—I have found the bicycle to be a passport to distant worlds every bit as delightful as a magic carpet."*

Beginning with *Biking with Bismarck*, in which he rides trains and his bicycle across France, Matthew Stevenson decided to marry his love of writing and trains with his love for cycling. He says, "I never learned very much belted up in a car, and there's no such thing as a bad bike ride."

After discovering that European trains require endless paperwork to transport a bicycle, Stevenson acquired a six-speed "touring Brompton" together with several saddle bags, and he has never looked back. He has taken the Brompton across the United States, to Crimea just before the war, up and down Vietnam, and, most recently, to Romania, Turkey, Georgia, and Armenia. He says:

"Traveling with trains and a folding bicycle has given me back the pleasures of travel, which I was beginning to loathe when on a discount airline or stuffed in a car. I am freed from taking taxis or hiring guides, and I can go wherever I want, especially after dinner in foreign cities when I wander on the bicycle through places I might not want to walk.

"I go in search of history—to this battlefield or that author's house—and I have found the bicycle to be a passport to distant worlds every bit as delightful as a magic carpet. To write about the Vietnam War, I rode (and took trains and buses) across Indochina. Yes, learning to ride in Saigon traffic was a nightmare, but I mastered the skill (which is never to turn sharply or abruptly), and I have since made endless bicycle-and-train journeys across Europe, where I have used the Brompton to track down aspects of the two world wars.

"To be sure, I get flat tires in inconvenient places (Crimea was notable in that regard), and I get caught out in the rain, but I patch the tires and my clothes dry, and I come back to my writing desk with the feeling that I am still a young boy, discovering neighbourhoods on my bike after school, and that's a thrill."

Stevenson is married to Constance Fogler, and together they have four children, all of whom have incorporated bicycles into their lives. His forthcoming books in this "Cycling Historian" series will cover the Vietnam War, British poets and writers of World War I, Crimea on the edge of war and peace, and history in Eastern Europe. But on his coffee table at home there are road maps about Cuba and histories of the 1848 Mexican-American war.

# ABOUT THE BICYCLE

This Brompton was made in 2014, and it has six speeds, a classic Brooks saddle, and touring butterfly handlebars. Ortlieb made the front bag, and it carries papers, tools, a book, maps, and a computer; the Dutch-made rear pannier has three days worth of clothes and some food. I wish I did not have to ride with a bulky lock, but not every museum wants visitors to drag in a folding bicycle.

# ABOUT THE BICYCLE

MY ADULT FASCINATION with bicycles began with a long-ago transit strike in New York City. (For some reason the city's mayor, Ed Koch, used the subway-less occasion to greet commuters trudging over the Brooklyn Bridge with a gleeful: "So how am I doin'?") To get around the shutdown city, I brought my childhood Raleigh ten-speed bike (made in Nottingham) into New York and pedaled around the mean streets, delighted to discover that cities and bicycles can be a great match.

After moving to Europe and getting around on trains, I often wanted to bring along a bicycle on my travels, and did, but quickly discovered that most European rail networks have more regulations for bicycles than does the New York City Department of Transportation. In Germany, for example, on the crack Intercity and Eurocity express trains, bicycles need both a ticket and a reservation; in France, you cannot buy a ticket for a bicycle after you buy your rail ticket.

I persisted with my bicycle travels (even using a bike to write a book about the 1870 Franco-Prussian war), but moaned about the ordeal whenever I returned home, assuming my family was interested to hear endless details about how hard it is to travel with a full touring bicycle from Krakow to Prague. They eventually tired of my whinging and in 2014 presented me with a touring Brompton bicycle, complete with six speeds, an Ortlieb front bag and a pannier, a Brooks saddle, and butterfly handlebars. In its folded state, it can ride free on any train in the world (although the fastidious Swiss and Amtrak in the USA demand it go into a bag).

Since then, the Brommie and I have been across the American Midwest, Vietnam, Russia, the Caucasus, and most countries in Europe, including to the Polish-Ukrainian border. At the same time I am not one to set off on a multi-day, cross-country ride. On the bike I am more a flâneur, happy to ride more modest kilometers to the places that interest me. Nothing pleases me more than to meander on the Brompton around unfamiliar cities, especially at night in summer, when even the most banal outpost can take on the magic of Venice, and I am pedaling a gondola.

Usually I pair the Brompton with trains and ferries, although I have taken it on the occasional flight, on which it weighs less than the normal baggage allotment. For me the pleasure of the Brompton is that I am freed from taxis, buses, subways, tour guides, and long walks in unfamiliar surroundings, and come the end of a day I feel in my legs the pleasure of miles ridden. On the Brompton, I am an immortal ten-year-old boy, wandering the (world) neighborhood after school.

Some of these Churchill travels predated the arrival of the Brompton, but not all, including the ride over that steep hill in Yalta on a hot humid day to find Livadia Palace and my wanderings in southern Belgium—in a cold winter rain—in search of what British soldiers called Plugstreet (aka Ploegsteert). That said, I don't associate Churchill with cycling, although in the archives I have come across a few pictures of him as a young man pushing the big gear. His early sporting loves, as a cavalry officer, were horseback riding and polo, and mostly, when he needed to get somewhere, he was driven around by chauffeurs. But I would like to imagine Churchill in another age embracing the pleasures of a bicycle, especially one British-made, as the Brompton represents many things he valued: independence of mind, the freedom to travel on your own, and seeing things for yourself. Of course, wet socks and flat tires come into the equation, but for them he would offer up an encouraging "K.B.O." or "Keep Buggering On", as life, on and off a Brompton, is a climb.

Milton Keynes UK
Ingram Content Group UK Ltd.
UKHW040424041024
449180UK00004B/112

# Love Thy Enemy

M.A. Nichols

Copyright © 2025 by M.A. Nichols

All rights reserved. No part of this publication may be reproduced or transmitted, in any form or by any means, electronic, mechanical, photocopying, recording, or otherwise, without the prior permission of the copyright owner.

The characters and events portrayed in this book are fictitious. Any similarity to real persons, living or dead, is coincidental and not intended by the author.

# Books by M.A. Nichols

## Generations of Love Series

With over 20 books published and more coming each year, this list is growing rapidly. For up-to-date information visit www.ma-nichols.com.

### The Kingsleys

Flame and Ember
Honor and Redemption
Hearts Entwined
A Stolen Kiss

### The Ashbrooks

A True Gentleman
The Shameless Flirt
A Twist of Fate
The Honorable Choice
A Light in the Dark

### The Finches

The Jack of All Trades
Tempest and Sunshine
The Christmas Wish

### The Leighs

An Accidental Courtship
Love in Disguise
His Mystery Lady
A Debt of Honor

### The Vaughns

Rivals and Roses
Marry in Haste
A Meddlesome Match
Love Thy Enemy

### The Vosses

A Knowing Heart

### Christmas Courtships

A Holiday Engagement
Beneath the Mistletoe
Once Upon a Winter's Eve

### Standalone Romances

A Tender Soul
A Passing Fancy
To Have and to Hold

## Fantasy Novels

### The Villainy Consultant Series

Geoffrey P. Ward's Guide to Villainy
Geoffrey P. Ward's Guide to Questing
Magic Slippers: A Novella

### The Shadow Army Trilogy

Smoke and Shadow
Blood Magic
A Dark Destiny

# Generations of Love Series
## Family Trees & Timeline

All of M.A. Nichols' romances take place within the Generations of Love universe; each book is a standalone story and can be read in any order with the titles grouped into family sagas.

To view the family trees and timeline visit www.ma-nichols.com/generations-of-love.

# Table of Contents

Chapter 1 . . . . . . . . . . . . . . 1
Chapter 2 . . . . . . . . . . . . . . 9
Chapter 3 . . . . . . . . . . . . . . 15
Chapter 4 . . . . . . . . . . . . . . 21
Chapter 5 . . . . . . . . . . . . . . 27
Chapter 6 . . . . . . . . . . . . . . 35
Chapter 7 . . . . . . . . . . . . . . 43
Chapter 8 . . . . . . . . . . . . . . 51
Chapter 9 . . . . . . . . . . . . . . 58
Chapter 10 . . . . . . . . . . . . . 67
Chapter 11 . . . . . . . . . . . . . 76
Chapter 12 . . . . . . . . . . . . . 83
Chapter 13 . . . . . . . . . . . . . 89
Chapter 14 . . . . . . . . . . . . . 97
Chapter 15 . . . . . . . . . . . . . 105
Chapter 16 . . . . . . . . . . . . . 113
Chapter 17 . . . . . . . . . . . . . 120
Chapter 18 . . . . . . . . . . . . . 127

| | |
|---|---|
| Chapter 19 . . . . . . . . . . . | 133 |
| Chapter 20 . . . . . . . . . . . | 142 |
| Chapter 21 . . . . . . . . . . . | 149 |
| Chapter 22 . . . . . . . . . . . | 157 |
| Chapter 23 . . . . . . . . . . . | 165 |
| Chapter 24 . . . . . . . . . . . | 172 |
| Chapter 25 . . . . . . . . . . . | 179 |
| Chapter 26 . . . . . . . . . . . | 187 |
| Chapter 27 . . . . . . . . . . . | 193 |
| Chapter 28 . . . . . . . . . . . | 199 |
| Chapter 29 . . . . . . . . . . . | 205 |
| Chapter 30 . . . . . . . . . . . | 211 |
| Chapter 31 . . . . . . . . . . . | 219 |
| Chapter 32 . . . . . . . . . . . | 227 |
| Chapter 33 . . . . . . . . . . . | 234 |
| Chapter 34 . . . . . . . . . . . | 242 |
| Chapter 35 . . . . . . . . . . . | 249 |
| Chapter 36 . . . . . . . . . . . | 255 |
| Chapter 37 . . . . . . . . . . . | 262 |
| Chapter 38 . . . . . . . . . . . | 268 |
| Epilogue . . . . . . . . . . . | 275 |

# Chapter 1

*Thornsby, Yorkshire*
*Spring 1854*

Was there anything more beautiful than balanced scales? Those brass arms polished to a brilliant shine and hanging equal distance from the table, each side resting in perfect harmony. All the adding and subtracting as one worked to achieve that all-important goal. Then there it was. Perfection. It was utterly satisfying.

Lifting his hand, Gregory Vaughn held the spatula steady, his finger poised to tap the edge and sprinkle it upon the waiting pile of powdered licorice root. Just a touch more, and he would have it—

"There you are!" bellowed Rodney as he shoved the workshop door open.

Gregory jolted, the spatula slipping from his hand and knocking against the scales, which set the powder flying into a swirling cloud that coated him and the table in a layer of beige dust. Rodney's brows rose, his eyes widening as he took in the film covering the workspace and his friend, and silence hung between them as palpable as the remnant powder floating in the air.

Rodney sniffed and said, "At least it is licorice root."

Leveling a hard look at his friend, Gregory didn't wish to admit that had been his first thought as well; there were a vast many more foul-smelling and expensive ingredients that could've been decorating the room now.

"And this seems a perfect time for you to come on a picnic with me and the children," added Rodney with a bright smile and an impish gleam in his eye.

"Now that my workshop is a mess?" asked Gregory in a monotone.

"Now that your task is complete."

Brows twisting together, Gregory considered the mess and then turned that incredulous expression toward his friend.

"Complete in a sense. As in needs to be restarted," said Rodney, stuffing his hands into his pockets. "Come now, the girls are eager to enjoy the beautiful weather. What else are apprentices for but to clean messes your friend unwittingly makes? You cannot rot away in this shop forever."

Before he finished speaking, a new whirlwind descended upon the workshop in the form of a small girl, her ringlets bouncing and skirts swaying as she rushed through the door.

"Mr. Gregory, come play!" cried Eva, throwing herself at him and wrapping her arms around his waist.

"I don't think Mr. Gregory likes playing," said Faith, hovering in the doorway as though uncertain whether she was welcome.

"He likes playing well enough," said Rodney, setting a hand on his daughter's shoulder to draw her into the workshop. "He simply feels the world will fall apart at the seams if he is not managing his business all on his own. Never mind that it does one no good to have assistants if you do not allow them to assist."

Faith frowned. "But he never smiles."

Gregory choked back a laugh, but Rodney didn't bother to smother his.

"Oh, he does, poppet. Just very carefully. If he does it too quickly, his face will crack," he said in a conspiratorial whisper. With arched brows, Rodney glanced at his friend before returning his attention to his daughters. "Perhaps we might convince him to come with us?"

Eva's gaze brightened, and she grabbed Gregory's hand, pulling him toward the door. "Come picnic with us."

Though Faith remained tucked beside her father, her expression took on a pleading quality, those large brown eyes (which were a mirror of Rodney's) begging with as much force as her younger sister's tugging. Gregory opened his mouth to give the usual excuses. He had work to be done, after all. Yet her eyes—so solemn and wide—held him fast.

With a sigh that was more for show than sincerity, he allowed a rueful smile to tug at the corner of his mouth. "I suppose Mr. Sparks can manage everything for an hour or two."

Eva squealed in delight and darted back the way she'd come, her curls bouncing with each step, and Faith's expression softened, as though Gregory's agreement had settled some upset inside her. But then, possessing a quiet disposition was an anomaly amongst the Stuart family, and an ally was always welcome when suffering through their exuberance.

"I have a mount ready for you," Rodney said, nodding toward the door. "I knew you would surrender eventually."

Gregory lifted a brow. "Am I so easily swayed?"

"Only when gang pressed by two sweet little girls," said Rodney, giving Faith a squeeze of the shoulder as they turned to follow Eva into the corridor.

"Give me a moment," he said, brushing himself off and depositing his apron on the table beside the now dingy scales. Stepping out of his private workshop, Gregory crossed to the room opposite to find his assistant and apprentices working through their tasks for the day; though the young men managed well enough in the confined space, he couldn't help but think (yet again) that they would fare better in a larger one.

Perhaps it was time to allow one of them to share his private workshop. Now that he had graduated from apprentice to assistant, Mr. Sparks deserved a proper place in which to work apart from the others. But the room was perfectly appointed, as it also served as a study in which to conduct his business.

But that was a thought for another day.

Explaining the mess and what needed to be done, he gave them their marching orders and followed the Stuarts into the apothecary shop. Though both the workshops and storefront were similarly designed, with shelving covering every vertical surface (every inch of which was filled with neatly labeled jars, vials, and boxes), there was an order to this public space that the others lacked. But then, customers needed to navigate the room without overturning the delicate containers.

Nodding to Mr. Guy, who was managing the counter at present, Gregory moved to the front door and stepped into the beautiful Yorkshire afternoon. And he couldn't help looking back at his shop.

The windows gleamed without a smudge, allowing the passersby to marvel at the pyramidal stack of amber bottles with their pristine labels and the marble mortar and pestle that Gregory had adjusted no fewer than three times that morning. Hints of aniseed, lemon balm, lavender, and licorice root hung in the air, as fitting as the scent of flour and sugar coming from the bakery two doors down.

"Are you going to stand about gawking all day?" called Rodney as he helped Faith into the waiting carriage.

Like the mother hen she was, Daphne settled her younger sister whilst calling for Eva to sit properly, as the child was hanging precariously over the side of the carriage, determined to examine the wheels beneath. In short order, the trio was settled (as much as they could be with the youngest still doing her utmost to cast herself from the carriage in her exuberance), and

Rodney swung up into his saddle as Gregory followed suit. Giving a nod to the groom, his friend set off down the street.

Shopfronts and cottages lined either side of the road, their window boxes overflowing with the early spring blossoms. Children darted between the buildings, their laughter ringing through the clear air, whilst shopkeepers lingered in doorways, exchanging news in low tones. Birdsong carried on the warm breeze as the church bell marked the half-hour, its deep toll echoing off the slate rooftops like a heartbeat.

Miss Higgins strolled down the lane, coming toward them, and Gregory tipped his hat. Just as he was about to offer a word of greeting, the lady's brows rose high on her forehead. Eyes darting away from him and fixing on the path ahead, she scurried past them without a backward glance, and Gregory frowned. Doubly so when Rodney cast him a glance from the corner of his eye.

"Another conquest, I see," said his friend. "If you aren't careful, every unmarried lady in the neighborhood will fall madly in love with you."

Gregory didn't answer: it was best to ignore the fellow when he was in a mocking mood.

Shifting in the saddle, Rodney glanced over his shoulder at the fleeing lady. "You look at them as though plotting their demise."

"I am usually thinking about dosages or ledgers," muttered Gregory.

Rodney grinned. "Exactly. Nothing romantic about laudanum ratios and sales tabulations."

"In my experience, profitable sales tabulations do wonders in attracting the fairer sex." And that was the trouble, wasn't it? The only ladies who didn't quiver and quake at the sight of his dour visage were those more interested in the size of his income.

"Perhaps if you let your hair grow out," said Rodney with feigned seriousness, glancing at his friend's close crop with an arched brow. "Longer hair is the fashion, and it might soften that stern visage."

Ignoring that jest disguised as a suggestion, Gregory forced his hand not to rub at the offending style, which was born more from necessity than preference. For all that ladies spend exorbitant amounts of time to get their locks to do what came naturally to his own, his curly mane made him look ridiculous, and soon the women of Thornsby would be laughing rather than fleeing.

No, it was better to keep his hair as short as short could be. Better to appear brooding than cherubic.

"You should try some cream on your face, Mr. Gregory," said Eva, resting her chin on her folded arms, which she propped up on the edge of the landau. The observation, stated so boldly and without explanation, caused all her companions to glance at her in varying states of confusion, and she gave them a gap-toothed grin.

"The maids use it to make their skin soft," she explained. "If you're afraid of your face cracking, you should try some cream first. Then you can smile more. Mrs. Todd says you're handsome when you smile."

Gregory stiffened in his saddle, forcing his gaze ahead. Rodney guffawed like the kind-hearted man he was, taking genuine pleasure in that discomfort and the old governess's secret tendre as only a true friend could. Even Daphne—whom Gregory had thought an ally just moments ago—covered her mouth to hide her grin.

"Faith, you are my favorite," he said with a sigh, and the girl, who had been watching the passing houses so keenly that she hadn't been listening, glanced over at him with a puzzled frown.

"Peace, Gregory," said Rodney—when he was able to speak. Drawing up beside his friend, he grinned. "Count yourself lucky. Marriage is a torture I wouldn't wish on my worst enemy. If not for my dear children, who came from that unlucky union, I would say it is the greatest regret of my life."

Despite the light tone and the tender smile he gave his girls, there was a heaviness to Rodney's tone that Gregory knew all too well; he had heard it many times in the past six years since the Stuart family settled in this quiet corner of Yorkshire. He counted himself lucky that he'd never met Mrs. Stuart; treating a lady with kindness was ingrained in his very soul, yet the thought of crossing paths with the harpy who had abandoned her husband and children tested Gregory's vast quantities of patience.

"Pay me no mind," said Rodney, glancing at his friend. "I see those cogs turning in your head, and you needn't fret. I cannot be unhappy on such a beautiful day, can I, girls?"

Turning to his daughters, he drew his horse closer, reaching to tug at Eva's curls. She squealed and pulled out of reach, throwing herself into her eldest sister's arms. Rodney laughed, the sound echoing through the air as he set his horse away from the carriage once more.

A crack sounded in the air, slicing through the quiet like the blast from a pistol, and Gregory's gelding jerked, his hooves dancing. Holding fast to the reins, he glanced toward the sound to see laundry strung up on a line beside the cottage, the petticoats bobbing and waving in the sudden gust that seized hold of them.

"Peace. It is just a bit of laundry snapping on the breeze," he murmured to his horse, but when another gust set the petticoats bouncing, the beast pranced backward.

A shriek sliced through the afternoon calm like a blade, and Gregory turned to see Rodney's mount rear, eyes wide with panic, forelegs striking at the air. The gentleman fought to hold the reins, but the horse had lost its senses. It surged sideways toward the carriage, and for a breathless instant, Gregory saw the collision coming. The groom fought his horses, keeping the pair steady—but the coach lurched when Rodney's mount lunged toward them, and the rider fought hard to keep the horse from striking the vehicle or his children.

The girls screamed, and Daphne held the others close whilst their father fought the horse as it reared again, shaking its mane as though desperate to be free of its rider and bridle. The driver shouted, but Gregory couldn't make out the words as he battled his own mount, who shied about, trying to avoid the others and the laundry, which kept waving at them. He held firm as his horse calmed, but his pulse quickened as his gaze locked on the madness unfolding just beyond reach.

And then Rodney was flung from the saddle.

Limbs flailing, he flew through the air, and Gregory watched as his friend struck the ground.

# Chapter 2

"Stay in the carriage, girls!" Gregory called back over his shoulder. A quick glance showed that the girls were merely frightened and that the servant had his team well in hand.

Jumping from his saddle, he tossed the reins to the groom and ran to Rodney—pausing only when the fellow's horse bucked, kicking out its legs at the intrusion. Breath caught in his lungs, Gregory watched with wide eyes as the beast stomped, his hooves narrowly missing his fallen rider before the animal took off at a gallop, racing down the lane.

"Rodney!" Gregory's knees hit the ground hard, but he barely felt it. Thankfully, there were no cobbles or stones along this stretch of road, leaving only the hard-packed earth. "Can you hear me?"

"Of course I can hear you," he muttered. "You're shouting like a madman."

"Do not move."

Gregory's vision tunneled, fixing on the task at hand, as he searched for injuries. His fingers trembled as they pressed along Rodney's scalp, down the curve of his neck, across his ribs. He couldn't stop seeing the way the fellow had fallen—

limbs loose, neck at the wrong angle, and the awful thud as his body struck the hard earth—and panic surged beneath the surface, cracking the veneer of calm he wore like armor.

This couldn't be happening.

There were few people in his life that Gregory Vaughn counted as friends, and he couldn't lose Rodney. Not like this. Not over a blasted petticoat flapping on the line.

Rodney groaned. "You do know I survived the fall."

Gregory ignored him. "You hit the ground hard."

"Yes, I was there. Everything still attached?"

"Apparently," replied Gregory, though he continued evaluating the damage.

Rodney flinched at a touch against his ribs, letting a sharp hiss through his teeth. "Tender. Not broken."

"You're not qualified to make that determination."

"I am not the one trembling."

"I am not trembling."

"Yes, you are."

Gregory stilled for a half second, jaw set. "If your ribs weren't bruised, I'd strike you."

"See? That's the Gregory Vaughn I know. Grave and slightly murderous."

Giving his friend a flat look, he resumed his examination, though more gently now. "You're fortunate the road was soft."

"I chose it intentionally. For your sake," said Rodney with a cocky grin.

With a sharp exhale through his nose, Gregory sat back on his heels, finally allowing himself a breath.

Rodney cracked one eye open. "If you're done poking me in the name of medicine, I'd like to sit up."

Bracing the fellow's back, Gregory helped ease him upright, and they sat in silence, Rodney hunched slightly forward, one arm cradled around his ribs. Then, with a glance toward the fluttering laundry still caught on the line, Rodney gave a faint, pained grin.

"It seems my mount is just as afraid of petticoats as you are."

Gregory huffed. "You are a lackwit."

"So I've been told."

Rising to his feet, Gregory offered a hand and helped Rodney up. Though his education lay more in medicine than surgery, a lifetime of assisting his father in doctoring had given him quite the experience—enough to know just how much damage could be done to a body without any outward indication. The fellow certainly was favoring his side, but as Gregory watched Rodney take a few cautious steps, he couldn't help but feel it was a good sign.

"You should ride with the girls," said Gregory, nodding toward the carriage. "We'll take you home and get you resting—"

"Don't be a spoilsport," said Rodney with a scoff. Turning a wide grin to his girls, he said, "We aren't going to allow a little accident to ruin our picnic. I am sore and bruised, but otherwise hearty and hale."

All three daughters watched their papa with watery gazes, the two younger girls clinging to Daphne. Limping over to them, Rodney caressed his eldest's cheek.

"All is well, darling," he whispered, and the young lady's chin trembled. Then, giving each a kiss in turn, Rodney teased and cajoled them into smiles once more. With a wink, he added, "Come now, we ought to enjoy the day while we can. We must give the boys a reason to be jealous when they arrive home from school on Saturday."

And despite his better judgment, Gregory found himself swept into the carriage as the group set off with his mount's reins tied to the back. A somber pall clung to them, yet like the magician he was, Rodney Stuart conjured a bit of laughter and levity, enlivening the party's spirits in quick order; a few jests and soon Eva was properly giddy once more, and between her and her papa, it was impossible to remain dour.

It took some time before Gregory could breathe easy again, and he found it difficult to think of anything else when his eyes insisted on scouring his friend for signs of hidden injury, but even he began to relax. And by the time they reached the grassy expanse chosen for their outing, all thought of the accident was erased from their minds.

The groom spread blankets beneath the shade of a sturdy oak, and soon hampers were emptied and treats passed around. Rodney reclined against the tree trunk, mindful of his tender ribs yet unconcerned when Eva cuddled into his side. He laughed softly at her animated chatter, brushing crumbs from her cheek with his thumb and smoothing her hair when the breeze tugged at her curls.

How quickly time had flown.

It seemed just a few months ago that Eva had toddled around this very patch of green in nappies. Then again, Daphne had grown in a blink from a gangly eleven-year-old into a proper young lady, ready to take her first steps into society. In fact, Faith was now the same age her elder sister had been when the Stuarts first arrived in Thornsby.

With book in hand, Faith straightened as she turned to the others, eager to read a passage aloud, and though Eva wasn't patient enough to sit through such things, Rodney kept her in hand and smiled as he listened. Faith's eyes brightened as she expounded on what she believed would happen next in the story, her expression glowing in a manner that only ever seemed to happen when her papa was around.

There, beneath the golden sunlight, sat an idyllic world. One that Gregory had been invited into but did not possess in his own right.

Shifting in his seat, he batted away the fleeting tickle of jealousy that tried to work its way into his heart—though that was not the proper word for it. He didn't begrudge his friend's good fortune, but it was difficult to see such happiness and not wish to possess a modicum of it himself.

Not that Gregory's life was empty or miserable. With parents who loved and respected one another, two younger siblings who boasted equally blissful unions, and seven nieces and nephews between them, Gregory Vaughn was a blessed man. He didn't want for anything.

And it wasn't as though marriage was a guarantee of happiness. Rodney's troubled history was proof enough of that.

Raising a hand to his head, Rodney rubbed at it, and though the fellow tried to hide a wince, Gregory couldn't help noticing that flash of pain. Chest tightening, he studied his friend. Rodney shifted again, his hand pressing against his ribs as a shadow of pain flitted across his face, though he tried to hide it—but there was no erasing the sheen of sweat gathering at his temples.

The earlier dread surged anew, coiling through Gregory's veins.

"We must return home. Now," he said quietly, barely controlling the strain in his voice.

Rodney glanced up sharply, his expression startled, though he quickly smoothed it away. "No need for dramatics. I'm a bit sore. That is all."

But Gregory shook his head, already rising, refusing to yield. "Please do as I bid."

Rodney met his gaze steadily, the silent exchange heavy with unspoken truths. Perhaps his friend understood after all, for his shoulders dropped slightly in acquiescence.

"Very well," he said softly, reaching out to squeeze Eva's hand reassuringly. "It seems Mr. Gregory insists our picnic is over."

Gregory's pulse raced as he hurried to gather their things, a sickening sense of helplessness gnawing at him. Likely, it was just a contusion. That was all. A few days of bed rest would set it to rights in a trice.

The laughter from mere moments earlier had faded, replaced by uncertain murmurs. Daphne's eyes followed Rodney's movements anxiously, Faith's book lay forgotten beside her, and Eva clung tightly to her father's hand, her cheerful chatter reduced to silence as Rodney's strained smile did little to mask his discomfort.

"Everything will be quite all right," Gregory murmured, forcing calm into his voice as he tucked a blanket around Eva's shoulders. He managed a reassuring nod to Daphne, though dread coiled tightly in his gut. He turned toward Rodney then, reaching down to help him stand.

"Slowly," said Gregory, masking the urgency beneath careful professionalism.

Rodney took his hand, his grip weaker than it should have been, and Gregory's heart clenched painfully as his palm registered the unmistakable chill of his friend's skin. Ice spread through his chest, settling deep into his bones as certainty gripped him. Something was terribly wrong.

# Chapter 3

At forty years of age, Gregory Vaughn had spent a lifetime learning. When raised in a family of physicians, surgeons, and apothecaries, the search for knowledge and understanding was highly prized—whether it was the years of studying at his parents' side as they plied their trade or the countless hours of rigorously searching through tomes and treatises on his own.

Though he had chosen to forgo a formal education in London, Gregory didn't feel his skill was lacking because he was a mere "Mr." and not a "Dr." The Vaughns had plenty of the latter.

Gregory knew how to mix and brew every common remedy by memory. He could identify and use every medicinal plant in England and many far beyond their borders, and if pressed, he thought himself quite the equal of any apothecary in the country. Perhaps not the best of his profession (for how did one measure such a thing?), but he had built his mother's small cottage shop into a thriving business through his talent and efforts.

Yet standing in the darkened corner of Rodney's bedchamber, Gregory wondered what good there was to be had in vast amounts of learning and experience when one could do nothing with it. His life's work granted him the knowledge of what was to come with no ability to forestall it, only illuminating the forthcoming horrors and ripping hope free of his grasp.

So much they could do—so many strides had been made in recent decades—yet all it had given them was the certainty that Rodney Stuart would not see the next dawn, and his doctor and apothecary could only watch as his strength ebbed.

Standing beside him, Edward watched his patient with a mask of calm concern, though Gregory sensed the sorrow simmering beneath the surface. A physician knew much about death and dying, yet Gregory didn't think his younger brother and father ever grew accustomed to the loss. The fellow looked upon his patient with a grave expression, and it wasn't difficult to guess that this young father's mind was on his own children, the heartache awaiting the little ones Rodney left behind, and the fickleness of life.

Rodney stared at the ceiling, his eyes fixing on the canopy draped overhead as night drew Gregory deeper into its embrace.

"This wasn't your doing," whispered Edward.

"I should've fetched him home immediately—"

"My fate was sealed the minute the horse tossed me," interrupted Rodney in a monotone as he turned his bleak gaze to the pair. When Gregory's brows rose, he added with a wan smile, "The room is small, and you two weren't whispering quietly enough."

Rodney's lips trembled, and he drew in a deep breath. "I am grateful we didn't return home. I was afforded a lovely afternoon with my daughters, rather than lying abed as I await the inevitable."

There was a hint of a question in his tone as though hoping one of them would rush forward with promises that something might be done, but there was nothing. Internal bleeding was a death sentence, and the poultices and medicines prescribed were effective in only the most minor of cases, and even those required a heaping dose of the miraculous. A ruptured spleen was anything but minor.

A knock at the door brought with it a flood of children, and though instinct pushed Gregory to calm the chaos they brought in their wake, good sense kept him silent. They couldn't do any more damage, and the smile that they brought to their father's face was well worth the intrusion.

Stepping forward, Edward helped his patient shift as the doctor placed another pillow beneath his head; Rodney's belly was too distended for him to sit up properly, but the fellow tucked one arm behind his head as though he were lounging by choice rather than necessity.

Eva squeezed close to her father on one side, and with his free hand, he tugged at Eva's curls whilst Wesley occupied the other side of the bed. The younger pair snuggled close, drawing winces from their father, but Rodney hid the pain away, welcoming the affection. The older four took up places around their father with Daphne clinging to the bedpost at the foot of the bed, her posture and expression strained as she fought to keep her composure. Clark stood beside her, his hands tucked behind his back like the young man he was becoming, whilst Faith and Jackson stood sentinel on either side.

"Faith." Though his breaths were shallow, Rodney kept his tone light and hid the pain that strained his expression as he eyed her with mock suspicion and examined the crumbs on her front. "Did you sneak one of the ginger biscuits from the kitchen?"

She blinked, eyes wide. "No, Papa."

"Then someone else has, and they placed the evidence of it upon your person," he said with a wry smile. "It must be that rascally groom. I have always suspected him of malintent, and I shall have to question him in the dungeon."

Eva giggled. "We do not have a dungeon."

"I beg your pardon," Rodney said, drawing himself up an inch before wincing and sinking back down again. "We most certainly have a dungeon. It is where we keep the vilest of villains. And if he doesn't confess, I shall place him in the stocks at dawn."

Wrinkling his nose, Wesley shook his head. "You hate waking early. You aren't going to rise at dawn."

Rodney gaped as though that were the greatest affront to his dignity. "I am known for my ferocity in the early morning. A goose once blackened my honor, and I had no choice but to call him out. Pistols at dawn, it was."

Eva's laughter doubled. "That didn't happen!"

"It did," he said gravely. "The feathered villain was a vicious creature. Never trusted geese since."

Wesley chuckled from his place beside his father, though when the lad shifted the pillows, Rodney's breath caught. Gregory made as though to move, but his friend lifted his fingers covertly, halting him. His arm trembled, but Rodney managed to shift it around his son's shoulders, holding him close despite the clear pain it sent pulsing through his abdomen.

"It is serious, isn't it?" whispered Clark, his head held high. Though Gregory couldn't say when the lad had come over, he stood there with a stony expression, his eyes fixed on the bed and his younger siblings. Though Clark attempted to keep the emotion from his voice, there was a catch that belied the act. "Father wouldn't have fetched us home from school if it weren't."

Gregory couldn't speak and settled a hand around the lad's shoulder as Rodney teased and twitted the others, brightening the somber feel of the sickroom. But the gentleman's arms trembled, his strength failing him as he struggled to maintain the facade, and Edward stepped forward, reaching for Rodney's hand to test his pulse, likely searching for something to do.

Rodney's chest rose and fell in panting breaths, his smile never faltering as he looked at his children. "I think it is time for bed, my little imps."

Eva and Wesley made their feelings known, though Daphne moved from her place at the foot of the bed to herd them and the others away. Rodney stopped each, giving them kisses on their cheeks and those tender affections that accompanied brief partings, but when Daphne moved to lead them away, he snatched her hand, drawing her attention back to him.

"Be brave," he mouthed with eyes so full of his heart that Gregory's vision began to blur. And with more strength than a child with only seventeen years to her credit ought to possess, she nodded and bent down to place a kiss on her father's cheek with only a slight tremble of her chin to betray the sorrow weighing her down.

"Off to bed," called Daphne with a forced smile as she followed after the others, sending them scurrying down the corridor.

With the younger children gone, Clark stepped forward, and with all the dignity his fifteen-year-old heart could muster, he bowed to his father—but Rodney seized the lad and pulled him down. Though Rodney hardly had the strength to make a leaf flutter, Clark allowed the tug to force him into his father's arms.

"I am proud of you, my boy," he whispered, and Gregory shifted in place, wishing he weren't intruding upon that private moment as the lad struggled to control his grief. Straightening, Clark nodded as he wiped covertly at his cheeks before striding out after his siblings.

When the door was shut once more, Rodney turned his gaze to Edward. "Dr. Vaughn, may I have a moment alone with your brother?"

Giving the gentleman a bow, Edward turned to the door, but stopped when his patient added, "And would you instruct the servants to keep the children from returning? I do not wish for them to see me as I decline. They do not need that memory haunting them."

Edward nodded and left, leaving the two alone.

His arm shook as he tried to move, so Rodney abandoned the attempt and glanced from his friend to the chair beside the bed. But Gregory didn't move. Every instinct urged him to retreat and join the children in the nursery, where the laughter still lingered and the air was lighter. Where the shadows were less cruel. But the thought of leaving Rodney—of walking away from the drawn face and trembling hand—was worse. The ache of it settled deep in his chest, sharp and heavy. To stay was agony. But to go? He could not bear it.

Gregory settled into the seat beside the bed, his shoulders sagging as he studied his friend. Rodney was the personification of light and laughter, and though his eyes still sparkled even in this terrible moment, his skin was clammy. The strain tugged at the corners of his mouth, but when Gregory reached for the bottle of laudanum, Rodney waved him away.

"Not yet. I feel myself drifting, but I need to speak to you while I am still lucid," he murmured, his brows pinching together. His eyes drifted to the canopy above him. "I don't know whether to be grateful or horrified that my end is so inevitable. Definitive. To have the time for final farewells is a blessing, but knowing what awaits is terrifying."

Rodney paused, halting as he slowly spoke the words that no one had been willing to say. "I am dying."

# Chapter 4

For all that Gregory had known that to be true, the bald statement felt like a knife in his chest.

"I...I am grateful for your friendship, Rodney. You have been so good to me."

A slight smile twitched at his friend's lips as his gaze swung to him. "If I hadn't known I was dying before, I would now. If you are growing sentimental and maudlin, I must be at death's door."

Gregory huffed, the instinct to turn his eyes to the heavens seizing hold of him. "It is like you to jest about this."

A twitch of his brows was the only sign of strain in the fellow's face, though Gregory suspected he clung to consciousness by the barest tips of his fingers.

"I would rather jest than cry," whispered Rodney, the corner of his lips trembling as his eyes met his friend's gaze. "We always believe there will be more time. Life can be snatched away in a moment, yet we never expect it will be *our* years that are cut short. And the thought that I will not be there to see my children..."

Rodney's voice caught as he whispered, "They are so very young."

Gregory's head lowered as pressure built in his chest, pressing against his heart until it ached. For all that his own pain pulsed through him, it was the thought of those little ones that felt like a leaden weight on his ribs.

"I named you their guardian in my will," said Rodney.

Eyes wide, Gregory's head snapped up, his brows climbing as he stared at his friend's ashen face. There wasn't even a hint of teasing in his expression. Rodney watched him with pleading eyes as his chest shuddered with his panting breaths.

"I settled everything long ago," added Rodney, a thread of iron weaving through his tone, though his gaze struggled to focus on the figure at his bedside. "The accounts, the house. Everything has been seen to, and they will be provided for handsomely. But they need a protector. A guide—"

Rodney's voice cracked, and he winced as his chest shuddered. Gregory reached for the tincture once more, but his friend waved him off.

"Please, not yet, Gregory. I need to hear you say you will do it," he said, reaching for Gregory's hand and holding fast to it. "Not because my will dictates it but because you willingly take them on. There is no one else I trust to watch over them. Please. I need to know they shan't be alone..."

Gregory wanted to nod and give him the answer he longed to hear, but the thought of such a responsibility held his tongue captive. To oversee their finances and the estate was one thing—something he would gladly do—but guardianship?

Rodney's eyes unfocused, sliding away as the haze drew over his mind once more. Gregory held his fingers to the fellow's pulse, though it was a struggle to feel the heartbeat, as it was as quick as a hummingbird's wing. Despite knowing that such signs were inevitable, his own heart seized, sending out waves of pain with each wretched beat.

"Will you?" asked Rodney, the strength entering his gaze once more as he focused on his friend.

"I am no father. How can I possibly raise your children?"

The corner of his lips twitched ever so slightly into a smile. "You will make a muck of it—as all parents do—but you will sort it out. If nothing else, you need Stuarts in your life to pull you from that solitary rut you enjoy far too much. Without us, you are bound to grow so dour that even the maid's lotion shan't be able to save your face."

Rodney smiled at the jest, but Gregory couldn't. That conversation seemed like some distant past, far removed from this moment.

"You will not do the job perfectly," added Rodney, as pain etched itself into the edges of his eyes and mouth, "but I know you will take the responsibility seriously. That is all any parent can do. And I know you will protect them."

"You don't believe—"

"I know my wife well," interrupted Rodney in a grim tone. Though his hold weakened, there was a strength that burned through the pain and fog, burrowing into Gregory as the man pleaded. "The moment she hears I am gone, she will reappear and do whatever she can to get control over the children once more. I have left a record of all that she has done, detailing the whole of her sins, as she could very well take the matter all the way to the courts."

"They will not go against a father's will," said Gregory with a frown.

But Rodney matched the expression. "There is precedence, and the laws are changing. She is crafty and excels at twisting people about, and I have no doubt she can bend the courts to her will if she puts her mind to it. Without me there to protect them, I fear for their future. But I know you will not be taken in by her wiles, and you will fight for my children to your last breath. I need you. Please. I have no one else I can entrust them to."

"I will do my best," whispered Gregory. There was no other answer to give, though his honor wove through every syllable, imbuing them with the sort of oath that had been made of old, binding one to the other with an irrevocable bond.

Rodney's hold slackened, his gaze growing unfocused, though a smile graced his lips. "I know you will. That is my only consolation."

Then there was stillness. The labored breaths, quiet and unsteady, were the only sign that the gentleman still lived. The candles burned low, their flames flickering each time the wind pushed against the windowpane, and Gregory sat there, hand wrapped gently around Rodney's whilst he listened to the soft, uneven rhythm of his breathing.

Eventually, Edward returned, taking his place on the other side of the bed for their silent vigil. The patient was beyond a physician's aid now, but Gregory suspected his brother remained more for his sake than Rodney's.

Minutes ticked by in fitful stretches. At times, Rodney roused, blinking blearily as though unable to recognize his bedchamber and the man seated beside him. Then a glint of recognition drew with it a few halting words about the children and happier days, his voice worn and thin but still threaded with warmth and hints of laughter, as though wishing to erase the truth of what was happening.

Gregory clung to those conversations, however fleeting. They were a lifeline. Each time silence reclaimed the room, it did so a little sooner, and a little longer.

And then Rodney slipped beyond the laudanum's tender touch, bringing with it a delirium and agony that burned into Gregory's memory. Every spasm. Every gasp. Every pleading look when snatched in the grip of suffering that was too great for him to speak. Those images would live in the corners of his mind for the rest of his days.

And when the last breath came—quiet, almost imperceptible—there was no grand final word, no dramatic sign. Just a hush so complete that the world outside quieted. Gregory didn't need Edward's confirmation that the pulse was now gone, for he could see the truth of it in his friend's visage.

The soul that had once resided there was gone.

It was some time before Gregory thought to move. Watching Edward as he set about the task of cleaning up, his thoughts couldn't drift past the fact that Rodney was gone. No amount of certainty had prepared him for it.

Rising to his feet, he murmured, "I need to see the children."

Edward's brows twisted as he studied his brother, and without a word, he came over and drew Gregory into an embrace. Vision blurring, he squeezed Edward tight, holding fast to him as though that might alter what had happened. And when they parted, his brother's eyes held all the tender concern and support one yearned for and shied away from all at the same time: the sympathy only made the loss all the more real.

Somehow Gregory found himself wandering through the corridors, uncertain what to say or do for the children. *His* children. Good gracious. With a hand outstretched, he leaned against the wall as his strength leached from him.

Forcing his feet forward, he climbed up to the nursery but stopped when he spied figures in the library. Though only a single candle flickered on the mantlepiece, the growing light of dawn on the horizon allowed him to see Daphne and Clark seated on the sofa, their rigid postures holding them like statues perched on the edge.

Neither said a word when they saw Gregory standing there, but they watched him with questioning eyes. What could he say? Though he knew the words, they would not come to his lips, and Gregory stood there, mute and unmoving. But that was answer enough.

Daphne let out a sharp sob, her hands flying to her mouth as that jagged breath ripped from her. All it took was an outstretched hand in invitation, and she threw herself into Gregory's arms, burrowing into his hold as she shook with tears.

Stiff and straight, Clark tucked his hands behind him. His chin trembled, but the lad tried so hard to be strong; though this would serve him well in days to come, he was still a lad of fifteen, and he came when bidden to his guardian's side. Once within reaching distance, Gregory tugged the lad into his embrace as well, engulfing the pair as their tears wetted his shirt. And his own joined with theirs, the little drops slipping free of his grasp as he considered the loss they all faced and the dark days ahead.

The promise he'd given rang through him, pulsing with each rapid beat of his heart. He would be as good as any father. Protect them as if they were his very own. No matter what was to come, Gregory would give his all for Rodney's little ones.

"I—" Daphne struggled for words, her breath shuddering as she forced them out. "I should tell the others."

"No," he replied, holding fast to the pair. "Let them sleep. Morning will come soon enough."

# Chapter 5

*Brackenfell, Yorkshire*
*One Month Later*

Silence wasn't a wretched thing. Not in the slightest. Quiet moments provided the soul an opportunity to settle and the heart to breathe. They were the essence of peace. A fertile world in which one's mind could wander, free to contemplate life's many mysteries. Silence was essential.

And though some disdained it, fleeing the quiet like a fox before the hounds, Theresa Stuart was one of the blessed who embraced both the chattering cacophony found amongst people and the peace that solitude afforded. One needn't choose one or the other, though far too many believed it to be so.

Granted, there was a time when Tessa had believed that suffering one's own company was the worst sort of punishment, but she'd come to appreciate the beauty of quiet contemplation. The pleasure to be found in the vast reaches of one's thoughts. When one was constantly occupied with others, it was impossible to truly know oneself, and that was a relationship one ought to nurture.

That said, there was a vast difference between quietude's gentle touch and the oppressive weight that choked this carriage as it swayed with every dip and bump of the dirt-packed lane.

Outside, sunlight flickered through the trees in golden patches as swallows dipped and darted across the open sky, and the fields that stretched out beyond the hedgerows shimmered with life as the breezes caressed the tall grasses and wildflowers. The window framed a world alive with motion, yet within the coach, everything remained thick and unmoving, cloaked in a smothering silence.

The gentleman hadn't spoken a single word since the journey began. Not a pleasantry, not an observation, not even a grunt of acknowledgment. Just that solemn, unreadable presence seated opposite her, arms folded and gaze fixed somewhere beyond the window, as though the scenery might rescue him from the inconvenience of her company.

Tessa might've been offended had not the fellow treated the others in the very same manner, ignoring everything and everyone. She hadn't minded it in the slightest when there were other passengers inside, but now they had alighted, leaving her and this stranger alone for the last leg of the journey, and his taciturnity was unbearable.

When one boarded a public coach, there was always the fear of the unknown. Would one's companions be delightful or disgusting? Entertaining or irritating? Gracious or demanding? Far too many cared more about their comfort, doing as they pleased regardless of how it might inconvenience the other passengers, snatching up more space than was due to them—though it did little to improve their comfort and did much to impose upon another's.

For all that the gentleman was large (as was evidenced by the breadth of his shoulders), he did not fling his legs outward as so many did, treating their limbs like Napoleon's forces, slowly marching into enemy territory to conquer and secure as much ground as possible. Tessa knew she ought to be grateful, but instead, she found herself wishing the portly gentleman, who had alighted a mere quarter of an hour ago, would return; he may have smelled like the kippers he'd eaten for breakfast and had a tendency to squash Tessa into the corner, but at least he had been a jovial sort.

Or frankly, it might be far more pleasant up with the rooftop passengers. Even if it meant an uncomfortable seat, those fellows had seemed a chatty lot during the last stop.

Shifting in her seat, Tessa resisted the urge to sigh. How was it that two people could share such a small space and still feel separated by miles? It might have been easier if he'd been unpleasant. A boor, at least, could be dismissed. But this brooding pillar of silence was infuriatingly inscrutable. And worse, he'd left her alone with her thoughts, which were far too numerous and loud at present for her liking.

Tessa's fingers curled tightly around one another, twisting and untwisting until the joints ached from the strain. She stared at the countryside streaming past the carriage window without truly seeing it, her gaze fixed somewhere beyond the gently rolling fields and hedgerows. Her pulse fluttered like a trapped bird in her throat, rapid and fragile, as the phantoms of the past whispered in her ears.

How many hours had she spent dreaming of this moment? How many years of waiting?

Those dear little faces filled her thoughts as Tessa tried to imagine how her children had altered in the past six years. One moment, she saw them as they had been—those rosy little cheeks, the tiny fingers wrapped tight around her hand, their laughter ringing in her ears. The next, that vision slipped from her grasp, replaced by stilted conversation and wary glances, as though she were a stranger encroaching on the life that had continued without her.

Tessa wanted to believe they would welcome her back. She needed to. But doubt clung to her, persistent and gnawing, whispering that too much time had passed for things to be made whole again.

Worse still was the quiet thrill buried beneath that silent unease. It slipped past her defenses and settled in her heart with a giddy little flutter. Rodney was gone. That part of her life was finished, shut like the cover of a book she had read too many times and never liked.

And yet, even as her shoulders relaxed, something sour twisted in her stomach. It was wrong to be glad. But what else ought she to feel? Grief? Sorrow? Her husband had earned none of that. Tessa's throat tightened. Thoughts of the past and what was to come twisted inside her like a knot, pulling tight around her chest until she couldn't breathe.

Enough.

Straightening, Tessa forced her gaze back to the window and tried to let the steady rhythm of the wheels remind her that time only moved forward. But thoughts of what awaited in Thornsby pestered and prodded, picking at the thin veneer of calm she had gathered close.

Quiet contemplation was a blessing, to be certain, but Tessa needed a distraction.

"What lovely weather we are having," she blurted. Of all the subjects to broach, it was the most obvious beginning, especially as it was an extraordinarily beautiful afternoon.

The gentleman's gaze turned to her, and Tessa forced herself not to shrink beneath his regard. Dark and watchful, his eyes scrutinized her with a quiet intensity that the Tessa of old might've found far too terrifying to ignore.

"Travelling in poor conditions can be so very taxing," she added. "Even if one is bundled up in wool and fur, it is nigh on impossible to remain warm. Especially in one's feet. So, I am very pleased that it is so nice today. I haven't required the extra shawl I packed in my portmanteau."

Nothing about the gentleman altered in the slightest as Tessa rambled on about the lovely countryside and the fresh air and all the useless nothings that one discussed when there was nothing of value to say. The fellow's expression grew no grimmer, nor did he ignore her by turning his gaze away; he simply watched her as she spoke.

There was something about the fellow that suggested he rarely spoke unless he had something worth saying, and she wasn't sure whether to be flattered or insulted that she hadn't yet warranted a single syllable.

Drawing in a sharp breath, Tessa studied the fellow. "Do you intend to let me babble on and on about the weather *ad infinitum*? Or am I to be graced with your brilliant insights into the state of the roads?"

Silence followed that. She felt the shift in the air that made this moment as vastly different from the earlier quiet as a funeral dirge was to a rousing reel. Nothing changed in his expression, but there was the faintest hint of amusement that brightened his gaze.

"Is this intended to be a conversation?" he asked. "You seemed quite content with monologuing."

Wrinkling her nose, Tessa winced. "Yes, I can be a bit of a babbler if not interrupted. I apologize if I am jabbering too much."

The gentleman turned his gaze to the window. "Nonsense. Some of the dearest people I know are babblers, and I'm rather fond of it."

"Then I am not intruding on your deep, morose contemplations?" she asked, lacing a laugh into her tone.

Silence followed yet again, and the gentleman considered the passing landscape whilst she studied his profile. It was difficult to discern much about the fellow in the best of circumstances, let alone with such an obstructed view, yet there was a weight to his presence. A sense about him. As intangible as air, yet just as real.

"Morose?" he asked, the faintest twitch of his lips betraying the solemnity of his tone. "My closest friend often tells me I look grim."

"And he is your closest friend?"

Again, the slightest twitch of his lips was the only sign of emotion from Sir Stoneface. "Isn't it the mark of a good friend that they tease and twit when needed?"

Tessa broke into a grin. "Too true. Then he must be a very good friend, indeed."

A shift in the air signaled a warning as the heavy weight settled back in place, and she sifted through her words to identify the source of that change. Though it was impossible to say what it was precisely, she felt something dark and sharp beneath the subject. Yet he had proven himself amenable to teasing, so Tessa quickly scoured for something with which to lure him back into the light.

Now that she had gotten him talking, she refused to slip back into silence.

Yet what could she ask? In such circumstances, inquiring about his destination was foremost on the list—as was the nature of the business that had drawn him from home—but that would only inspire him to ask it in return, and Tessa couldn't bear to broach the subject of her children. Even to a stranger.

"Are you an avid reader?" she asked, nodding toward the book that Sir Stoneface had abandoned on the seat beside him.

The gentleman's hand darted over, snatching it up and tucking it out of sight. "Isn't everyone?"

"No, in fact," replied Tessa, her eyes narrowing as she studied his expression. Nothing had altered there. No hint of movement to betray his feelings. Yet there was the slightest touch of pink to his cheeks, which, paired with the frantic movement, made her reconsider him. "I know many who cannot be bothered."

Sir Stoneface didn't react, and Tessa wondered if she dared prod him further. Perhaps she might've abandoned the subject if not for the fact that she couldn't bear to return to the silence.

"And what were you reading, sir?" she asked with a challenging raise of her brow.

"Nothing of importance."

"As was clear from your determination to hide it from sight like a schoolboy caught in some mischief by his headmaster. Entirely unimportant. Hardly worth noting." Threading her tone with all the innocence such a ridiculous statement deserved, Tessa folded her hands primly in her lap as the gentleman turned a gimlet eye on her.

"It is a novel. That is all," he said.

"An *unimportant* novel," she corrected. "And we needn't discuss it any further, as it is so unimportant that it hardly warrants a second thought. Yet just important enough to be tucked out of sight at the first notice."

Sir Stoneface sighed. A genuine sigh. Though so quiet that she might've missed it had she not been paying such close attention, it was unmistakable. As was the hint of humor in the sound.

"If you must know, I am reading..." His jaw tensed, his eyes fixed on the window. "*A Lady's Honor.*"

Tessa's brows jerked upward. "By Helen Gardiner?"

A quiet hum was the only reply he gave.

And heaven help her, Tessa tried to keep hold of her emotions. She truly did. Speaking to Sir Stoneface was difficult enough, and risking what little progress she had made was a dangerous game, especially when there were still hours of travel before them. Yet a spark of a laugh escaped her control, bursting out of her.

Tessa tensed and watched with wide eyes as Sir Stoneface turned a grim expression to her again. Those commanding eyes were half-masted, watching her in a manner that dared her to laugh again. Which only made it all the more diverting.

"I apologize, sir. It is not amusing in the slightest. One's reading preferences are one's own..." But try as she might, Tessa couldn't help another chuckle. Especially when the gentleman offered another of the slightest sighs ever known to man.

"Yes, I realize the ridiculousness of it," he murmured. "What gentleman reads novels with love stories?"

"Now, now, my good sir," said Tessa with an impish grin. "You make it sound as though it is grand literature with a dash of romance. Gardiner's works are sweeping romance stories, the likes of which are guaranteed to make ladies swoon with delight."

Sir Stoneface gave a silent harumph at that, turning his gaze to the passing landscape once more, and Tessa's thoughts whirled with what to say that might draw the gentleman from his window.

"You needn't feel embarrassed. I understand why you feel a bit sheepish, but there is no reason to, in my eyes." Then, with a prim tone, she added, "I will have you know that I admire your choice. Not only do I adore Helen Gardiner's work, but I think it is brilliant for you to indulge in pastimes, regardless of others' opinions. I do hate it when I am judged for my own."

Sir Stoneface's eyes swung back to her, the challenge rife in his gaze, though he said not a word.

"I am a painter," she said.

"There is nothing odd about that."

Tessa nodded. "But my preferred subject is executions. Anne Boleyn, Charles I, Thomas More, the Cato Street Conspirators, I have captured them all in their gruesome glory. I must have a dozen different paintings of Guy Fawkes and William Wallace, as I cannot decide if I prefer to capture the drawing or the quartering."

Silence fell once more as Sir Stoneface stared at her, and Tessa wondered if she had stepped too far into impropriety by making such a dark jest. But with a low hum, the gentleman turned his attention back to the window.

"There is no need to mock me, madam," he said.

"I am not," she said, leaning forward. "I—"

The coach lurched sharply, the wheels dipping into unseen ruts with a jarring thud that rattled through the frame. Wood groaned beneath the strain, the whole conveyance rocked as though it might tip altogether, and Tessa had no time to brace herself as the motion pitched her forward.

# Chapter 6

The gentleman lunged forward, his hands moving to keep Tessa in her seat and restore her balance. His fingers wrapped around her arm, halting her descent with ease, his other hand braced against the wall for support. For a moment, they hovered in that suspended stillness, the closeness unexpected and unsettling, before he released her with quiet precision and sat back without a word.

"I never would've guessed that being crushed into a carriage would be a blessing in disguise," she said with a self-deprecating laugh. "But when one is wedged between the wall and another passenger, such jostling is hardly noticeable."

But Sir Stoneface returned to his quiet contemplation, leaving Tessa growling at herself for her previous misstep. Not every jest hits the mark, and there was nothing to be done but offer a bit of honesty to balance the scales.

"I meant what I said. You needn't be embarrassed," she said, brushing off her skirts and setting them to rights once more. "All jests aside, I am well-acquainted with having interests that do not align with expectations, and I learned long ago to give others' opinions no weight."

Wrinkling her nose, Tessa considered that. "Or rather, I attempt to do so. If I were to be entirely honest with you, I am not always successful."

"Is this a situation of 'do as I say, not as I do'?" he murmured, his eyes remaining fixed on the window.

Humming to herself, Tessa realized he wasn't going to believe she was in earnest unless she confessed the whole of her sins. Though it mattered little whether or not he approved, she didn't wish to subject herself to the condescension that usually followed.

"If you must know, I happen to adore ledgers, investments, and anything else to do with finance," she said, lifting her chin.

Brows lowering, Sir Stoneface turned his attention to her.

Holding up her hands, Tessa hurried to add, "As a young lady, I never thought myself particularly interested in sums, but through a series of decisions and happenstances that are too numerous to discuss at present, I discovered I have a head for business and used that to build a bazaar in Leeds."

Bracing herself, Tessa wondered what the fellow would say to that. Heaven knew she had heard it all. In general, people greeted that information with polite but dismissive smiles as they immediately categorized her business as a mere hobby. An eccentric manner in which to pass her time. And of course, there were those who were shocked, horrified, or disbelieving.

"Is that so?" he asked.

Tessa's breath stilled, her heart pleading with all its might that he wouldn't prove to be amongst the worst set: those who belittled and condescended. For some bizarre reason that she could not comprehend, those people viewed her mighty efforts as meaningless and insubstantial, yet they deemed it a good use of their time to ensure that she understood just how meaningless and insubstantial she was. Ignoring her wasn't enough.

"I do not know many women who boast professions of any sort, let alone finance. How did you settle on that business?"

Brows rising, Tessa considered that question and the tone with which it was asked. Sir Stoneface seemed genuinely interested in her answer, which made her reconsider it. Speaking of money was gauche at the best of times, yet it was impossible to reply to his query without addressing that all-powerful resource.

"I found myself without an income, and in desperation, I sold some of my things to a stall in a local bazaar," she said, forcing her hands to relax in her lap. "Though there aren't as many women in trade, it isn't uncommon for stalls there to be owned by women, and I met a lovely widow who had begun selling there after her husband's passing. We became partners and built it into a thriving business, eventually expanding it into our own bazaar."

Such a succinct accounting of the last few years of her life, skirting around the strain and effort expended over the past few years with those restless nights and the nagging worry that rarely let her be.

"I imagine there is far more to the story than that," said Sir Stoneface, the faintest hint of a smile showing at the corners of his lips. "I oversee my family's business, which was well-established before I took the reins, and my friends would say I spend far too much of my time fretting and fussing over it. I cannot imagine the effort it took to build up such a venture on your own."

Something inside Tessa uncoiled, loosening so that she could relax into the seat once more. "It has been an ordeal, to be certain, but it is exciting as well. Whenever I feel as though I have sorted matters, things change, leaving me to adapt to the new way of doing things. It's like navigating a maze that is forever shifting."

Sir Stoneface's brows rose at that. "I know precisely what you mean. I am a trained apothecary, quite able to manage producing whatever medicines our shop sells, but more and more, the business draws my attention. I cannot simply follow a recipe as I do with my tinctures and powders."

And now Tessa's expression shifted to match his, though for entirely different reasons. Not only did his posture relax as he settled into the subject, but there was no judgment in his tone. No wisdom he felt necessary to share. Simply an exchange of opinions and experiences. It was rare enough to find anyone who wished to discuss the subject, let alone speak to her as though they were peers. Equals. Not someone wishing to bestow his great intellect or show her the error of her ways.

The conversation unfolded like a dance. For all that men led and women followed, the best pairings required give and take on both sides. A perfect understanding as they moved through the steps with ease. A partnership.

Tessa found her conversation adjusting as she refined her arguments with each of the gentleman's questions and verbal thrusts as he pressed her—not to dominate, but to understand. To test the strength of her thoughts and offer his own in return. It required effort to keep pace, but the challenge was invigorating. There was something deeply satisfying in matching wits with someone who made her think more sharply, more precisely.

The gentleman didn't speak over her or dismiss her thoughts; he listened, then countered with his own. Sometimes she held her ground. Sometimes she didn't. And more than once, she was forced to reconsider her perspective, the shape of it shifting beneath his careful questioning.

It wasn't a battle, but the same sort of energy thrummed beneath the words. Rather than forging weapons, they forged ideas, striking at the other with calm consideration. And when his head tilted to the side, his eyes falling away as he considered her latest point, Tessa knew he had conceded defeat.

Yet this wasn't about victory. It was about discovery. Tessa's heart lightened as they wandered deeper and deeper into the subject of finance, customers, and the art of the sale.

...

There were benefits and drawbacks to travelling by public coach. Amongst the former, there was the joy of being conveyed about the countryside at a fraction of the price, and as Gregory considered that, he realized it was perhaps the only blessing. The pitfalls, on the other hand, provided far more fertile ground.

Not only was one subjected to long bouts without food or drink, but one was battered by rain, nipped at by frost, and burned by the sun. To say nothing of being crushed into a tiny box with the other passengers, many of whom gave hygiene a passing nod. Then there were the snorers, the foot-tappers, the pokers, the loud chewers, the know-it-alls, the weak-stomached, and the busybodies who made the hours creep by until one was certain that walking was preferable.

And if all that was not enough of a megrim, there was the added frustration of being stranded on empty stretches of country roads or tossed into a ditch when the vehicle, tack, or animals failed—all of which were common enough occurrences.

Usually, Gregory despised the moments when passengers inside and up-top were forced to alight so that the luggage-laden carriage could make it to the top of a hill without the added weight to further fatigue the horses; the added time of waiting for all the passengers to make their way up the rise was highly vexing. But now, Gregory found himself lingering at the end of a string of passengers, who waddled their way after the carriage like a family of ducklings, grateful to stretch their legs. With plodding steps, he walked alongside his companion, his gaze more fixed on her than on the carriage that awaited them as the others crested the hill.

For all that she appeared to be of similar age to him, Mrs. Chatterbox had an energy that was far beyond anything Gregory's forty-year-old spirits could muster. Though some might consider her too plump for fashion's sake, the fullness of her cheeks made her dimples more pronounced, which only enhanced the bright joy that sparked in her dark-as-night eyes.

And with that humming energy, she bounced from subject to subject with all the gusto of a puppy exploring its new home, sniffling about and pawing at topics here and there before darting on to the next. Once the common interest of business had been broached, there was no stopping Mrs. Chatterbox. Even if he had wanted to.

Gregory supposed he ought to know her proper name by now, but enough time had passed since their first conversation that asking would be uncomfortable, as he hadn't been listening when the lady had introduced herself to their other travelling companions at the very beginning of their journey. Besides, he rather liked the moniker. It suited her.

Despite being a touch short, Mrs. Chatterbox carried herself as though meeting him eye to eye. It was the sort of confidence that one could only attain after decades of experience. The surety of someone who had carved out her place in the world. Who knew herself and felt no need to twist into knots to please another.

"I am going on and on, aren't I?" she asked with a wince. Then, seeming to shake off that concern, Mrs. Chatterbox squared her shoulders and gave him another of her wry smiles. "But I suppose it serves you right for broaching the subject of business. Few people ever wish to speak about such things, so when I find an eager listener, there is no stopping me."

"Then I am the author of my demise?" he asked in a monotone.

"Do not feign injury, my good sir," she replied with a laugh. "I saw you during the first leg of our journey. You are quite capable of avoiding conversation when you wish, so you needn't act like the victim of my babbling."

Gregory bowed his head in acknowledgment, and the amusement coursing through him drew forth a confession. "In truth, I have enjoyed our conversation. Though my family adores the medical aspect of the business and will discuss it at great length, the rest is far less appealing to them. It is rare to find someone who is as intrigued by the whole thing as I am."

"I know precisely what you mean."

"Speaking of which, I know many swear by magazines and periodicals, but what have you found to be the most effective manner of advertising?" But when Gregory glanced at the lady, she was suspiciously silent.

"I own a small bazaar. I hardly think I am in a position to lecture an apothecary, with all your skills and learning, on how to best advertise your business," she said, her eyes widening. "It sounds as though you are far more successful than I."

"Nonsense," said Gregory. "Though I have a hand in the production, at its heart, my business is selling a product—and that is no different than what you do. The core principles are universal."

"Then I fear I have no good answer to give you, for I do not focus much on advertisements per se. I prefer to use my limited time and funds on improving the shopping experience for my customers, as they are far more likely to spread the word on my behalf—"

The lady's foot slipped, and Gregory's hand shot out to steady her. Mrs. Chatterbox graced him with another smile, and despite her handing them out at every opportunity, he found himself quite taken by the sight.

Tucking her hands into the folds of her cloak, Mrs. Chatterbox glanced at him from the corner of her eye. "Please do not think me forward, but may I offer a piece of advice?"

A chuckle sounded in his memories. The sort Rodney had always given when he was being even more "Rodney" than usual—most especially when he asked just such a question, which was more a warning that he was about to say something irritating than it was a genuine request for permission.

The thought made the corners of his lips twitch upward. Before they fell again.

The moment passed like a shadow drawn over sunlight, leaving only the hollow behind. The sound wasn't real. His friend wasn't there. And no amount of imagined laughter would bring him back.

The ache that followed was sharp and immediate, stealing the warmth from the smile before it ever fully formed. Grief had a cruel way of threading itself through the ordinary, quiet moments in unexpected ways, and it didn't matter how often it happened. The absence still landed like a blow.

## Chapter 7

Forcing his thoughts back to the present, Gregory questioned whether it would do any good to deny Mrs. Chatterbox. The lady couldn't seem to help herself. For all that she claimed that his knowledge and skill dwarfed hers, she was quick to offer her opinions. But in truth, that inevitability had nothing to do with the nod he gave her: Gregory truly wished to hear what she had to say.

Over the past few hours, the lady had proven herself to have a fine head for business, and though he knew nothing about bazaars (beyond being a customer), Mrs. Chatterbox clearly did.

"I fear you are losing sight of your clientele," she said. "It is imperative to keep them firmly in your mind when you are making decisions concerning your business."

With raised brows, Gregory said, "I am an apothecary. Everyone is my clientele."

"True," she conceded with a nod. "However, how one sells to a woman is far different than how one sells to a man. And what appeals to a young lady may not catch a matron's attention. If you fix your intention on far too broad a range of customers, you will end up appealing to no one."

Glancing at him, Mrs. Chatterbox smiled in that free and easy manner of hers. "In the beginning, I hoped all and sundry would patronize my bazaar, and while I still do, I discovered it was far more useful to keep the needs of my ideal clientele in my mind. From the types and quality of goods sold to the stall aesthetics and the sellers themselves, I aim for those that will lure in my ideal customers. It is a slower process than relying on advertisements, but I find it makes for much more loyal customers."

Silence fell between them as Gregory considered that pearl of wisdom. It wasn't as though Vaughn & Co. was floundering. Far from it. Mother—the great apothecary that she was—had opened the shop to assist Father's doctoring, and her talent for medicine had all but guaranteed that it flourished under her watch.

Yet in the ten years since Gregory had stepped into her shoes, the business had expanded far beyond the reaches of Thornsby and Danthorp. Even Leeds. This country apothecary shop had the potential for something far bigger if he fostered its growth.

The pair strode up the hill, not bothering to hurry as the others began to take their seats on the roof. It was silly to wander slowly along as they were; it wasn't as though their conversation would be interrupted with only the two of them inside. Yet for once, Gregory found himself wishing the journey might take a bit longer.

But there were so many who needed him in Thornsby.

"Have you considered settling the base of your operations in Leeds?" asked Mrs. Chatterbox, stumbling upon the very subject that was haunting the shadowy recesses of his mind. "It seems as though that would be far more conducive to your growth than remaining in the country."

She took his proffered hand when they arrived at the carriage and accepted his assistance, and when Gregory took the seat opposite, he found her watching him expectantly. Clearly, still awaiting an answer to her question.

By even the broadest of definitions, Gregory would never be considered a chatty person. It wasn't like the Vaughns to air their thoughts. Except Edward, of course, but where his younger brother had garnered that trait was a mystery to the rest of his family. Likely, it was Mother's family influence.

Yet sitting with a stranger in a carriage as it carried him toward all those responsibilities and concerns, Gregory found his tongue loosening. Perhaps it was Mrs. Chatterbox's bright nature that pulled it from him, or simply the desperate part of him that required perspective, but regardless, Gregory answered.

"I would like to work from Leeds. Though I adore my home, there are more opportunities in a city."

Even before Stuart's passing, leaving Thornsby had been an impossibility. As the eldest, he had far too many responsibilities to abandon his family for the sake of ambition, and now, with those six dear children awaiting him at home, Gregory was needed more than ever. He couldn't uproot them from the home they loved so dear.

"But you cannot?" she prodded with a sympathetic twist of her brows.

"I have responsibilities. People who depend on me." Though he did not begrudge either the responsibilities or the people attached to them, the words settled like a lead weight on his shoulders. A burden he would have to bear on his own.

Gregory forced his thoughts away from that. Not only did it do no good to dwell on that which he could not change, but it was unfair of him to think of the people he loved as "burdens." The children and his parents were the people who mattered most to him in this world, and thus, they weren't a punishment to endure or a hardship to bear. And no aspirations could ever be more important than them.

"That is good of you to place them first and foremost in your thoughts. Not everyone is so conscientious." Mrs. Chatterbox's tone drew Gregory's attention, but her expression was placid as she studied the passing landscape. There was such a heaviness to it. The same sorrow that he heard in his family's voices when speaking of the darkness that had stolen away their father's vision. A finality. The hollow echo of a lost hope.

The lady stiffened, her eyes swinging to him as if surprised that she had spoken, and curiosity twitched in his heart, prodding him to delve deeper into the subject.

"We cannot have our cake and eat it, too, as they say," she said, easing back into her smile. "Every choice in life requires us to sacrifice other things we desire—goals that are diametrically opposed—and which path we choose to chase says much about a person."

That struck him. More than it ought to have. The words were too polished to be accidental, too practiced to be theory alone. The lady spoke like someone who had lived it. Whatever *it* was. And though she tried to hide it behind the curve of a smile, Gregory heard the wear in her voice, the weight of it slipping through the cracks.

This conversation, though far weightier than the others, slipped out just as readily as their discussion of business and finances. There was a rhythm to their words. A cadence. Something comfortable and familiar as the lady spoke without calculation, listened with intent, and met his silences without flinching. Somehow, impossibly, she understood how to fill the space without crowding it. And all while wheedling him into saying far more than he intended.

There was something familiar about this. About her. It unnerved him more than he liked to admit. Yet it stirred something inside him. A gentle warmth that settled into his chest.

The carriage rocked, swaying with each bump of the road and jerk of the horse. The clatter of hooves and the jingle of tack punctuated the laughter that echoed from the passengers above. While those outside seemed to be enjoying the raucous environment of a public house, inside, the air felt closed off. Not stifling but secluded. Like the hush of a library, where thoughts were meant to be heard and studied.

Words flowed, not for the sake of filling the air but because they each had ideas that needed to be shared. And every turn of phrase seemed to open a door neither of them had known was there, leading down new paths. It was easy. Natural. The connection of two souls who fit snugly together like two puzzle pieces.

And Gregory hadn't realized just how much he'd missed that.

Studying the lady opposite, he had to amend that thought. Rodney had felt like a long-lost brother the moment they'd met six years prior, and there was nothing fraternal about Mrs. Chatterbox. Gregory's eyes traced the sweep of her neck, and his fingers longed to reach out and caress the dark brown locks that peeked out from beneath her bonnet. Were they as silky as they appeared?

At that thought, he swore he felt Rodney at his elbow, ready with a quip about Gregory's history with women, but he batted it away: Mrs. Chatterbox seemed at ease in his presence.

However, one could hardly take her bright expression to mean anything particular, as it was clearly her natural state of being. However, there was comfort in her mannerisms and conversation that indicated she wasn't liable to clutch her skirts and flee.

Glancing at her hand yet again, Gregory wondered if he could trust the ringless finger he'd spied when she had removed her gloves. From her conversation, he guessed that Mrs. Chatterbox was a widow, though she never touched upon the subject of her husband and family.

A flash of a church spire drew Gregory's attention to the window.

"Thornsby," he murmured.

"Pardon?"

He nodded toward the village and fought to keep his shoulders from sagging as his heart fell to his toes.

"Is that Thornsby?" she asked, perching on the edge of her seat as she stared at the approaching buildings. "The time passed so quickly."

Was there a thread of disappointment in her tone? Gregory perked at that, his pulse quickening as he considered the implications. Doubly so when he realized that this must be her destination as well. In quick succession, his mind cobbled together possibilities. If she were merely awaiting a connecting carriage, then he could keep her company until then. If this was her final stop, then something more was surely possible.

"Are you stopping in Thornsby?" he asked.

Mrs. Chatterbox perked at the question, turning her gaze to him with what he liked to think was an extra dose of brightness in her eyes. "I am. And from your tone, I gather you are as well?"

Gregory nodded. "It is my home."

The light in her expression flickered like a candle caught in a draft. She adjusted her gloves, then her skirts, then her gloves again, her movements just a touch too brisk to be idle. Her gaze darted back to the window, then to the floor, then briefly to him before slipping away. But before Gregory could question why his being nearby made her uneasy (for that boded ill), Mrs. Chatterbox straightened again, shaking free of whatever darkness had flitted through her for that briefest of moments.

"Wonderful," she said, pressing a hand to her heart. "I am here for a visit, and it will be such a pleasure to have a friend nearby."

"Friend" wasn't such a terrible start. Not bad at all.

"Most certainly. I would be quite happy to introduce you around, Mrs…" Drat his wretched tongue! At least he stopped it from calling her that nickname, though that was of little consolation as it put his ignorance on full display.

Mrs. Chatterbox arched a brow at him. "You haven't the slightest notion what my name is, do you?"

"You do not know mine," he retorted.

"Only because you ignored the rest of us when the introductions were being handed around, Sir Stoneface." Then, with more than a hint of a challenge in her eyes (which was tempered by a heaping dose of teasing), she added, "That is what I have been calling you in my thoughts."

Gregory huffed. "Sir Stoneface? That is far worse than Mrs. Chatterbox."

Gaping with all the melodrama of a stage actress, the lady gave a feigned scoff of indignation that melted away almost the same moment she gave it. With a laugh, Mrs. Chatterbox shook her head before extending a hand.

"Mrs. Theresa Stuart," she said.

The surname sent a jolt down Gregory's spine as he shook the proffered hand. "Mr. Gregory Vaughn."

Stuart was common enough. Perhaps not in the same league as Smith, Jones, or Thompson, but it was an everyday sort of surname. An entire royal dynasty bore it, after all. Nothing of note.

Still, the name rang louder in his ears than it ought to have.

It was a coincidence. Of course it was. He told himself so twice in the space of a breath, even as a faint tension began to creep across his shoulders. There were likely dozens of Stuarts scattered throughout Yorkshire. Dozens more in the surrounding counties. He was borrowing trouble. Inventing ghosts in the shadows.

Gregory scoured his memory for Rodney's wife's given name. Surely it had been Jane. Or Louisa. Something like that. The fellow had so rarely spoken it, but surely, he should be able to recall it. After six years of friendship, this was a piece of information he ought to know. And it would easily erase any question.

Not that he needed to worry, for this Mrs. Stuart was far too pleasant. Too warm. Too conscientious. This engaging creature couldn't be the harpy that had plagued his friend and abandoned her children.

Gregory drew a slow breath and offered the faintest of nods, his fingers releasing her hand with care. No need to leap to conclusions. Stuart was just a name. Nothing more.

And yet, as the village came into full view and the coach began to slow, that tight coil of apprehension refused to unravel.

"What brings you to Thornsby, Mrs. Stuart?" asked Gregory. No doubt there was a simple—and satisfying—answer.

"I am visiting family."

Though it was a simple answer, there was a heaviness to her tone that settled in his stomach like a stone dropped into the darkest depths of a lake. And Gregory couldn't stop the question that slipped past his tongue.

"Your children?"

# Chapter 8

Tessa's breath caught, and prickles ran down her spine like a lightning rod. She blinked once. Twice. Everything inside her yearned to move, but she sat still—too still—as though the slightest shift might betray the surge of surprise that coursed through her veins.

Surely, Mr. Vaughn hadn't known Rodney and her family. But as quickly as that thought popped into her mind, Tessa brushed it away. In a village like Thornsby, everyone knew everyone. No doubt, Mr. Vaughn had heard of Rodney's passing and connected it to Tessa's surname.

Yet what had her husband told the others about their situation? One's good name was a commodity as precious as gold, and Tessa could well imagine the questions that had arisen when he established himself in the village without his wife—and the stories that Rodney had spread as a result.

Heat licked at her cheeks and swept through her, and Tessa fought to steady her pulse. "Then you know my family, Mr. Vaughn?"

All the light and warmth of a moment ago vanished like a snuffed candle. The gentleman didn't speak, and she felt him withdraw inside himself as the silence that followed took shape and sharpened like a blade. This wasn't like the quiet that Sir Stoneface had once preferred; it hummed with unease as his eyes narrowed on her.

Good gracious. He'd known Rodney.

Tessa felt it in the intensity of his gaze as it bore into her, and she tried to remind herself that this was to be expected. Rodney wouldn't have lived there for years without weaving some version of his story into the local fabric, and he'd never been the sort to keep his opinions to himself, especially when they cast him as the injured party. And from the moment Tessa had planned this journey, she'd known her reception would be cold. Frigid, even.

Yet how much had Rodney told them? How much kindling had he laid for her pyre? And what could she say or do to keep the sparks from igniting it?

Tessa schooled her expression, her pulse quickening until she felt it in her neck, and forced herself to remain calm. This conversation was no different from the one they'd shared over the last few hours. She would not flinch. But oh, how she wanted to know what Mr. Vaughn saw when he looked at her now.

Shifting slightly in her seat, Tessa cleared her throat and pondered what to say to secure his good opinion. The moment she set foot in Thornbsy, turmoil would follow. It was inevitable. Regaining her children's affections would be an ordeal, and having even a single ally in Thornsby would be a great blessing.

"Mr. Vaughn," she said, smoothing her skirts, "I won't pretend to misunderstand your reaction. Clearly, you are familiar with my husband and may know something of our troubles. However, I would have you know—"

"No, Mrs. Stuart," said the gentleman with a tone that was as unyielding as Sir Stoneface's expression had been. All traces of Mr. Vaughn, affable businessman, vanished as cold seeped into the carriage. "I do not need to know anything you have to say."

His tone felt as final as a death knell, marking the end of her hopes. Mr. Vaughn's reaction spoke of one far more familiar with the "situation" than was good for Tessa. This was not the firmness of one who had heard whispers or had noted the blaring absence of the Stuart matriarch and leapt to conclusions. The level of marked disgust that curled his lips and sharpened his gaze was reserved only for the truly appalled.

Whatever rapport they'd shared vanished, swept aside in the wake of her husband's gossipmongering.

"I do not know what you mean to accomplish in Thornsby, Mrs. Stuart," he said, spitting out her surname with such venom that it struck Tessa to the heart, "but you had best take the first carriage back to Leeds and abandon your games, madam."

"This is no game," she replied, forcing her spine up. "My children reside in Thornsby, and I am here for their sake. Not that it is any of your business, for all that you have strong opinions on the matter, sir."

Fingers strangling the fabric of her skirt, Tessa felt an old familiar stirring in her chest; like an anxious puppy, it scratched and clawed at the barriers she'd placed around it, locking it firmly out of sight. But she wouldn't give in to it. After having allowed it to shape far too much of her life, Tessa wouldn't allow her temper free rein again. She was better than that.

"For your children's sake, do not seek them out," replied Mr. Vaughn. "They have suffered enough and do not deserve to have their pain compounded by you making them a source of speculation and gossip."

That clawing feeling intensified, scratching at her chest. He knew no better. That was all. She'd known Rodney would spread lies about her, so there was no point in losing her composure when she'd known the battle to follow would be difficult to win.

But she hadn't anticipated a skirmish so soon. And with a passing villager.

Tessa met the gentleman's eyes, refusing to shrink away from the fire burning in those dark depths. "I do not know what my husband has said, sir, but there are two sides to every story—"

Mr. Vaughn scoffed. "Is there any version in which I will feel empathy for a woman who abandons her children?"

The walls of the carriage rattled, shaking as thoroughly as Tessa's heart. Clenching her hands, she forced her anger to remain within the bounds she'd set. She was the ruler of her feelings. Her own mistress. She would not allow another to gain control over her. But as much as she tried to reassure herself of those truths, she felt her hold slipping.

"Again, I do not know what you have heard, Mr. Vaughn, nor do I comprehend what business it is of yours to treat me so abominably, but you haven't the foggiest notion what transpired between me and my husband or what I have suffered—"

Mr. Vaughn gave another heavy huff as he gazed upon her as though she were the vilest of creatures. "There may be two sides to every story, and I will concede that there is often truth to be found in both, but if even a fraction of what Rodney told me was true, you deserve that 'suffering.' I have no patience for those who abandon their duties for their own selfish desires."

Turning his gaze back to the window, he clenched his jaw. "And spare me your justifications, Mrs. Stuart. Rodney was a good man who doted on his children—whose very last thoughts were of them and their well-being. You are the woman who made a mockery of your marriage and abandoned your children to gallivant about the country. So, do not think you can appear after so long an absence and demand my respect and understanding. I know what you are, Mrs. Stuart, and I will do everything in my power to protect the children from you."

Tessa stared at the man, the shock of his words ringing through her. Truly, fate could not be so cruel as to place her in this situation. Surely it could not. Yet as she examined his words and tone, her temper drifted into the nether as realization settled heavily in her heart.

This was her children's guardian.

The roundabout manner in which she had heard of Rodney's passing hadn't included any insight into who it was, except that it wasn't her. And Mr. Vaughn spoke as one who was intimately aware of the situation. Rodney certainly wouldn't have spared his friend all the sordid details—most especially those that painted her in a poor light.

Mouth agape, Tessa struggled to gather her wits, but before she could settle her control back in place, the carriage pulled to a stop. They had arrived.

The door opened, and Mr. Vaughn emerged, leaving her gaping at the carriage wall. She couldn't leave it like this. Of all the people in Thornsby, this was the one she needed to win over. The man who controlled her children's very existence. Who had the power to keep them from her, no matter what she or they wished. Who could move them to the farthest reaches of the globe if it suited him.

Pushing herself forward, Tessa scrambled out of the carriage behind him, emerging to see him engulfed by three girls. Her heart stuttered to a halt, freezing between one beat and the next and holding her in place as she watched the trio greet their guardian.

It had been six years since she'd laid eyes on Faith, yet the quiet and self-contained child Tessa had known remained. Grown, to be certain, but she clung to Mr. Vaughn's coattails as though hoping to disappear into his shadow. And Tessa couldn't help smiling at the sight of the book in her hands; she couldn't say what the title was, but the tightness of Faith's grasp and the worn edges of the cover made it clear she hadn't grown out of her love of stories.

And Daphne. The child she'd known had been replaced with a young lady, full of the bashful grace of one on the cusp of adulthood. Having inherited her father's height and frame, she was elegant even as she corralled Eva, doing her best to keep that little whirlwind in order as she bounced around the others, words flowing from her mouth with such rapidity that she more than made up for Faith's taciturnness.

To hear little Eva speak drove daggers into Tessa's heart. The last she'd seen of the child, Eva had only begun to form proper words and small sentences. Yet it was so entirely fitting that the babe who had spent her days babbling nonsense at everyone and everything had continued to do so once she possessed the words to properly speak.

But where were the boys? Tessa glanced about, searching the crowd for their familiar faces—only to realize that they were of an age where they must be at school. Her boys.

"Aren't you surprised, Mr. Gregory?" asked Eva, bouncing on her toes as she threw her arms around the gentleman's waist. "Faith said we ought to wait until you arrived home, but I thought it would be a great surprise to meet you here. Aren't you glad we did?"

"You ought to be home with your lessons," said Mr. Vaughn, and though there was a coldness to his expression that set Tessa's pulse racing, Eva met that with a laugh as she spoke of the governess they'd escaped for the afternoon. And for all his stony mannerisms, Mr. Vaughn watched her with a warmth in his gaze that settled deep into Tessa's bones. If nothing else, her girls were loved.

"What is she doing here?" demanded Daphne.

Stomach sinking to his toes, Gregory motioned the girls toward the carriage; he needed to get them away from here before Mrs. Stuart caused a scene, but Daphne refused to budge as she stared at her mother.

Seeing the pair in such proximity, Gregory wondered how he hadn't guessed his companion's identity. Though Daphne boasted her father's height and thinner frame, her features and coloring were so very like her mother's—more so than the others, though Faith had Mrs. Stuart's rounder visage. And with Daphne's temper sparked, the similarities were even more pronounced.

"Ignore her," said Gregory.

Those eyes, which were the same unfathomable brown as Mrs. Stuart's, turned on him, and the temper within crackled and sparked like the first flames of a brandy-soaked Christmas pudding.

"Did you bring her here?" demanded Daphne.

Gregory held up his hands. "Of course not. And I will make certain she doesn't plague you. Do not fret—"

"Please, Mr. Vaughn," said Mrs. Stuart, drawing closer, and it took all of Gregory's composure not to bark at the lady and drag the girls out of arm's reach.

"Do not speak to them, madam," he said, forcing his voice to lower. Mustering every ounce of determination and strength he possessed, Gregory infused his gaze with steel.

"But I am their mother," she hissed.

Stepping between her and the girls, Gregory scowled. "You gave up that title when you tossed them aside—"

"I didn't, you great lummox!" shouted Mrs. Stuart. "I would never do such a thing!"

"Which is why you haven't set foot in Thornsby until today. I assure you that Stuart's money is out of your grasp, no matter how much you feign interest in your children. You will not get control of them or Stuart's estate."

"I—"

"Leave!" Daphne stiffened at her outburst, her hands flying to her mouth, though her eyes continued to burn as she glared at her mother. When she lowered them again, she spoke softly as she held Eva's hand tight within her grasp. "Please leave. We do not want you here."

# Chapter 9

Mrs. Stuart stilled, the fury seeping from her as she stared at her daughter. If Gregory thought the woman possessed a heart, he might've thought the glimmers at the corners of her eyes were the beginnings of tears. But she didn't, so they couldn't be.

Nodding toward the carriage, Gregory motioned for Daphne to take the others, though he remained where he was until they were safely tucked away. Turning back to Mrs. Stuart, Gregory studied the lady. Her shoulders sagged, those false tears gathering in strength as she watched the girls.

Dash it all, the lady was talented. Gregory clung to his promise and Rodney's various confessions over the years. Whatever image she'd presented during the journey here, Mrs. Stuart did not deserve sympathy, and he would not bend.

"As I said, madam, I will not allow you to plague these poor children. They have suffered enough, and I will not tolerate anyone adding to their pain," he said, infusing his tone with the steely promise that he'd made to his friend. "I gave Rodney my word that I would protect them, and you may shirk your responsibility, but I do not. Take the first coach back to Leeds, and do not return."

And with that, Gregory turned on his heel and strode away, climbing into the carriage. In a trice, the groom had them on their way, leaving Mrs. Stuart far behind them. Though the air filled with the squeak of the suspension springs, the jangle of the horses' tack, and the groan of the wood as the carriage rocked, there was a pronounced silence inside the vehicle.

Glancing at her elder sisters, Eva settled into the seat beside them, her legs swinging with each bob of the carriage. No doubt she sensed that something was amiss without understanding the breadth of the troubles that surrounded them.

"She isn't staying, is she?" asked Daphne, her hands twisting in her lap.

"We have no control over what that woman chooses to do," he said. "I have warned her away, but I cannot force her from Thornsby. However, you needn't fret. She is my problem to solve, and I will ensure she does not pester you."

Gregory yearned to know what to do in such a moment. He felt a prodding instinct that warned that he needed to do more than simply reassure them, but it didn't offer any insight into what that ought to be. As a close friend of their father, he was something of an uncle to them, but despite the girls' effusive greeting moments ago, these heavy, sullen moments made him all the more aware that he was not their father.

Daphne nodded in acceptance before her gaze turned to the window, and Gregory couldn't help feeling as though he had failed them. And Rodney.

...

"The bank stocks haven't performed as anticipated," said Mr. Copps, his bushy brows pulling low as he studied his notes. "Which is disappointing, but the consols' steady interest annuities have made up the difference."

"Do you think we ought to sell?" asked Gregory, rubbing his forehead.

"Not yet. There is still a chance that they might recover. But the railway stock, on the other hand, ought to be disposed of," replied Mr. Copps before detailing the various investments and financial interests the Stuart family boasted.

Leaning back in Rodney's armchair, Gregory intertwined his hands and rested them upon his stomach, his eyes tracing the walls of the study and the rows of books resting there; the scent of Rodney's cigars lingered, absorbed by the paper and mingling with the leather covers. Despite having spent countless hours here with his friend, the room felt foreign from this vantage. But then, Gregory had never sat behind Rodney's desk before his passing.

Forcing his attention to the ledgers before him, Gregory fought to focus on Mr. Copps' information. A businessman he may be, but Gregory Vaughn had never developed an interest in investments, interest rates, and annuities. Yet despite Mr. Copps' stellar abilities, any gentleman of sense knew one ought to be familiar with his man of business's goings-on.

"All in all, the investments are healthy and well-appointed," said Mr. Copps, glancing up from his notes. "As they stand, the children are more than amply provided for."

Gregory nodded, though that was never in question. Regardless of Rodney's financial stability, the Vaughn family's resources were thriving and could easily support the children as well (though not to the degree to which the Stuarts were accustomed).

"My thanks, Mr. Copps," said Gregory, rising to his feet and extending a hand.

With a nod and a shake, the fellow strode from the room, and the moment the door shut behind him, Gregory sagged into his chair. He was by no means a dunce when it came to such matters, but his finances were far simpler to manage. Thank the heavens that Rodney had a man of sense and integrity like Mr. Copps managing the bulk of it.

Another rap on the door had him straightening once more before he called out for the person to enter.

"Mr. Vaughn, sir. I must speak with you," said Mrs. Ferrell, bustling in with all the determined vigor a housekeeper must possess. "There are several items of concern that require your attention."

Yet again, Gregory found himself inundated with information, but rather than figures and business plans, it was linens, household accounts, and staffing shortages. Though he would rather simply place the entirety of the decisions on Mrs. Ferrell's shoulders, a wise master kept a weather eye on the goings-on of his home, and it would not do to shirk his responsibility.

And that was doubly true of someone who was a mere guardian. Clark was the master now, and it was Gregory's duty to ensure that his inheritance was properly maintained until the lad was old enough to manage it himself.

Which was when Gregory realized he ought to be taking note of what was being decided—with both the household and the investments. At fifteen years of age and occupied with his studies, Clark wasn't prepared to shoulder those burdens, yet that time would fast approach, and Gregory ought to ease him into the matter.

Despite his lack of expertise on domestic matters (as his own household was so small that he had only a single servant, who managed quite easily on her own), Gregory handed off the housekeeper's marching orders before he relaxed once more into the chair.

Only to shoot upright when another knock sounded at his door.

Gregory muttered an oath that would've made his mother box his ears and prepared for more dire business that required his attention—only to see Mrs. Todd sweep in and stand before his desk.

"There is an issue with the girls' lessons," she said with a curtsy.

The devil take her and all the rest! What good was it to have an army of retainers on hand if they required constant supervision?

But yet again, Gregory settled into his seat with the calm reassurance that it was the responsible course of action. If one did not oversee one's interests, one might wake up one day to discover that one's investments had failed, the household accounts were in shambles, and the children's education was severely lacking.

With a nod, he listened as Mrs. Todd detailed the future curriculum, her concerns about the girls, and the supplies they required. Thankfully, Rodney was a wise master who had hired people with good heads on their shoulders, bringing forth only the truly demanding issues and doing so in a succinct manner. That was a blessing.

"Buy Faith as many books as she wants," said Gregory, his fingers drumming against the table. Though Eva was in danger of growing into a coddled and spoiled child, her elder sister was more of a mind to be overlooked and ignored. If a personal library made the child happy, he wouldn't begrudge her that.

"Education is important," he added. "I know her father would agree with me in saying that her intellect needs to be encouraged and cultivated."

Mrs. Todd gave a sharp nod before pausing, her lungs drawing in a sharp breath as she considered her words. "And Daphne?"

Gregory's brows rose at that.

"Before his passing, Mr. Stuart and I discussed what was to come next as the young lady is ready to be out." Mrs. Todd paused, her brows furrowing. "Though I suppose with this unfortunate business, it is best that she does not attend her first public ball this summer."

Those words struck Gregory, pinning him to his seat like an insect put on display by a naturalist. His throat clamped shut, squeezing the moisture from it as his tongue cemented itself to the roof of his mouth.

Daphne stepping out into society? Of course, he'd known that time was fast approaching, but with all the various troubles that had arisen in the wake of Rodney's passing, Gregory's mind had been too full of the here and now to consider what was yet to be. Daphne was practically grown—ready to take her place amongst the young ladies at the balls and parties—but how was *he* supposed to guide her through it?

Gregory was no chaperone. Rodney hadn't been any better equipped to ease a young lady into society, but at least he was her father. This transition was such a topsy-turvy time for anyone, let alone someone without the comfort of her parents to assist her.

Fighting the impulse to groan and rub at his head, Gregory considered Mrs. Todd. "What did you two discuss?"

The governess's expression softened, her eyes filling with sorrow. "Only that it was an issue to address. He wished to put it off."

Rodney had prepared for so many things—the guardianship of his children and their inheritances—and this was what he dropped in Gregory's lap? Money was easy enough to manage. Even the guardianship could've been secured without the will, for Gregory would've claimed the children with or without Rodney's explicit instructions. But playing mother and father to a young lady during such a turbulent time?

Venturing amongst the ladies of Thornsby and Danthorpe was a major undertaking. Gregory had watched his sister suffer at the hands of those harpies that were found in even the smallest corners of society, and he couldn't bear the thought of Daphne following in Sadie's footsteps whilst still reeling from the loss of her father.

Gregory's pulse quickened as he considered that it wasn't just society he had to consider. Being "out" meant a young lady was old enough to entertain gentlemen callers. Daphne wouldn't likely find a beau or marry right away (most didn't, after all), but she was fetching and possessed a sizable dowry, either of which was enticing to potential beaus. Especially those of the unsuitable variety.

How would he navigate that?

Unable to help it any longer, Gregory rubbed his forehead, wishing he could knead out the knots forming in his brain. Thankfully, his family boasted ladies to play the role of chaperone and social guide. Granted, both Joanna and Sadie were occupied with their growing broods, and Mother had her hands full with Father, but between the three, they might just manage.

"I will take that all into consideration, Mrs. Todd. Thank you for bringing it to my attention."

"Very good, sir," she said with a bob. "Do you wish for me to continue my reports?"

Gregory straightened. "Of course. How often did Mr. Stuart wish to be apprised of their lessons?"

"Fortnightly."

Giving her a nod, he waved her off. "Then so do I."

Another bob, and Mrs. Todd exited the same way Mrs. Ferrell and Mr. Copps had, leaving him blessedly alone once more. Having been absent only a few short days, he hadn't thought so much work would be waiting for him—but then, he supposed that with all the upheaval of late, the staff hadn't been pestering him about these matters as much. Apparently, that was to change.

To return home or not to return home. That was the question.

Though managing Rodney's legacy was a high priority, it wasn't the sole object of his attention. There was Vaughn & Co., and despite having a good number of apprentices and clerks to manage much of the day-to-day business, just as the house and investments required a master's overview, so did his business. As he had been absent for several days, they required him. Even if that absence had been related to said business.

But with the evening waning, it was entirely logical to remain at Eden Place. Especially with Mrs. Stuart skulking about. Rodney's final plea rang in his ears, and Gregory couldn't bear the thought of leaving the children alone. Though they were hardly alone. With a governess, housekeeper, and many servants on hand to see to their every need, the girls did not require his presence.

Leaning into his chair, Gregory longed to kick his feet up on the edge of the desk. Had it been his, he would've done precisely that. Instead, he rose from his seat and crossed to the armchairs seated before the empty fireplace, casting off his frock coat and settling into the place that was far more familiar to him before propping his feet up on an obliging ottoman.

The world looked better at this angle. As though it had twisted about and then righted itself once more. Except that the chair beside him remained empty.

He ought to send word to Walter and give the headmaster a warning about Mrs. Stuart. Though she likely didn't know where her boys were housed, it was information she could easily wheedle from some well-meaning villager, and Gregory could easily imagine her descending upon the school just as readily as she had descended upon Thornsby.

For all that the boys had wanted to return to Reed College, Gregory still couldn't help wondering if it had been wise to keep them enrolled. Not that he doubted his brother-in-law's talent at molding the lads, but having never attended boarding school himself, he couldn't help thinking it was an odd practice (even if the majority of the gentry employed such institutes). At least the lads were close enough to return home for the Sabbath and their half-days, but he would feel much better if they were under his roof.

But those ponderings led his mind into a place he did not wish to venture.

The vibrancy of Mrs. Stuart's expression as she spoke so passionately about her business. The wry smile that graced her lips when needling him to respond. The warmth in her voice as she commiserated over his troubles, matching his stories with her own as they shared their insights and experiences.

For the briefest of moments, it had felt as though Rodney had returned. So much of their easy conversation reminded him of that which he had shared with his friend. Though different. More.

# Chapter 10

Ludicrous. Gregory huffed at himself as he tossed those thoughts aside. Crossing his ankles, he sank lower into his seat, his head resting against the back as he propped his interlocked hands on his stomach, his eyes turning toward the heavens.

Mrs. Stuart was simply good at feigning kindness. No doubt she'd known precisely who he was the moment he stepped into the carriage and had used the situation to her best advantage.

Yet even as his bitterness longed to embrace that, logic couldn't. As Gregory himself hadn't known he would be taking that carriage until boarding it, there was no reason to believe Mrs. Stuart could've planned their meeting. The only reason the girls had known when he was to arrive was because he sent a message ahead at Brackenfell.

Unless Mrs. Stuart had discovered he was in Leeds and followed him about the city. But if that were true, the lady would've hied to Thornsby all the quicker to insert herself into the children's lives whilst their guardian was absent.

Gregory straightened, his arms falling aside as he considered just how close he had come to leaving them in Mrs. Stuart's clutches. If he had taken the next carriage, she would've arrived before him. The thought sent prickles along his skin, and he forced himself to relax once more.

His family had been watching over them. The entire household as well. He hadn't left them unprotected, and there was no need to work himself into a dither like Sadie or Joanna; he adored his sister and sister-in-law as much as any brother could, but he needn't mimic the easy manner in which they fretted, quick to imagine the very worst coming to pass.

Turning his thoughts backward, he tried to recall precisely when he'd veered into the ridiculous... The carriage ride with Mrs. Stuart.

Gregory's heart panged, but he ignored it. When testing the popularity of a product or marketing strategy, one couldn't evaluate efficacy on a single point of data; an array of information was required, and the same could be said of first impressions. Though a decent metric for determining a person's character, they were only to be believed when supported by additional evidence.

And Rodney had provided enough information to prove that Mrs. Stuart's behavior this afternoon had been an outlier. An anomaly. Even the worst of people could be pleasant at times.

Of their own volition, his eyes turned to a section of books stacked in the corner of the bottom shelf beside Rodney's desk; the spines were blank, giving no indication as to their authorship or subject, but Gregory was familiar enough with the volumes. Having not opened the journals, he couldn't vouch for their subject matter precisely, but a letter jutted from the top, peeking up from between the pages.

As investigating Mrs. Stuart had seemed unnecessary when she was safely tucked away in Leeds, Gregory hadn't bothered diving into the "evidence" that lay within. Between funerals, wills, seeing to the children, and his own business's demands, there'd been precious little time to bother with such things. Gregory had hoped Rodney had been wrong in his prediction, but clearly, the fellow had been generous in his assessment of his wife's character.

Despite having suffered such a great blow, the children were now to be subjected to their mother's antics. Heaven help them all.

Rising to his feet, Gregory strode to the bookshelf and drew out the book that held the letter, settling back into his seat once more. For all that he'd been privy to many of Rodney's darkest secrets, it was unnerving to have those most private thoughts available at his fingertips. One did not intend for one's journals to be explored by anyone other than oneself, and although he'd been directed to this very moment by his friend, Gregory still felt like an interloper.

The book opened to where the letter sat as a bookmark, and the script pulled his attention to the page.

*Faith has developed an obsession with the hallway rug. Every morning without fail, she toddles down the corridor and stops at the fringe. She crouches, inspects it like a scholar poring over a scientific treatise, and straightens every last tassel. Woe betide the person who walks across it afterward. Though she says not a word to anyone who dares disturb her work, the heated glare she levels upon them makes one afraid that one will spontaneously combust at the sight. Then, silent as a wraith, she smooths the whole thing again, patting each corner as though sealing a deal...*

The entry was dated some nine years previous, meaning that Faith would've been about two years of age, and the corner of Gregory's lips lifted into a half-smile. He'd met her when she was five years old, and the child had grown out of such peculiarities by then, but he could well imagine her quietly flitting about the house and setting the rugs to rights.

But as much as he enjoyed the happy peek into the Stuarts' past, it did not serve his purpose, and there was no point in wasting his time and avoiding what needed to be done.

Breaking open the seal, Gregory unfolded Rodney's letter:

*If you are reading this, I am no longer here to speak on my behalf...*

How could just a few words cause his heart to twist so completely? His friend was gone. Gregory had seen his passing with his own eyes. Heard his last breath. Seen his casket lowered into the ground. Yet reading those stark words written in Rodney's hand sent new sparks of pain skittering through him.

*...and so I must bear witness from beyond the grave—plainly and without embellishment—about the woman who bears my name.*
*I married Theresa Rush in 1836, and in the naïveté of youth, I believed that charm and beauty were virtues enough to build a happy life. And perhaps they would have been, had they not been accompanied by pride, discontent, and a tendency to incite conflict. From the earliest days, Tessa found fault with everything I did. No mistake went unpunished, no failing unremarked. Her criticisms were constant and, more often than not, public. She relished in her dissatisfaction.*
*When sorrow visited our household in the form of a stillborn child...*

Gregory straightened, his brows rising. Despite such things being commonplace, such a loss could never be deemed insignificant. And though Rodney had told him so much about his life, he hadn't shared this detail—which told Gregory just how greatly the loss had affected his friend.

*...I did what I could. I tended to the household, our children, and all the daily burdens that required attention. I did not collapse. I could not afford to, yet she called me heartless for it. Claimed I abandoned her, leaving her to suffer alone. I did not, but it suited her to say so.*
*I worked. I provided. I endured. She sulked, needled, and withheld her affection from me, though she was quite willing*

*to entertain the attentions of other men. What began as petty flirtations to provoke me soon became something far more serious, and when Tessa announced she was expecting, I had every right to question the legitimacy of the child she claimed was mine.*

Too right. Despite knowing how that portion of the story ended, reading it in black and white was still jarring. Infidelity of any sort within a marriage (either husband or wife) was inexcusable. One's marriage vows were not to be broken. But at least a woman couldn't be tricked into believing that her husband's byblow was her own—raising, providing for, and even loving a child who was the evidence of her broken marriage.

But for all that this was compelling reasoning for their estrangement, Gregory wasn't certain such hearsay would be accepted in court. Perhaps he ought to hire someone in Leeds to dig into Mrs.Stuart's affairs. No doubt there was ample evidence of her infidelities, which would secure their case and the children's safety.

*With her sins brought to light, Tessa fled our home and rushed into the arms of her paramour, but she did not leave empty-handed. She stole many items of great monetary and sentimental value, which she sold off to line her pockets, as she deemed the allowance I granted her was insufficient for her needs.*

*Yet even that wasn't enough for her.*

*As I didn't wish to embarrass our children by securing a legal separation or petitioning for a divorce (both of which were well within my rights because of her immoral behavior), I was unable to protect myself or our finances from her wrath. Tessa accumulated massive debts that, as her husband, I was legally responsible to settle, regardless of our living arrangement. Without an official separation in the eyes of the law, my wife could spend me into debtor's prison.*

That devious minx.

Gregory had often wondered why anyone would make their separation known publicly by formalizing it in the courts. Living apart raised speculation, but society would accept the idea without complaint as long as the couple went about their business in private. Once they stepped into the courts, the gossipmongers feasted upon the scandal for years to come, tainting them and their families.

Yet here was a prime example of why such a thing might be not only desirable but necessary. A wife's debts were her husband's responsibility, after all.

*With those ill-gotten funds, Tessa had established some disreputable bazaar in the city without any regard to how her inappropriate behavior would reflect on either her family or mine...*

Gregory's brows continued to climb his forehead. His lips curled as he stared at the words, reading them once more, but Rodney's meaning was clear enough. That business of hers—the bazaar of which Mrs. Stuart was so proud—had been built through thieving?

*As Tessa had deemed it her right to use the law to punish me with debts, I saw no reason not to use it to protect myself. So, I exercised my right as her husband to seize the income produced from that business venture, which in the eyes of the law belonged to me.*

*Realizing we were at a stalemate (or more likely, Tessa knew I could take control of her business at any point, should I wish to), we settled into an uneasy peace. Or ceasefire, rather.*

*Throughout this time, I did not keep her from seeing the children. No matter how much I detested being near her, I made certain they were available when she wished to visit and that I was present to ensure she couldn't corrupt them. It was well within my right to deny her even that kindness, but I could not deny my children when they wished to see her—*

The study door creaked open, and Gregory jolted. The journal fell from his lap and clattered to the ground, and he glanced over to find Faith standing in the doorway. The child didn't look at him. Her eyes were fixed on the desk and the chair her father usually occupied. She clutched a book to her chest with one arm as her eyes drifted over the shelves of books and fell to Gregory on the sofa.

Faith's gaze held his for a long, silent moment before he motioned for her to join him. She shut the door behind her and climbed onto the sofa beside him, settling into the cushions.

Gregory sat stiffly, spine ramrod straight. His hand hovered for a moment over the back of the sofa, unsure whether to rest it there or let it fall around her shoulders. The child didn't lean against him—didn't even glance in his direction—and his chest ached with the absence of something he couldn't name. He watched her out of the corner of his eye, trying to make sense of the book she clutched or the way she stared straight ahead, but there was no clear answer.

Every word that came to mind felt awkward. Every movement felt clumsy. Gregory wasn't made for this—whatever "this" was—and the longer they sat, the more certain he became that he was going to fail her. His fingers twitched, restless with the need to fix something he didn't understand, and the longer they sat, the more the room seemed to press inward, too quiet, too still.

Gregory tucked the letter out of sight and turned the book toward her. Clearing his throat, he forced himself to speak. "I was reading your father's journal. He wrote about you."

Faith straightened the tiniest bit, and Gregory opened the page he had been reading. Leaning closer, she fairly tucked herself into his side as she studied the writing. Returning to the start of the passage, Gregory read aloud the portion about the rug, and a faint smile graced the child's lips.

"'But then, I suppose such peculiar behavior ought not to be surprising, as she has an ongoing feud with the ottoman—'"

But Gregory's reading was cut short when Faith giggled. It was a tiny little thing—hardly more than a chuckle—but he forged ahead.

"'As she toddles around the parlor, Faith points to it and scolds the poor article in a string of incomprehensible babble, which is made all the more surprising by the fact that the child tends to speak little in general. For reasons known only to herself, she lectures it, deems it "naughty," and banishes it to the corner. It takes all her might to push the thing there. Heaven forfend anyone who dares to move or use the footstool.'"

As he read, Faith settled her weight into his side, cuddling into him until Gregory felt free to rest his arm around her. She remained tucked beside him as Rodney's words filled the air, his love evident in every syllable as he described the goings-on of his children and all those little things that brought light and laughter to their days and made the sacrifices and anxiety their parents suffered worth the effort.

"'Though Tessa continues to be miserable—'" Gregory's voice cut short, though his eyes swept over the rest of the passage.

*She is determined to blame me for all her troubles—as if it is my fault her figure hasn't returned to what it was before the children. Of course, I've held my tongue and pretend I do not see the alteration…*

Gregory shut the book and turned a smile to the little one who had seen far too much unhappiness in this world and did not need a glimpse into the tumultuous thing that was her parents' marriage. Whatever was to come, there was no reason to fill her head with such terrible things.

"Perhaps we ought to read some of your book," he said, nodding toward the one she clutched tight.

Without a word, she offered it to him, and Gregory flipped open the cover to find illustrations of princesses, castles, and witches.

"Fairy tales, is it?" he asked with raised brows. "I thought you read nothing but astronomy at present."

"I like the happy endings," she whispered, and Gregory couldn't help it as his arm tightened around her.

Holding her fast, he nodded. "As do I."

# Chapter 11

Narrow lanes criss-crossed through the village, cutting paths around cottages of weathered stone. The little patches of earth that abutted the buildings were bursting with color, brimming with hollyhocks, delphinium, and lavender, which added their heady fragrances to the scent of hay and sun-warmed earth that permeated the air.

The village felt as though it had grown from the grey stone that jutted from the surrounding fells. A part of the very ground beneath their feet. Cultivated like a flower in a garden, it had been pruned and guided to suit the needs of its inhabitants, yet it still felt as natural as anything found in the meadows and forests.

Thornsby did not bustle. It breathed. And that peace nestled beneath Tessa's ribs, making itself at home in her heart. Having spent her entire life in Leeds, she'd been unprepared for the beauty of this quiet corner of Yorkshire.

But no amount of quaintness and calm could withstand the sight of the shopfront before her.

A sign hung above, and just like its proprietor, it eschewed the usual flourishes and embellishments, proclaiming in simple block letters to all and sundry its owner and purpose. Tessa did not require the latter, but she most certainly needed to speak with the former.

The freshly painted trim and spotless windows stood out smartly against the aged buildings that lined the street, and the careful arrangement in the display window (with a perfect pyramid of bottles and a marble pestle poised just so) spoke of a man who valued order over ornament. Even from the outside, the place exuded discipline.

Everything inside her clenched, pushing her nerves to the very edge of their endurance. Two days was hardly anything at all, yet it had felt like a lifetime to her. Now that she was in Thornsby, Tessa couldn't bear to wait, but neither would it do to rush matters. Clearly, Mr. Vaughn required time to acclimate, and if she pressed the issue too aggressively, all would be lost.

After so many years of hoping for the opportunity to heal the breach, having the possibility lying just within reach was a temptation the likes of which she hadn't faced in years. Yet to let things lie as they did might allow resentment to fester and misunderstanding to grow.

Touching a hand to her forehead, Tessa considered her course of action. Business had taught her to barter. Marriage had taught her patience and self-control. Surely, together they provided enough experience to manage the forthcoming conversation. Yet this was no contract negotiation, and the man inside that shop held all the power over her children's future.

She straightened and drew in a deep breath. Mr. Vaughn had seemed a level-headed fellow. Before the unfortunate ending, their conversation had been lively and cordial, and Tessa had to hope that without the years of resentment and bitterness festering between them, they might come to a more amicable arrangement than she and Rodney had ever managed.

Negotiating from a place of desperation or antagonism did nothing to further one's goals. Yet as Tessa reached for the door handle, she couldn't help the frisson of fear that settled into her stomach and made her muscles jittery. Losing in business only meant risking money. A frustration, to be certain, but not devastating. But to lose her children once more? She refused to contemplate failure. Success was the only possibility.

The chime of a bell announced her arrival, and Tessa examined the shop interior, which matched the pristine and orderly exterior. It was the sort of business that invited confidence, demonstrating in a visual manner the meticulousness of these medicine makers. There was no clutter, no frippery, only purpose and order. Not fussy, but intentional. Just as the owner himself seemed to be.

That knowledge settled into Tessa like a warm coal on a frigid winter's eve. Carrying on a conversation with Rodney had been impossible, but Sir Stoneface (née Mr. Vaughn) was levelheaded. Logical. Tessa was certain that if she approached the situation with caution, she could win the day.

"May I be of assistance, madam?" asked the apprentice. Shelves lined the walls behind him and the counter he stood behind. Bottles and jars filled every space, the sides neatly labeled, though the words meant little to Tessa.

"I wish to speak with Mr. Vaughn."

"I assure you I am well-trained—"

Tessa held up a staying hand. "This does not concern a medical matter. I have business to discuss with him."

The apprentice nodded and ushered her through the shopfront and into a corridor that sprouted from the back, which led to two doorways that stood opposite one another. One room held several other young men, who were grinding and boiling various ingredients, but the other was closed, and when the apprentice knocked on the door, a voice called from within for them to enter.

Tessa drew in a steadying breath.

Mr. Vaughn stood over a countertop with more jars and vials neatly arrayed along the shelves beneath. His attention was fixed on a book that stood open, his weight propped on his hands, which were planted on either side, and Tessa gave a start as she realized he was standing in his shirtsleeves, the cuffs rolled up to his elbows.

"Sir—" began the apprentice, but when Mr. Vaughn glanced in his direction and spied Tessa, he jolted upright and lunged for his frock coat. The gentleman tried tugging it on, but his rolled cuffs caused the sleeves to bunch awkwardly, forcing him to tug it back off and straighten his cuffs.

"Mr. Caney." The name came out like a censure, and the young man glanced between his master and Tessa, his eyes widening as understanding slowly dawned; the apprentice nudged her back into the corridor and shut the door behind him as his cheeks blazed a bright red. "Mr. Vaughn will be a moment."

Soon the door reopened, and the gentleman in question appeared, his apron gone and his frock coat in place. Giving the young man a nod, Mr. Vaughn sent the lad scurrying away before leveling an inscrutable look at Tessa as the silence stretched out.

Clearing her throat, she attempted a smile. "We need to finish our discussion, sir, and I thought it best if I approach you here, where there is no chance the children will overhear."

"I wasn't aware there was anything more to discuss, madam," said Mr. Vaughn with raised brows. "If I wasn't clear enough, I am certain Daphne was."

Those words cut straight into her heart, digging deep with their sharp claws. Her eldest daughter's fury and cold expression still haunted her, plaguing her day and night, but Tessa refused to allow it to cow her. No doubt the children were confused about everything that had passed between their parents and were understandably overwrought after their father's passing.

When Mr. Vaughn tried to shut the door, Tessa stuck out a hand to stop it.

"I understand this is all very confusing and even upsetting, sir, but I have traveled a good distance to see my children, and I will not leave until we discuss this."

The gentleman did not force the door closed (though his expression said he wished to do just that), but it was clear that an abrupt approach was doing her no favors, so Tessa added something that needed saying.

"And I wish to apologize, Mr. Vaughn."

Her words made Gregory pause with the door caught halfway between open and closed. Barely holding back a scoff, he studied her expression, but her earnest tone matched the openness of her features as her eyes pleaded with him to forgive her. No doubt it was a trap.

"I fear my temper got the best of me the last time we spoke. I believe I called you a 'lummox,'" she said with a grimace that was, no doubt, intended to make her appear sweetly coy with its amusing dash of self-deprecation. Yet there was a ring of truth to the affectation that made it difficult for him to dismiss her apology so readily.

"It was unkind of me," she continued, "and I am ashamed that I allowed my shock to loosen my tongue. I thought I knew better. I have tried so very hard to curb my temper, but it appears there is still much improvement to be made."

Mrs. Stuart shifted from foot to foot as she seemed to struggle for words. Gregory didn't think himself a savant when it came to comprehending human nature, but he possessed the ability to see beneath veneers. It had aided him many a time during his professional career when taking on clerks and apprentices, to say nothing of the various actions he'd taken to broaden his family's business. Such matters always required an ability to see the truth veiled beneath the polished lies.

And every instinct within him believed this apology to be genuine.

"The only excuse I can offer is that I was startled to discover that the gentleman with whom I had been speaking was the very same guardian I was so anxious to meet," she said, wrinkling her nose. "Since hearing of Rodney's tragedy, I have wondered about the man he entrusted with our children, and it never crossed my mind that he was the source of such a diverting conversation on the road to Thornsby."

Drawing in a breath, Mrs. Stuart steeled herself, and Gregory sensed what she would say next a mere second before she spoke. Any hint of softening in his heart fled as she arrived at what she truly wished to say.

"Please, Mr. Vaughn. I know my arrival must've been a shock to you as well, and I can well imagine that my husband has said some..." Mrs. Stuart sucked in a sharp breath, "...colorful things about me and my past, but I assure you that I am not some villain wishing to swoop in and pester my children. I only wish to see them again."

"Colorful?" he repeated, latching onto the word that fell so terribly short of what ought to be said. Rodney's letter still burned bright in his memory, helped along by multiple rereadings, and "colorful" was not the word Gregory would choose to describe the Stuarts' past.

Mrs. Stuart's gaze dropped away, her cheeks pinking. "I can well imagine that my husband has told you much, and I assure you that it is not as terrible as it appears—"

"Then the business of which you so proudly spoke wasn't financed by selling off stolen heirlooms?" he asked with raised brows, his eyes scrutinizing every detail of the lady who stood before him.

With her hands clenched in her skirts, Mrs. Stuart's gaze fell away from him, dropping to the floor as the pink in her cheeks deepened. No doubt she was furious at having her sins spoken of so plainly. The little shift in her weight as she moved from foot to foot and the way she pressed her lips into a line testified to her annoyance at having been found out. Her posture screamed of one steeped in discomfort, and Gregory could well imagine that she had thought a few bats of her lovely eyes and a little flirtation would be enough to ensure his cooperation.

And now, with her plans stymied, the lady was in a fluster to change course.

"I did steal from Rodney," she whispered.

# Chapter 12

Gregory's brows snapped upward, but thankfully, the lady's gaze was affixed to the ground, thus missing that flash of weakness before he was able to gain control of his features once more. A small admission was hardly a sign of good character, as she likely employed it only to gain his sympathy. Just as she had apologized to soften his heart.

"I wish I could deny your accusation, Mr. Vaughn," she continued, her hands twisting the fabric of her skirts. "Or I wish I could claim I was in dire straits and had no other choice—"

Gregory scoffed. "There is always a choice. You may dress it up in whatever justifications you wish, but just because you do not care for the options before you, doesn't mean you were forced to pick the worse of the two."

Mrs. Stuart's chin jerked up, her eyes rising to meet his. "I know that, sir. I did not say otherwise. I said I *wished* I could claim such a thing. Not that I was claiming it."

Ah, the righteous indignation. Gregory struggled to keep his reaction in check, as engaging with a stubborn fool would only earn him a megrim. But surely she did not think him such a simpleton that her mock affront would soften his heart?

Relaxing her hands, Mrs. Stuart changed course once more, lifting them in placation as she affixed a pleading smile on her lips. "Please, Mr. Vaughn, I do not wish to fight. Surely, we might put the past aside and do what is best for the children."

"As if you know what is best for the children," he muttered.

Despite the quiet of his retort, Mrs. Stuart's lips thinned even further, though Gregory refused to spare even a fleeting flash of guilt at having been overheard. If the lady didn't wish to be painted a villainess, she ought to give more thought to what was best for her children rather than feigning an interest when it suited her.

"I know you are distraught. You are mourning the loss of your friend just as my children are mourning their father," she continued, drawing in a deep breath, though the edges of her temper were making themselves known in the tightness of her syllables. "With him gone, I am all they have left."

Gregory wasn't easily riled. With a younger brother like Edward, patience was something one learned at an early age, and though he'd heard Mother speak of her fiery temperament once upon a time, he couldn't imagine her in a rage. None of the Vaughns boasted tempers.

Yet hearing Mrs. Stuart say such a thing made the pressure in his chest build like steam in a locomotive engine. Feigning concern for her children was infuriating enough, but hearing her speak of Rodney—the man whom she had tormented for years—was like dumping shovelfuls of coal into the firebox.

*"Gone."* As though her husband had simply stepped away for a bit. Gregory couldn't say whether that blasé statement was more or less provoking than the implications running through the rest of her words.

"I assure you, madam, they are not alone," he said, resting a fist against the doorframe. "As long as those children breathe, they will always have me. What they do not need is an absentee mother making an appearance simply to stoke her vanity."

Mrs. Stuart sucked in a sharp breath, her muscles tensing, though Gregory had thought the description quite gentle compared to that which he wished to say.

"Even when his body was wracked with agony, and every lungful caused him excruciating pain, he pleaded with me to watch over them," he added. "Rodney knew he was dying, yet he didn't fear for himself. He feared what would happen to his children when he was not here to protect them from *you*. I gave my word that I would stand in his stead, and I will not break my promise. I will do everything in my power to keep them safe and happy."

One could sense trouble afoot before it happened. The more observant one was, the more readily one could discern what was to come. One need only be aware (both of oneself and human nature) to predict such things. It took no power of premonition to know one ought not to hand a delicate teacup full of liquid to a young child. Experience was power enough.

And when Tessa had boarded the coach to Thornsby, she'd known that approaching her children's guardian would be an arduous task—one fraught with misinformation and bias that would take time to overcome. Mr. Vaughn's hostility was understandable, given that he'd had years of Rodney filling his ears with poison, and in many respects, Tessa was grateful her children's guardian took his duty so seriously. Doubly so, as it was clear that he harbored affection for them.

What she hadn't predicted was her behavior.

Even with two days to steel herself, Tessa's control was quickly fraying. Forcing herself to breathe, she pushed against the tension that had her chest tightening as Mr. Vaughn's gaze hardened.

"And you view it as your duty to protect them from me?" she asked in a clipped tone. "I am their mother."

The gentleman didn't go so far as to scoff, but his tone was steeped in ridicule. "That well may be, but I am their guardian, and in the eyes of the law, my claim trumps yours. Rodney was clear in his desires, and I will not blacken his memory or fall short of the duty I owe him and his children."

"*My* children." Tessa forced her mouth closed, breathing through the feelings that yearned to be set free. It would not help matters. She had spent so many years learning to rein in her tongue, which too often bolted free of her control, and she was not going to be undone by Mr. Vaughn. "I assure you, sir, that neither Rodney nor my children require protection from my care and affection."

"From what I understand, your definition of 'care and affection' is something the children can do well without," he retorted, stepping back into his workshop. "Now, please take your leave. There is much I have to do today—"

"No!" Gritting her teeth, Tessa forced in another breath, only then realizing that she was scowling. Thankfully, her features were far more obedient than her temper, for they relaxed the moment their mistress commanded it. Even if her expression felt unnaturally stiff.

Having Mr. Vaughn stand there, watching her with that stony expression of his, did not help matters.

Thankfully, this was a familiar position. How many times during the course of her business had she spoken with men whose condescending manners left much to be desired? This was simply another negotiation between business associates, and a level head must prevail. Tessa had managed precarious deals before.

Focus on that. And not Mr. Vaughn's impertinence.

"Forgive me, sir," she continued, managing a far more politic tone as she stepped further into the room. "I know this is a difficult situation, but surely that is precisely why we ought not to rush matters."

"But that is the very heart of this disagreement, Mrs. Stuart. I do not believe this 'situation' is difficult at all. It seems quite clear to me. Rodney's final wishes were explicit, and I will not go against them. I will protect those children—"

"From what? A mother's love?" Tessa spoke, her fists settling on her hips before she knew what she was about, but it was difficult to muster enough sense to care that she was slipping into old habits. And just as she was grasping onto her control again, Mr. Vaughn spoke.

"If they had a mother who loved them, I wouldn't hesitate to allow her into their lives."

"How dare you!" she said through gritted teeth, fighting against the instinct that had her hand wanting to slap his face. "You haven't the slightest notion of what I feel for my children."

"They say actions speak louder than words, madam," he replied with a challenging glint in his eye. "And your abandoning your children speaks volumes."

Tessa straightened. "Rodney forced me from the house and threatened to cut off his own children if I did not leave them be—and all because he got it into his head that I was unfaithful, though I never was."

For all that her fury burned in her veins, those four words (tacked on the end before she could think better of it) singed her mouth. Breath catching, Tessa tried to keep her eyes fixed on the man before her, but they darted away as the past flooded her mind. A hesitation. A momentary flinch that she smothered as soon as it appeared. Forcing herself to meet his gaze, Tessa straightened, but the silence that followed hung between them like a miasma, clawing at her skin as she tried to ignore the bitter taste the words had left on her tongue.

"I am certain you were a perfect saint, and your husband was the devil incarnate," replied Mr. Vaughn in a dry tone.

"Hardly—"

"And what reason would Rodney have to threaten his children like that?" he demanded, speaking over her.

Tessa considered that question, though she knew he wouldn't care for the answer. "He despised me and knew it was the only way to keep me from them."

Silence fell, and Mr. Vaughn stood there, his arms folded as he studied her. Tessa scoured his features for some sign of the gentleman she'd come to know during their trip to Thornsby. Quiet he may have been, but Sir Stoneface had been kind. Despite so many men dismissing her business acumen, he had spoken to her as an equal, which was a rare treasure. And what he had shared of his dealings had shown him to be insightful and intelligent.

Surely he would see the truth.

Drawing in a deep breath, Mr. Vaughn let it out with a halting chuckle. "If you are going to lie, you had best make your tales more believable. A grave misunderstanding between spouses is one thing, but you are a fool if you think I will believe Rodney would threaten his children's welfare like that. Whatever his flaws, he was a doting father. Almost to a fault."

Mr. Vaughn leaned against his desk, those frustrating arms of his still folded. "You, on the other hand, abandoned your family for a fling with a paramour, choosing your pleasure over your children—"

"I did not!" Tessa forced in a breath, but it did no good. Her tentative control was slipping, and she felt herself sliding into old habits. It was as though the past had opened up like a gaping maw, swallowing her whole. Gone were all the years of effort she had put forth to keep her temper in check, and she was reverting once more to the Tessa she despised. The Tessa who had landed her in this trouble in the first place.

It was time to retreat.

"I understand your skepticism. I hadn't thought him capable of such a thing either, yet it happened," she managed before stepping toward the door. "But clearly, we are getting nowhere today. Perhaps I should return another time to discuss this further."

"There is nothing to discuss," he said.

Tessa paused, her muscles tightening, straining at the fraying edges of her self-control, and then, forcing one foot in front of the other, she fled the apothecary shop.

# Chapter 13

The sun—a rare and welcome sight—draped its golden light across the churchyard as the parishioners spilled out the front doors and into the yard, turning their faces to that blessed sun like flowers lapping up its life-giving rays. Voices filled the air as the worshipers gathered into conversations, blending with the birdsong that echoed from the eaves of the church, where swallows flitted beneath the stone archways.

Gravestones, worn smooth by time and weather, stood in quiet rows across the green, their shadows stretching long and soft in the afternoon light, and a scattering of daisies and wild clover peeked between the markers, lending a gentle charm to the solemn setting. The old yew trees, bent and bowed with age, rustled faintly in the breeze, their dark branches casting lacy patterns across the footpaths.

It was a place meant for quiet reflection, but on such a bright day, the air thrummed with eager fellowship. Yet the beauty of the atmosphere evaporated like a puff of smoke at Daphne's declaration. Staring at his eldest charge, Gregory couldn't make sense of it.

"Pardon?" he asked, for though he had understood her

words, his mind couldn't grasp their meaning. Not in their entirety.

"The Billings have invited me for a card party on Thursday next," said Daphne. "I know I am not out in company yet, but it is a small affair with a few close friends, so it is hardly a public function, and Mrs. Billings said it is entirely acceptable for me to attend such a gathering, especially as her daughter will be in attendance as well."

Daphne paused long enough to catch her breath, and Gregory could do nothing but stare at the girl as she launched into another rambling exposition. "And I believe they invited your brother and his wife, so I shan't be unchaperoned. I am certain Mrs. Joanna would be eager to serve in the role. She has told me so already—"

Gregory's brows rose at that, but Daphne didn't pause as she fairly begged him to agree. Though she affected an expression of polite disinterest, her words came in such a flurry that it was impossible to overlook the eagerness seeping through the apathy.

And Gregory didn't know what to say. Of course, there was no reason to deny the girl if she wished to go (assuming she was correct about Joanna being in attendance), yet he longed to flee from the question.

Daphne was a young lady. Gregory had spent far more time thinking about the boys' futures, as they were far more immediate. To build any sort of decent profession required early planning and education. Of course, Clark had the estate, so Gregory simply needed to see him through his education, and then he and Mr. Copps would undertake his higher education in matters of business and investments.

Jackson was another issue altogether. As the boy was fourteen years of age, a course of action must be chosen. His inheritance wasn't grand enough to forgo a profession, but was university in his future? Or a clerkship? An apprenticeship was a bit beneath him, but not out of the realm of possibility. Either way, a decision needed to be made, though Gregory hadn't the slightest notion what it ought to be.

Rodney may have provided funds enough to secure whatever path was chosen, but a young man required money *and* connections to establish himself in a proper profession, and Gregory's were rather limited.

Thankfully, Wesley was young enough that such matters needn't be considered at this juncture—especially when there were so many other considerations to tend to first.

Such as their eldest sister's coming out.

Even the thought was enough to give Gregory palpitations as readily as some fractious lady in a Gothic tale with all her fluttering handkerchiefs and vapors. Did being a guardian to a young lady mean he had to invest in a bottle of smelling salts? At the very least, he might need to secure a batch of ginger lozenges. The manner in which his stomach churned was bound to give him a severe case of indigestion.

Daphne was only the beginning. Faith was six years her junior, so it would be some time before she entered the social fray, yet many ladies did not marry in the first years of their coming out. It was entirely feasible that just as he had Daphne settled, Gregory would have to endure the whole mess again with Faith. Or fate may be truly set against him and have them overlap, leaving him with two young ladies to protect from the hordes.

And of course, Eva would grow in the blink of an eye.

Heaven help him. Gregory felt as though he were sinking into the deep end of a pond, the water rising over his head. How was he to protect them from the ills of the world and those immoral people who thought nothing of using others for their own good? Or ensure the children's happiness when life rarely unfolded according to plan?

And Daphne stood there, waiting so patiently, though with each passing moment, the brightness in her eyes dimmed. The girl asked so little and did so much for the family that Gregory couldn't deny her this joy. Yet to speak the words felt like stepping over a line he wasn't ready to cross.

But before Gregory could think what to say, Daphne's brows rose as her gaze fell to the black ribbon pinned to her neckline. Each of the children bore those little signs of their mourning, and her shoulders fell as Gregory saw the realization dawning upon her.

"I ought not to be thinking of card games and parties," she whispered.

No doubt some preferred to follow rigid strictures of mourning, but just as Rodney hadn't wished his children to be bedecked in black, Gregory knew he wouldn't want them to forgo the little pleasures of life in some misguided effort to place their sorrow on display. He had helped the children through enough tearful moments to know just how much they were all suffering, and they needn't prove their heartbreak to society.

"That has nothing to do with it," he insisted. "Your father would wish you to be happy, not to sit about weeping over the loss. He loved you too much to see you miserable and alone. I am simply not certain about allowing you to go to a card party. That is all. I need a little time to consider the situation before I decide."

And to discuss it with someone who knew far better than he about the appropriateness of a young lady attending a card party without her guardian. And to confirm with Joanna if she truly wished to play the chaperone for the evening. And to speak with the Billings to ascertain whether or not the guests were appropriate company; Daphne and their daughter may be friends, but Gregory needed to do his due diligence before any decision was made.

Shoulders drooping, Daphne nodded, and Gregory nearly conceded the whole issue. Though she tried so hard to retain a calm expression, she couldn't hide the sorrow brimming in her eyes as she turned back to her friends.

"I will consider it, Daphne. I promise," he said, and though she nodded again, the words did little to lighten her spirits as she drifted back into the crowd.

Had he made the wrong choice? Delaying a decision often

brought unforeseen consequences, yet something about this moment felt far more monumental than he was prepared to face at present.

The children tore across the churchyard like water from a burst dam, all pent-up energy and shrieking laughter as they raced between crooked headstones and leapt over low stone borders without a care for decorum. Their voices rang out bright against the quiet hum of post-service conversation, a joyful chaos that belonged wholly to this day. And despite the strain surrounding Daphne's request, Gregory found himself smiling at the sight.

Until his gaze fell on Mrs. Stuart.

Her bonnet tilted back slightly as she spoke with another parishioner, her smile faint but present. Nestled amongst the congregation, she was deep in conversation with several matrons, speaking with a comfort and ease as though she had always been amongst them, rather than a recent addition who had hardly been here for more than a fortnight.

Though Gregory had done his utmost to ignore her presence as she lurked about the village, the sight of her set his teeth on edge. What was she saying to them?

According to the ladies in his life, little was being said about the Stuart family beyond a general surprise that their matriarch chose to reside at the inn, rather than her children's home. Thornsby didn't even find it odd that she reappeared after such a prolonged absence, as it was only natural that their remaining parent would come at such a difficult time. So, the speculation was mostly innocent.

For now.

Gregory watched her closely and determinedly ignored the way his stomach tightened at the sight of her. Speaking the truth was hardly a reason to feel guilty; what he'd said to Mrs. Stuart was quite kind, given the situation, and he doubted many would've been so circumspect.

Yet his words replayed in his mind, needling him with a skitter of unease that prickled along his spine.

"Come now, we should be on our way," called Gregory, motioning the children toward the gate that separated the churchyard from the rest of the world.

In his forty years, he'd often heard people speak of the difference between boys and girls. While there were always variations that proved generalizations weren't sacrosanct, they existed for a reason and held more than a grain of truth. Thus, dismissing them as wholly wrong was silly.

And Gregory had heard time and time again that boys and girls each presented difficulties to their caregivers, with people always claiming one side or the other was the "easier" to manage. In his limited experience, there was nothing easy about parenthood, but anyone who claimed that boys were the more difficult to herd about had never dealt with girls entrenched in conversations with their friends after Sabbath services.

Gregory called to the children, and though the boys chose roundabout paths like bees in a field of wildflowers, they were pointed in the direction of the gate. The girls chose outright rebellion.

Eva ran after a gaggle of girls who moved deeper into the churchyard in a flurry of muslin and ribbons, and Daphne was no better, remaining with her friends and their conversation. Even Faith—sweet, quiet Faith—ignored him, her attention fully fixed on the book she held propped in her lap, giving the pages her full attention; he wasn't certain how she had secreted it here, as Mrs. Todd had assured him that she had checked before bundling them into the carriage.

"*Et tu*, Faith?" Gregory mumbled to himself.

Thankfully, his mere presence at the edge of their circle was enough for Daphne's friends to hurry her along with assurances that they would speak again soon, whilst dropping a few pointed comments in Gregory's general direction, expressing their hope that Daphne would be allowed to join them for the party. Eva was quick but couldn't match Gregory's long legs, and snatching the book from Faith's hands, he secured her attention quite thoroughly.

But by the time he fetched the girls and set them on their course, the boys were so far ahead that Gregory called to them to slow. And now that their sisters were complying, the lads seemed determined to careen ahead with the thoughtless abandon that only the young possessed whilst living in that strange little world where they were the center of everything and nothing bad ever happened.

"Boys!" Gregory bellowed when Wesley veered in front of a carriage. Thankfully, the driver was aware and kept the horse at bay. "Wait there!"

Though he saw the temptation to run stir within Wesley, the older two did as ordered, which allowed sanity to prevail, and all three remained where they were.

But that was when he heard his brother-in-law's voice calling for him to wait, and Gregory couldn't help wondering if the lads had actually obeyed him or simply hadn't wished to misbehave in front of their headmaster. Turning to see Walter striding toward him, he motioned for the girls to continue.

"What are you doing in Thornsby?" asked Gregory. "Has Bonnie's cough returned?"

His brother-in-law shook his head. "No, thank heavens. Edward and Joanna invited us for a repast this afternoon, so we attended here, but I sent Sadie and the children ahead in the carriage so that I might speak with you about the boys. You have so many things occupying your time that I haven't wanted to call you out to the school."

Walter tucked his hands behind him as the two strolled along. Gregory looked ahead, but with Daphne there to keep the dervishes in line, he turned his attention back to Walter.

"How are the boys faring?" asked Gregory.

"About as well as one can expect, given the circumstances," said Walter with a frown, his gaze turning to his pupils. "Such active boys require challenges and tasks to keep them occupied, and though you likely would've preferred to keep them close while they are mourning, being at school is good for them. It is as much home to them as Eden Place now, and I believe the routine is beneficial."

Gregory nodded. Though the decision hadn't been easy, keeping them enrolled had felt like the proper course. It wasn't as though they were abandoned to some far-distant institution, and with his sister and brother-in-law to watch over them, the boys couldn't be in better hands.

"In all honesty, you are better prepared to manage the boys than I am," admitted Gregory. "I haven't the slightest notion what to do with them or the girls. Especially in this difficult time."

"I don't think any parent does," said Walter, slanting a look at him from the corner of his eye. "However, I would suggest introducing Jackson to your work the next time he is at home. He has an aptitude for science and may do well in your profession."

Gregory straightened at that, his mind racing with the possibility.

"In fact, I was hoping you might allow his class to visit your shop in the next few days for a practical demonstration. We've been speaking of chemistry, and you are in a prime position to teach them all about it in a more direct manner," added Walter, and though that certainly sounded intriguing, there was a cautious note in his brother-in-law's tone.

When Gregory had first met the fellow, Walter Reed had hardly been able to string more than a few words together (unless it was to a classroom of students), and in the intervening years, that taciturn nature had shifted. Walter would never be gregarious, but he was quite capable of speaking when necessary. However, he still tended to beat about the bush when having to broach difficult subjects.

"What is it?" asked Gregory, glancing at the fellow.

Drawing in a deep breath, Walter forced it and his words out. "I am concerned about Clark and this recent *development* with his mother."

## Chapter 14

"Is Mrs. Stuart causing trouble at the school?" asked Gregory.

"Heavens, no," said Walter with a vehement shake of his head. "If that was it, I could manage it well enough. I will not allow anyone to disturb my students. However, her reappearance has had an effect on his studies over the past fortnight. And what with the gifts—"

"Gifts?" asked Gregory, jerking to a stop.

"I didn't realize who the sender was until after they'd already been given the packages," said Walter as he came to stand before his brother-in-law. "Wesley and Jackson were quiet about it, and I didn't see a need to demand answers or insist they surrender the trinkets, but Clark said he destroyed his. The lad has grown so angry of late. Ever since his mother arrived, his marks have slipped, and his aggression toward the other students has increased."

Gregory's chest tightened. Doubly so when he spied the hesitation in the fellow's expression. "And?"

Drawing in a breath, Walter straightened. "If not for his extenuating circumstances, his behavior would warrant expulsion, but the lads involved and their parents are sympathetic concerning Clark's loss. They are patient now, but if matters grow worse, I cannot in good conscience allow him to stay—and I fear the damage such an action might do to him."

When Rodney had asked Gregory to be his children's guardian, the answer had seemed so clear. Simple. Not only had he adored their father, but he'd known these children for most of their lives. Yet he couldn't help but wonder if he would've accepted the position had he recognized the difficulties ahead.

Heart shuddering, he shook away that thought. There was no good to be had in considering that question. Especially with Mrs. Stuart lingering in the shadows, waiting to pounce.

"That woman," muttered Gregory, shaking his head as the pair continued down the lane. "I will do my utmost to force Mrs. Stuart back to Leeds, and then I hope that Clark will settle, but do keep me apprised. No matter how busy I am, send for me if matters grow worse. I do not want Clark or your school to suffer because of this."

Walter nodded, and the pair followed after the string of children.

Just ahead stood Hawthorne House—that old, familiar place that he knew better than any other. The building in which he'd taken his first breath. His first steps. The home of his childhood. His youth. For all that he had settled into his own rooms above the apothecary shop some years ago, this was the building he still thought of as his.

The gate latch still stuck, and the flagstones bore the same uneven tilt. The ivy, thick and resolute, had climbed a few inches higher along the timbered corners, but the plaster remained whitewashed and bright, its surface catching the sun just as it always had. Roses still draped over the trellis by the door, their petals caressing the frame.

Little had changed in the years, yet it felt wholly different somehow.

Of course, some of that had to do with its new master and mistress. With the local physician stepping down and his son taking over his work (and Edward's brood growing too numerous for their former rooms), it had been practical for them to exchange homes with Mother and Father. The smaller quarters were better suited for the older couple. Or so they claimed.

Gregory couldn't help wondering how difficult it was for Mother to see her home now in the hands of another. Even if Joanna was like her own flesh and blood.

When the children arrived at the front gate, the younger three charged through with shrieks and gales of laughter, which earned an echoing chorus from around the side of the cottage. Along the back sat the large kitchen and physic garden that supplied the herbs and vegetables required for the house and Edward's medical practice, but lawn covered the rest, and his brother and sister-in-law had placed chairs along the side, providing a respite for those who did not wish to run about the grass.

Before Gregory could say a word, Eva stripped off her shoes and stockings, her bare toes digging into the lawn as she chased after little Caroline. Edward's eldest gaped at the display for only a moment before Caro and her sister tore across the grass, eager to keep clear of Eva's grasp, lest they be caught and lose whatever game they had decided upon without any clear coordination.

Meanwhile, Walter's eldest tried to follow after, though she and her cousins, Oscar and Marianne, were a touch too young to keep up with that elder group.

With his thoughts still spinning with news of Daphne and Clark, Gregory considered whether or not he might sneak around to the back of the house; a few moments splitting wood always helped to clear his head and to keep the fires fed. No one ever seemed to notice that the Vaughns never wanted for kindling, and Gregory was quite happy to leave his habit unnoticed.

But thoughts of the axe and logs fled as his family approached to greet him.

"Darling," called Sadie with little Maxwell on her hip as she strode to her husband and greeted him with a kiss on the cheek before turning to her brother, bestowing another buss on him. "It is good to see you, Gregory. How are you faring?"

"As well as can be expected," he said, though his answer drifted off into a questioning tone when Mother came forward to greet them as well.

Mrs. Violet Vaughn was a formidable lady. Her height was not as recognizable when amongst her brood, yet still, there was a power to her presence that spoke of one who would ensure that everything was spit-spot and ship-shape. Yet her usual smile was absent from her face. Or rather, it was fleeting, appearing when her children approached and fading just as quickly. There was a tightness to her features and dark circles beneath her eyes that lent a haggard edge to her appearance, and Gregory could well imagine the strain she was bearing.

"I miss your visits, my boy," said Mother. But the moment the words fell from her lips, she waved them away. "I apologize. I did not mean that as a condemnation. I know you have more pressing matters to attend to, but your father and I simply haven't seen you in a while. That is all."

Edward and Joanna gave their greetings from afar as they waded through the horde of children, and Walter held out his arm to his wife, leading her into the fray to give some semblance of order to the fracas, whilst the maid set out the tea and cakes.

But Gregory didn't see his father amongst them. Turning about, he searched for the gentleman in question, but he was nowhere to be seen.

"Where is Father?" he asked, and the exhaustion redoubled in Mother's eyes, her smile tightening at the edges.

"He decided it was best to remain at home. He was fatigued," she said in a tone that Gregory knew all too well.

In his younger years, he would've dismissed it as nothing important, but with forty years to his credit, Gregory had learned much about his parents. His mother had always seemed stalwart and invulnerable, ready and eager to overcome any obstacle that came her way, and though he still knew that to be true, there was another truth sitting right below it: Mother took too much on herself. Given her parents and brother, it was little wonder, but she needn't manage everything on her own now.

But before he could say a word, Faith appeared at her side. No doubt the child would've stood there all day long, silently waiting for someone to acknowledge her, but Mother was quick to notice the intrusion and bestowed a genuine grin on the child.

"Well, hello there, Faith. Is that a new book?" she asked.

Faith nodded, her eyes brightening.

With a gentle smile, Mother asked, "Will you read it to me?"

Such a little question, yet the girl beamed as though that was the greatest gift she had ever received. Taking Mother by the hand, she led her to a pair of chairs. Being eleven years of age, the girl was far too large to cuddle upon the lady's lap, though Gregory could see the desire to do just that. But Faith settled her own chair close beside her and leaned the book on the arms between them before resting her head against Mother's shoulder.

The younger children continued their frantic games whilst the elder set settled in with the adults, and seeing his family welcome the Stuarts so readily into their midst set Gregory's heart burning. It wasn't as though they'd discussed his situation and come to an agreement that the children were now Vaughns; his family had simply enveloped them, accepting them as their own.

Going over to where Eva had shed her shoes and stockings, Gregory picked them up and placed them on one of the seats so that they wouldn't be forgotten, alongside the doll that Eva had abandoned during their play. And a bit of Walter's conversation snapped into place as he stared at the poppet.

Hadn't Mrs. Stuart sent the boys gifts? Would she show the lads such favoritism, or would she have sent all the children something to win them over? Surely, the staff would've alerted him if the children had received something from Mrs. Stuart. They knew she wasn't permitted to contact them.

Gregory stared at the doll, uncertain whether or not this was the usual one Eva favored, but for the life of him, he couldn't recall what that one looked like beyond the fact that it existed. Poppets all looked alike, after all.

Yet Eva didn't carry them about. So, why was there one here, now?

"Eva," called Gregory, his gaze fixed on the toy. Better to be certain.

It took a few calls of her name before the child realized he was speaking to her, but she dashed across the lawn and settled to a stop before him, her hair pulling free of its ribbon.

"Yes, Mr. Gregory?" Eva bounced on her toes, her eyes darting toward the others, her thoughts only partially on her guardian.

"Where did you get this poppet?"

"It was a present," she said, reaching for it.

That was clear enough, for the child hardly had the money to buy such a thing. "From who?"

Eva darted forward, snatching up the doll and squeezing it to her chest. "Mama."

Gregory stiffened, his brows rising as his gaze darted to the others. Though the elder children didn't seem to notice, little Faith stiffened in her seat beside Mother. Carefully, she closed the book and drew it to her chest as well with a wary look at Gregory.

"May I see it, Eva?" he asked.

Shaking her head, the child clutched the toy tighter as she inched away. "It's mine."

"Please, I just wish—"

"No!" She clung to the doll and glared at him before scurrying out of reach. A hush stole over the garden as the others became aware of the tension between the pair, and though the adults attempted to draw the children's attention away, Eva made that impossible.

"It is mine! I won't let you take it."

"I didn't say I would. I simply wish to see it." Though in truth, Gregory wasn't certain why he wanted the doll so much. It wasn't as though Mrs. Stuart had poisoned the thing, yet just the thought of her having given it so secretly sent a rippling wave of unease through him. A feeling that grew as the child stubbornly refused to listen.

Eva turned, placing her back between him and the doll, and all thoughts of Mrs. Stuart fled as a greater issue arose to the forefront.

"I told you to give me the doll," said Gregory, infusing his voice with the sort of command that usually inspired obedience, but she fled instead. "Eva!"

Frustration bubbled in his chest, causing his jaw to set, and Gregory tried to hold fast to his patience, but the issue of Mrs. Stuart was no longer the center of his concern. Eva glanced back at him, her chin jutted out as she once more ignored him and did as she pleased.

"Eva, you little brat!" barked Clark, stomping over to his sister. "Give that ratty thing to Mr. Gregory. You don't want anything from that woman."

"Clark!" called Gregory, following after the lad, but he was on his sister in a flash. As Clark was so much larger than her, it wasn't hard for him to pin her down, and Gregory rushed over, lifting him off her. "Stop that. I will handle this."

The moment he released the boy, Clark spun about and shoved at him. "I am trying to help!"

"I do not require your help," barked Gregory. "You do not hurt your sister. Or anyone. Ever. That is not how you behave. Do you hear me?"

Now, both Clark and Eva were glaring daggers, their eyes burning into him as though he were the worst of villains. Glancing between the pair, he didn't have the slightest notion what to do. Having led his family's business for so many years, Gregory knew well enough that ignoring disrespect and rebellion only fostered more. Such things festered, destroying everything they touched.

Yet these weren't insolent apprentices whose family had hired him to lead and guide them. These were children. Rodney's children. Whom he had valued most in the world and had entrusted to Gregory's care.

Rubbing his forehead, Gregory considered what to do—but what could he do? He could bully them into submission, but the thought sat sour in his stomach. And what was their crime? Mourning their father? Struggling with a major shift in their lives?

"Did your mother give you the doll?" asked Gregory.

Eva refused to answer, but Daphne gave a single, nearly silent word. "Yes."

Glancing between the children, Gregory brushed off his frockcoat and wandered over to his mother. "Is Father at home? Would you watch over them while I pay him a call?"

The lady nodded, but when he moved to leave, she grabbed him by the arm, tugging him to her. "Running away isn't going to solve the problem, love. Stay and speak with the children."

But when Gregory glanced about and spied the varying shades of anger, disgust, and fear, he squeezed his mother's hand and strode toward the front gate once more. With each step, he felt the pall lifting from over the party, and his shoulders fell at that.

How had things spun so quickly out of control? That question hung in the air, poking at him and prodding his feet forward. A modicum of the strain left him as he put distance between himself and the children, but it was of little comfort as the weight in his chest redoubled as he considered how quickly his temper had gotten the better of him.

Those children deserved better.

# Chapter 15

Arriving at what used to be Edward and Joanna's entry door, Gregory slipped in and climbed the stairs that led to their home above the draper's shop and was quickly ushered in by the maid-of-all-work.

Despite the rooms retaining the same configuration as when their former master and mistress had lived here, Mother had transformed the parlor into something that felt altogether new. The familiar wall hangings and decorations from Hawthorne House had found a home here, nestled along the walls and shelves.

But Gregory's attention was on the gentleman sitting alone on the sofa beside the window. A cane was propped up within reaching distance, and Father's attention was fixed ahead, though he looked at nothing.

"Gregory?" asked Father, his face turning toward the noise as his eyes searched about, though they could not see him.

"It's me," he confirmed, stepping around the armchair to sit on the sofa beside his father. "I was at Edward's for the afternoon, but heard that you had chosen to sit here, alone, rather than spend time with your family."

A slight smile twisted the corner of Father's lips, though there was nothing amused about the expression. "I thought your mother deserved an afternoon on her own without an invalid demanding her attention."

As Father couldn't see his expression, Gregory felt free to show his disappointment with a frown, but before he could say a thing, the gentleman waved it away, giving a self-deprecating laugh.

"I apologize. It has been a difficult day, and I thought it would be best to keep my dark mood tucked away. Despite having years to acclimate to the growing darkness, I still find myself overwhelmed by it."

"Everyone is allowed those sorts of days, Father. It is simply part of being human. But I wish you had been there, for you could give me some advice on how to refrain from causing irreparable damage to the children in my care."

Father gave a considering hum. "'Irreparable damage' is inevitable. I am certain every child blames his fears and shortcomings on something his parents did. Each generation instills troubles for the subsequent ones."

With a huff of laughter, Gregory settled into his seat and watched as the tension in Father's shoulders eased. "And what damage did Grandfather and Grandmother do to you?"

For all that it had been a jest, Father's tone was far too serious to be ignored. "They are good people, and I adore my parents, but they certainly left me with a few ghosts in my attic."

Gregory's brows rose at that, for he couldn't imagine his father struggling in any fashion. Certainly, the blindness had caused its fair share of heartache and difficulties, but such was the nature of unforeseen circumstances. It wasn't the same as what they were discussing.

"Now, what supposed damage have you done to those children?" asked Father, turning his face toward his son.

By even the greatest stretch of the imagination, Gregory wasn't a gregarious sort. That was Rodney's forte. And Edward's. Yet even the most insular of people required the occasional listening ear, and as this was the exact reason (or one of them) that he'd sought out his father, Gregory required no further prodding to explain the whole of the situation.

Beginning with Mrs. Stuart, of course. The lady hung over every conversation now. The silent thread that wove through their lives, whether they wished it or not.

Gregory didn't bother to edit his words. Giving his father a partial truth wasn't helpful, but even he cringed a touch when divulging their last conversation. Had he known the lady would be so sneaky and manipulative as to send her children presents, he wouldn't have felt the slightest bit guilty—though he supposed that was untrue, for he felt it anew when he recalled the precise words he'd said to her.

*"If they had a mother who loved them, I wouldn't hesitate to allow her into their lives."*

Father winced. "Oh, that was badly done, son."

"I am well aware of that," said Gregory with a sigh. "The lady is so infuriating, but that doesn't justify my poor behavior. It was true but uncalled for. Yet the more I learn of her, the more angry I become."

With that, he pulled the letter out of his pocket. Why he had taken to carrying it with him, Gregory couldn't say, but he read it to Father. There was nothing in it that couldn't be shared with a gentleman of discretion such as Arthur Vaughn.

*"Life continued in that fashion until I had a chance encounter with Tessa and her daughter. Eva favors me in looks so completely that one couldn't deny that she was mine, though Tessa attempted to do just that. Hiding her from me for the first two years of my daughter's life wasn't enough. That jezebel wished to steal my own child from me. To keep me from my dearest Eva."*

Pointing to that section, Gregory straightened. "What sort of woman would keep such a secret for years? To separate a father from his child?"

Father's brows rose. "Likely the same sort of woman who was afraid that the father would snatch the child away as he had the others."

"You do not understand," said Gregory, shaking his head. "Rodney separated them to protect the children."

Turning again to the letter, he continued:

*"Never have I witnessed such a heartless deceiver. In one breath, she claimed the child wasn't mine. The next, she claimed Eva was proof of her fidelity. But neither was true. I do not know what possessed her to spin such lofty tales, but I have the evidence of my own eyes to prove her inconsistency in our marriage.*

*"At that moment, I knew my kindness and generosity would be my children's undoing. There was no good to be had in allowing them near their mother. So, bundling up Eva and the rest, I fled Leeds and settled in Thornsby."*

Gregory turned his gaze to his father. "It wasn't cruelty that made him do it. Rodney wanted to protect them from a poor influence."

Nodding, Father considered that. "There are often two sides to every story—"

"Yes, but Mrs. Stuart admitted to stealing from Rodney," said Gregory. Father moved to reply, but he knew precisely what the gentleman was going to say, so he rushed to add, "And yes, people do change, but I hired a man to investigate her after their separation, and she was arrested for grand larceny less than a year ago. Mrs. Stuart is just as deceitful as ever. And she has no interest in the children."

Nodding toward the letter, he continued reading.

*"Tessa wrote only once in the six years that followed our move to Thornsby, but it was a long letter full of hollow apologies and revisionist history."*

"Once," repeated Gregory. "She only wrote once. If a mother cared about her children, why would she send only one letter? And why wait until her husband has passed to appear on their doorstep? Had I been in her shoes, I would've hounded Rodney until he relented. I wouldn't have surrendered so easily."

Pointing to the last few paragraphs, he read:

*"Tessa is many things—charming, clever, tireless in her efforts—but I would never entrust her with anything fragile. Not hearts. Not homes. Certainly not children. She is the kind who ruins and then rewrites the ending to suit herself. Remember the theft, the manipulation, the disloyalty. I bore it for years so my children wouldn't have to.*

*"Do not be deceived. I leave this as a warning, not out of vengeance, but out of love for those who cannot yet protect themselves."*

Father's brow arched at that. "Didn't you chastise Mrs. Stuart for painting herself as a saint and her husband a devil? I fear you may be doing the opposite. Most broken marriages are the fault of both parties, so I would be cautious in assuming that Rodney's was the exception. People love to believe themselves the anomaly that exists outside the bounds of law and morality, but there lies madness. The lure of justification has led many a man into ruin."

"True, but nothing I have seen of Mrs. Stuart recommends her as a mother," said Gregory, though he paused as he considered the woman he'd met before the truth had emerged. That lady had much to recommend herself, if Gregory were honest with himself. And he always tried to be.

But honesty or not, Gregory didn't wish to admit why the lady had taken up residence in his thoughts—for it had more to do with himself than the children. Of course, he was concerned about their well-being, but Mrs. Stuart could be dealt with. At the very least, the law was unlikely to step between a guardian appointed by a father's will and a mother who had abandoned them.

*"I didn't, you great lummox!"* Mrs. Stuart's voice rang from his memory, and he couldn't help wanting to know more, though he also knew the lady had too strong a hold on him already. Gregory couldn't erase Mrs. Chatterbox from his mind or the possibility she had presented. But it hadn't been genuine.

Holding up his hands in surrender, Father said, "I am not saying you must welcome her into the bosom of the family, simply that you are too quick to condemn her. I doubt she was the sole source of disquiet in their family, yet you are determined to tie her to a pyre. Truth be told, several of the things I heard your friend say about his marriage over the years gave me pause—"

"Rodney was a good man."

Father nodded, his tone growing tentative. "True, but being a good man and an excellent father doesn't mean he was a decent husband. And mind you, I have no concrete evidence, so I am speaking only of my own impressions, but I found his criticism of her unsettling."

"With her behavior, is it any wonder?" asked Gregory, but that earned him a censorious look from the old man.

"Again, I am not advocating for Mrs. Stuart or casting aspersions on your friend," said Father in a tone that demanded his son listen. "I am simply suggesting that you need to accept the possibility that not everything he said was wholly accurate. He may have been a victim of her cruelty, but more often than not, the truth is complicated."

Once more, the image of the lady he'd met in the coach rose to his thoughts. Mrs. Chatterbox had been well worth knowing, but truth be told, Gregory had fancied more than merely knowing her, and perhaps a touch of disappointment played a role in his reaction now.

He'd best mull over that thought for a bit.

"My feelings toward Mrs. Stuart are complicated, to say the least," said Gregory for the sake of honesty. But shaking free of that, he continued, "But I am primarily concerned with the children. I do not know what to do with them. Rodney had few others he could entrust with their safekeeping, and I fear he made the worst possible choice."

Father's brows furrowed, his empty eyes turning toward Gregory. Though they could not see any longer, they were filled with emotion, showing quite clearly his concern for his son.

"You are like your mother, my boy. Taking the whole of the world upon your shoulders and expecting too much of yourself," he said, reaching for his son's hand and giving it a squeeze when Gregory took hold. "You went from being a bachelor to a father of six children. That alone would be difficult enough for anyone, let alone with the added stress of their broken hearts and this business with Mrs. Stuart. Give yourself some grace."

"What grace is warranted if I ruin the children?" blurted Gregory, sinking into his seat. "Managing the boys' future will be difficult enough, but how can I oversee Daphne's coming out if I haven't the slightest notion of how to guide a young lady through courtship? For goodness' sake, I haven't even navigated one myself."

"Yes, you've certainly made a muck with the ladies," replied Father in a wry tone. "I fear you bear the Vaughns' curse for difficult courtships. Heaven knows your mother made a muck of ours. As did your brother. Though Sadie's troubles stemmed more from Walter than herself."

"Mother mucked it all herself?" asked Gregory with a hint of a smile. "Ought I to ask her about that?"

Father held up a staying hand. "That is threat enough, sirrah. I am properly cowed."

Leaning forward, the gentleman angled toward his son and reached out, seeking Gregory's knee; with a slight touch to guide him, Father found it and smiled warmly.

"Your concern for the children is proof enough that you are the proper guardian for them, my boy. Children do not need much. Affection and a good example are all they require, and you are quite capable of providing both."

"But—"

Father squeezed Gregory's knee again, silencing him. "Parents fret and fuss over how to teach and guide their children, but the truth is, they needn't worry about teaching anything. Simply live the upstanding life you wish the children to have and demonstrate the joy it brings you—that motivates them far more than lecturing. And if you are living as you ought, lessons will flow from you to them in a natural fashion without the need to fabricate moments."

"Live a good life? That sounds far too simple," muttered Gregory.

Father huffed. "There is nothing simple or easy about being a good person. If it were, far more would do it. Unfortunately, the 'do as I say, not as I do' method is far too prevalent, and parents think they can simply teach their children to be better than themselves without having to sacrifice their favorite flaws."

With a wry smile, Father added, "Children test your patience again and again, and you have to remain strong against that baser self that wishes to rail against them or ignore the problem and let them have their way. But I am certain you will sort it out, Gregory. You are a good man, and you adore those children. They are blessed to have you."

Though the affirmation warmed Gregory, he couldn't help wondering how much of the fellow's certainty was due to a father's blind faith in his child. But one way or another, the Stuart children were his. He would sort this out.

And the first thing that required addressing was their mother.

## Chapter 16

The fields surrounding Thornsby stretched wide, their gentle slopes bathed in honeyed light as the grasses bobbed up and down in slow rhythm with the breeze. Dry stone walls cut through the expanse in tidy lines that were softened by moss and time, and beyond them, sheep moved in lazy clusters. The world felt unrushed here, suspended in that quiet hour before dusk, when those who claimed daytime were settling in for the evening before the creatures that ruled the night rose from their beds.

Just beyond the village's edge, Eden Place rose from the grasslands, the warm brown stone looking as though it had sprouted from the soil, and the last rays of sunlight gleamed off the polished windows like flecks of gold. The gardens had softened in the fading light, the breeze that stirred the hedgerows carried a coolness that promised dew by morning, and somewhere near the orchard, a thrush sent up a few final notes before settling in for the night.

The sun slipped lower, and one by one, windows began to glow from within, candle by candle, lamp by lamp. Though the hour was quiet and the world seemed momentarily still, Eden

Place was very much alive. Watching. Waiting. Holding its breath as night settled.

And Tessa stood at the gate, wondering if this were a mistake.

She was simply following Mr. Vaughn's summons, yet staring at the building that had once been her husband's home, Tessa couldn't help the twist of dread that sat heavy in her stomach, though her pulse quickened at the thought that perhaps—just perhaps—this was a good thing. Surely the gentleman wouldn't send for her simply to chastise her.

Drawing in a deep breath, she forced her feet to close the final distance, and she was ushered into the house. The servant led her through a maze of corridors and stairs, though Tessa hardly noticed it as she scoured every chamber they passed. No doubt Mr. Vaughn had the children tucked out of sight, but it didn't stop her from searching.

Then, with a bob, the servant motioned for her to step through a final doorway. Despite her having never set foot in Eden Place, the study felt so familiar. Of course, there was something to say about the utilitarian nature of such masculine spaces, which varied little from one to the other, but as Tessa stood on the threshold, it felt as though she were transported back in time to their home in Leeds. For all that Rodney had been gone some weeks now, the space still smelled of him, and she half expected to see him seated behind the desk on the far side of the room.

But Mr. Vaughn occupied that place. Though there was something of Rodney in the hard set of his jaw.

Tessa held a steadying breath and reminded herself—once again—that the best course was to be civil. Obliging. Obsequious, if necessary. Aggravation would only be returned tenfold, and for her children, she needed to keep a level head. For them, she could sacrifice her pride. She must.

"What do you mean by sending presents to the children?" he demanded as she came to stand before him.

As Tessa refused to look like an errant child receiving a lecture, she lowered herself into the chair facing him. "I wished to give my children presents. That is not out of the ordinary."

"I have made my feelings clear on the subject, and if you think going behind my back and being secretive about it will win you any goodwill, you are sadly mistaken," he said, leaning his weight on his forearms.

Tessa straightened. "I hardly went about it in secret. As I knew you would not wish me to meet with them alone, I sent the gifts by messenger. I did not hide my identity nor indicate that they must keep it from you. As I have been clear about my intentions, I have broken no trust."

"I have been clear on my position regarding your relationship with the children," said Mr. Vaughn. "That alone is a breach of trust."

Pain sparked in her chest, and it prodded her to speak—to defend or attack, it mattered not which—but Tessa forced the instinct down. She would not allow her emotions to run roughshod over this moment.

Besides, Mr. Vaughn wasn't wholly wrong. The tiny voice of reason that had warned her about acting so rashly made itself known once more, and that niggling of guilt held her tongue in check.

Another calming breath, and Tessa asked in as calm a tone as she could, "Did you send for me to give me a tongue lashing? Or to warn me away from the children again? Or to dole out more threats?"

"I wish to ensure that you will not continue to cause them more heartache."

"I have never set out to cause my children any heartache."

"Yet you have done so all the same." Mr. Vaughn's voice was cold and hard, slicing through her words with a quick flick of his tongue. "Are you trying to buy your way into their good graces? Did you think that a poppet or a few trinkets would heal the breach between you after all the heartache they've suffered because of you?"

Try as she might, Tessa couldn't help gaping at the accusation. The heat in her cheeks grew, creeping down her neck and prickling beneath her collar. Her throat tightened, and she pressed her lips together as if that might keep the rising flush from blooming any brighter, but she felt his gaze upon her like a spotlight, highlighting every flaw and foolish decision she'd made in her youth.

Her spine stiffened reflexively, her hands clasped so tightly in her lap that her knuckles strained white. Words clawed at the back of her throat—half defense, half disbelief—but all of them tangled together the moment she tried to summon them.

"I am trying to make up for the time I have lost with them," she said.

"Come now, Mrs. Stuart. If you continue to speak as though you had no hand in this separation, it will only strengthen my fears surrounding you," said Mr. Vaughn.

Shoulders dropping, Tessa drew her brows together as she stared at the stony visage glaring back at her. "Nothing I do will ever be enough, will it? You are determined to hate me."

The moment she said the words, Tessa felt the truth of them. The hardness in his features strengthened and twisted, his eyes boring two judgmental holes into her flesh, burning through her with all the pent-up fury of her former husband. Mr. Vaughn had made up his mind about who she was and would not be swayed.

"Have you done anything to earn my trust? For I have plenty of evidence to the contrary," said Mr. Vaughn, motioning to the books along the side of the room. Rodney had always been such an avid journalist that she recognized the personalized bindings the moment she spied them. They stood there like little soldiers, ready to combat any move she might make.

"So, it is my word against Rodney's," she said.

"And your own behavior, madam. Abandoning your children—"

"I never abandoned my children!" Tessa's voice rose of its own volition, and she fought to keep herself in check, but the words began flowing forth, slipping out of her grasp. "I was forced from my house by my jealous husband, who convinced himself I had broken my vows. He stole my children and kept me away by threatening to disinherit them."

"Not this again, madam," he said with a sigh.

"Believe what you will, but it is the truth! I kept my distance to protect them from my husband's anger. He may have loved them dearly, but he hated me more."

Mr. Vaughn's expression remained unmoved. "Perhaps he hated your thieving ways. One might explain away taking money from your husband if you required financial assistance, but that isn't the extent of your sins, is it?"

Tessa straightened. "Pardon?"

"I know about the larceny charges," he replied with a challenging raise of his brows.

"And any lady will attest that you cannot trust larceny charges," she replied with a scoff.

Mr. Vaughn leaned back, folding his arms. "Ah, now, are you going to blame the entire judicial system as well as your husband for the ills in your life?"

Jerking up to her feet, Tessa was standing upright before she knew what she was doing, her hands hitting the desk with a crack. "No, but I will blame corrupt shopkeepers, who are known to slip extra bits and bobs into a lady's purchase in order to extort her for a few extra coins under threat of a ruined reputation. I refused, fought the charges, and was found innocent. Something your spy in Leeds, whoever he is, ought to have known if he'd bothered to do proper research!"

That temper slipped through her fingers once more, but Tessa hadn't the strength to care. With this unfeeling, wretched man standing between her and her children, there was no reason to play nicely any longer.

Stomping over to the journals, she jerked out one of the volumes, checking the year before tossing it aside and going to the next. Mr. Vaughn leapt from his chair and hurried over to her, but when he yanked the tome out of her hands, she simply went to the next one. Finding the proper era, she spun to face him, shoving the book into his chest.

"You want to see how terrible and wretched Tessa Stuart is? Read it in his own hand," she said, jabbing the cover with her finger. "But be warned: Rodney had a talent for twisting a narrative with each retelling. I doubt the stories he shared with you bear any resemblance to what he recorded here."

Forcing her feet away from that odious man, Tessa hurried out of the room.

The study door slammed shut behind Mrs. Stuart, and Gregory moved to the sofa. Sinking onto it, he rubbed his face with a groan. That hadn't gone as he'd hoped, though he also couldn't say how it ought to have gone differently when that infuriating woman was determined to lay the blame on anyone and everything but herself.

As his friend of some years, Gregory was very familiar with how mercurial Rodney's moods could be and how bright his anger flared—Mrs. Stuart's matched it—but the fellow hadn't been this vengeful, cruel being she claimed him to be. And with each explosive interlude, Gregory rather thought his friend had been charitable toward his wife.

Most men wouldn't have minded taking the vixen to court and legally separating the moment the infidelity was known. Without the right Parliamentary connections, a divorce was nigh on impossible, but a legal separation would've been simple enough; then his finances would be protected and his children safely kept out of their mother's reach. And though they couldn't remarry, they would be individuals once more for all intents and purposes.

Yet Rodney had protected his family's reputation. And Mrs. Stuart's.

Setting aside the journal, Gregory tugged the letter from his pocket, rereading the lines he knew all too well. In Rodney's own hand, it spelled out the facts: Mrs. Stuart had been unfaithful and left the family for her paramour, contacting the children only when it suited her and not at all when they weren't within easy reach. Gregory knew the details, yet Mrs. Stuart claimed them to be false.

Did she truly believe he would take her word over his friend's? A stranger over someone he'd known for years, who had been like a brother to him, the father of his wards?

Gregory glanced at the book Mrs. Stuart had shoved at him. For the briefest moment, he wondered how it might exonerate the lady. But there was no reason to read the thing. These were Rodney's personal musings. Beyond those few entries he'd glanced over a few weeks ago, Gregory felt no need to intrude further into his friend's privacy. The letter alone was evidence enough.

*With the courts swaying more and more in favor of the mother—despite a father's right to decide what happens to his children and most especially his heir and the family holdings—I fear for the future. This letter is but a small record of what passed between us, and should a more detailed record be required, look to my journals for the entirety of the story. Surely that should be sufficient to keep my children from her clutches.*

Even Rodney, himself, was telling him to read the book. Yet it felt like an invasion. It was bad enough that Gregory slept in the fellow's bed and used his study. Was there nothing of Rodney's that would remain his and his alone?

Yet he was charged with protecting the children. That was the most pressing issue. More than safeguarding Rodney's privacy. If Mrs. Stuart was lying, then it was time that he armed himself with the truth.

Not *if*.

Mrs. Stuart was lying. And clearly, the lady wasn't going to leave Thornsby of her own volition. Understanding one's foe was paramount, and Gregory needed all the ammunition and weapons he had to defend his charges.

# Chapter 17

Flipping open the cover, Gregory glanced through the first few pages. This was long before their paths had crossed, and he found himself enjoying the glimpses into the Stuarts' life in Leeds. But this was not the purpose of his scouring.

Forcing himself to concentrate, Gregory scanned the pages.

*I smell him on her. I see the imprint of his lips upon her flesh. I sense his specter hovering at her elbow, taunting me. I have tried so hard to ignore it. To be a good husband till death do us part. Our vows were not contingent on both of us remaining faithful. I promised to be a stalwart husband no matter how she behaves, and I will be.*

*I am so very tired of being the source of all her troubles. I am the reason our marriage is failing. I am the reason her figure is gone. I am the reason it rained during her picnic. I am the force behind every ill in her life.*

*Yet I am not the one who has changed. Where is the witty, tender woman I married? I feel like a widower, and the woman I married is dead and gone, yet I am not free to seek happiness elsewhere.*

*I will not break our marriage vows. I will not stoop to her level.*

Gregory's heart shuddered on his friend's behalf. Thankfully, his parents and siblings all boasted the sorts of marriages that grew stronger with each year, but he'd seen enough of the other variety to know that not everyone chose their spouses so wisely.

Courtship was such a strange thing, a time when couples attempted to discern the truth about the other's character whilst trapped in a fishbowl, having all and sundry examine every action and behavior. To say nothing of the blinding flush of attraction that precipitated such pairings. That alone was bound to make people behave irrationally and choose based on their hearts alone, without any thought for what the future would make of this pairing.

What would it be like to marry, only to discover that the person to whom you were irrevocably bound was an imposter? A fraud?

And then Gregory spied another passage a few entries after:

*Trevor Gooding. So many weeks of searching—so much effort expended—and her fancy man is that peacock? Tessa must be desperate to welcome the advances of such a ridiculous fellow. Apparently, he adores her. But that is only because he hasn't the misfortune of living with the woman.*

*Every time I attempt to show her husbandly affection, she shies away with all sorts of wailing and moaning about her figure as though I am the reason she grows rounder with each child, when it is she who indulges in anything and everything she wishes. Tessa hasn't a shred of self-control and then lays the blame on me and our children when it rests squarely on her shoulders.*

*I try my best to see her as she once was. But that portly creature isn't the woman I married.*

Gregory's brows rose at that, a frisson skittering down his spine. After so much difficulty, it wasn't as though Rodney didn't have every right to be jaded and frustrated, yet there was a darkness to the words and the criticisms that settled uneasily in his heart.

A bachelor couldn't claim to be an expert on women. Though he may know much about the fairer sex, one could not say one truly comprehended a thing if one hadn't lived with it. Especially when one was speaking of a wife: a type of woman that was vastly different from a sister or a mother.

Yet even his bachelor mind recognized the folly of criticizing a woman's weight.

Bringing children into this world was called an "ordeal" for a reason, and any man of sense knew that it wrought great changes in a woman's body. And no one ought to begrudge a woman for that fact—let alone a husband, who ought to adore his wife regardless of the alterations that time and children brought about. Love that was contingent on outward appearances was not love at all.

Gregory read the passages again and again, trying to ascertain the tone with which Rodney was speaking. Or writing, rather. It was so difficult to discern emotional intent in a pen. Wit and sardonicism were often lost.

Then, of course, there was the context of the writing to take into consideration. At this point, they had been married some ten years, most of which had been difficult. And people often spoke more harshly than intended when under such strain. Doubly so when it was in one's journal, which was merely an extension of one's own private thoughts.

To say nothing of his wife's infidelities. To endure such a thing—

Straightening, Gregory turned his ear toward the door and heard the faintest touch against the wood.

"Is someone there?" he called.

The door inched open, and Daphne peeked through. "Mr. Gregory?"

Snapping the journal shut, Gregory set it aside and rose to his feet as he stuffed Rodney's letter back in his pocket. "Come in."

But though she did as bidden and shut the door behind her, Daphne drew no closer. Hands clasped before her, she shifted from foot to foot.

"What is the matter?" he asked, ushering her toward the sofa, though the young lady didn't sit. Standing by the mantlepiece, she glanced at the unlit fireplace.

"I..." But nothing else emerged as she continued to shift about, her eyes darting around the room. "Was she here? I thought I heard her voice."

Gregory didn't need further explanation to know who "she" was. "I needed to discuss something with her in private. I thought this was the best place as my workshop is empty at present, her inn provides only the appearance of privacy, and it isn't appropriate for her to pay a call on a bachelor in his rooms."

Daphne nodded but said nothing more. Nor did she settle. Gregory longed to sit, but with her on her feet, he couldn't bring himself to do so. She may be his ward and hardly more than a child, but those hard-won manners his mother had instilled in him wouldn't allow him to take that liberty. So, he stood and waited.

His eyes tracked her as she paced before the fireplace, and it wasn't long before she paused and turned to face him again. Jerking her hand forward, Daphne opened it to reveal a brooch resting on her palm. Though he was no expert in jewelry, Gregory could see that the piece was quite fine: a flower formed from silver, the leaves and petals spiraling out like a sunburst from the blue stone set in the center.

"This was the gift she gave me."

Gregory glanced at it and then at Daphne. "It is lovely."

The young lady peeked up at him as though expecting something more, and that hesitancy made understanding dawn.

"You may keep your mother's present if you wish, Daphne," he said, pausing to consider how to explain his thoughts without leading her deeper into her parents' discord. "I was surprised that she sent you gifts, and I was concerned about how it impacted you children. That was all. I will not begrudge your keeping it."

Gregory doubted he could pry the doll or book from Eva and Faith. Not that he wished to. He hadn't even asked the boys what Mrs. Stuart had sent them; Walter hadn't thought the presents inappropriate, so they were free to keep them if they wished.

Daphne shook her head, though she also tucked the brooch into her pocket. "Her note claimed that it is an heirloom, passed down the family line to the eldest daughter."

When she paused, Gregory felt as though she expected a response, though he couldn't think how to do so.

"That is nice," he said at last, but she shook her head again.

"No, it is not." Daphne continued her pacing, her words growing more heated as she continued. "It is naught but a bribe. Something to make me believe she thought about me over the years, holding onto this bauble in hopes of giving it to me someday. It's likely just a trinket she couldn't sell at her *business*."

She said the final word with such a sneer, as though trade was beneath her.

"Providing for oneself is nothing to disdain," said Gregory, the defense springing to his lips. "However wrong her other behavior may be, starting a shop and building it into a success is something to applaud. Unless you disdain me and my family as well."

Daphne paused and turned to face him, her eyes wide with surprise. "But you know she stole from Papa to finance the whole thing—"

"How do you know that?"

"Papa told me," she said with a dismissive wave of her hand, though Gregory didn't think that was worthy of overlooking. Just how much had Rodney told the children of their troubles? "If this brooch is genuine, it means she kept it. Sold off his things to spare hers. And somehow, she believes that will soften my heart toward her?"

"Or it means that not only does the brooch matter dearly to her, but that it was important for her to safeguard it for you. Perhaps she wished you to have a piece of your family legacy." Again, Gregory didn't know what possessed him to defend Mrs. Stuart. Surely her behavior didn't warrant his support, yet hearing Daphne's sweet voice speaking such hard things demanded a retort.

Turning away from him, she retrieved the brooch again, staring at the jewelry. "It's just something she purchased."

Yet even his uneducated eyes saw the way the silver gleamed as only silver could, and the style was old enough to give the appearance of having been from a few generations ago. Gregory doubted it was the sort of piece that found its way to bazaars.

"At church, the ladies were speaking of her," she said, staring at the piece in her hand. "She's already received invitations from several families. They all seem to think she's delightful."

It had been only a fortnight since the lady's arrival, and it was easy enough to maintain a good reputation for such a short time, but even Gregory couldn't deny just how quickly the parish had embraced her. Despite whispering about the notorious Mrs. Stuart for years, the villagers were eager to ignore the past and welcome her into their circles.

But Gregory's own doubts weren't for Daphne to hear. The poor dear had heard enough of the bickering and backstabbing between her parents, and he wouldn't allow this to continue.

"If she truly cared about us, she would've come the moment Papa passed," she said, tucking away the brooch again.

"He didn't wish us to post an announcement in the newspapers, but from what I gather, she came the moment she heard." Again, it felt odd to defend her, but Gregory wasn't going to allow the children to continue in this festering mess of misunderstanding and speculation. Just as he wouldn't tell them that Rodney hadn't wanted his death made public to spite his wife.

Straightening, Daphne turned her dark eyes to him—those eyes that were a mirror of her mother's.

"This is still a trick," she said, though there was a hint of doubt in her voice.

There were too many questions. Too many attempts to paint the picture in black and white, but life was rarely that stark. Or clear. Glancing at the journal he'd abandoned, Gregory considered Rodney's words and all he'd learned, and he gave Daphne the only answer he could.

"I don't know if it is genuine or a manipulation, but I think you should keep the brooch safe until you know for certain one way or another."

# Chapter 18

The sun had slipped just below the hedgerows, leaving the sky streaked with dusky gold and purple, and the crickets began their chorus in the fields as a bat flitted overhead, barely more than a blur against the fading light. The grass edging the lane whispered with every swish of her hem, and the earth beneath her feet was dry and uneven, beaten down by cart wheels and foot traffic over countless seasons.

Tessa folded her arms tightly against her ribs, more to contain the roiling within her than to brace against the evening chill, and she hurried along, desperate for the refuge of her bedchamber. Dragging in a breath as she scurried down the lane, she held it for several long moments before letting it seep from her nose.

But it did no good.

Her fingers curled into fists, nails biting into her palms as her thoughts circled back to that wretched exchange. How effortlessly Mr. Vaughn had stirred her up. How smug he'd been, how quick to pass judgment. And worst of all, how easily she had fallen into old patterns—snapping, bristling, defending with too much heat and not enough grace.

The path narrowed as Tessa reached the village proper, the lane hemmed in by the storefronts and houses. Lamps were lit up and down the row, their light flickering through the edges of the shutters, and the inn's chimney puffed steadily in the distance, a faint haze curling above the slate roofs.

Tessa forced her steps to slow, though the frustration hadn't drained from her limbs. Instead, it simmered low, threatening to rise again.

She hated this. Hated feeling like she was unraveling. She was stronger than that sharp-tongued girl, who bristled at slights and lashed out when cornered. She'd worked so hard to soften those edges—to respond with composure and grace—but every time she spoke to Mr. Vaughn, Tessa fell right back into those old habits. Rising to the bait. Snapping when she ought to walk away. Losing her temper. Lashing out, not in defense but because she yearned to win the argument.

All it had taken was one man with a sharp tongue and a colder stare, and Tessa regressed to that creature she despised. The version of herself she'd tempered and contained. That pigheaded woman who had done her level best to destroy her marriage.

Pausing at a street corner, Tessa gazed heavenward to see the first stars of the night. She pressed her hands to her face, willing herself to calm. This wasn't who she wanted to be. Not anymore. Not ever again. But here she was, heart pounding, teeth clenched, and fury burning holes in her stomach.

The years fell away, and Tessa felt as though she had stepped into the past. To that moment where her stubbornness had finally crumbled to dust, allowing her to rebuild her broken heart. That vulnerable moment, after she'd lost everyone and everything, finally recognizing the pit she'd dug for herself. The darkness had been so thick that she could finally see that pinprick of light shining above her like the first stars that glimmer in the night's sky. The climb out hadn't been easy, but she'd managed it.

Only to be undone by the man determined to keep Rodney's spite alive.

Gritting her teeth, Tessa chided herself as she continued her journey. Accepting responsibility for one's own actions was paramount to gaining control over oneself. No matter what anyone else did or did not do, one could always maintain control. In theory, at least.

Tessa sighed to herself and reviewed her conversation with Mr. Vaughn. His opinion mattered only because it stood between her and her children; all else was immaterial. And her pride needed to remember that before she found herself cut off once more.

The scent of roasting meat met her as she turned the last bend, the glow of lanterns spilling across the packed earth outside the inn. A pair of stable lads loitered by the hitching post, voices low, while a dog nosed about the stoop, tail thumping lazily against the worn stone step.

And then she saw him.

A lone figure stood beside the inn's front wall, half in shadow, half lit by the flickering lantern overhead. Tall and lithe, Tessa knew that silhouette. For the briefest moment, she thought some mistake must have been made: Rodney was standing there. But then he shifted. Turned his face slightly. And her breath caught.

Clark.

Tessa slowed, her pulse hammering in her throat as she tried to warm her icy hands. He'd always taken after his father, but the round face he'd inherited from his mother had faded as age had transformed him from a child to a young man.

Her son didn't smile. Didn't speak. Just stood there, his expression unreadable in the gathering dark, the space between them stretching taut and brittle.

"You've grown." Such a silly statement, but Tessa couldn't help it. Six years had turned the lad she'd known into a young man, complete with frock coat and hat. A gentleman.

Clark strode toward her, his hand outstretched, and Tessa rushed forward, her arms wide; tears blurred her vision as her mind rushed ahead, imagining the feel of her son in her embrace once more. But his hand remained wedged between them, keeping her at a distance as he shoved several objects at her. Tessa fumbled to keep them all in hand, hardly able to recognize the sack of marbles and silver penknife for what they were.

"We do not want anything from you," he said, and every muscle within her clenched. Hands trembling, she struggled to keep a hold of the gifts, and it felt as though she were standing on the front drive once more as Rodney cast her luggage out onto the gravel.

"They were gifts. That is all," she whispered.

"We both know that isn't true," he replied, lifting his other hand, which held the remnants of the pocket watch she'd given him. The metal was twisted and the glass shattered, as though he'd taken a hammer to the thing.

"That was your grandfather's. He wanted you to have it." Tessa didn't know how she managed to speak evenly, but seeing her father's beloved pocket watch mangled and her son's face distorted by fury broke something within her. Like a spring wound too tightly, it snapped. But rather than heat and fire surging forward, Tessa felt the strength seeping from her.

"I do not want it, you jezebel," he snapped. Though Rodney had called her that name often enough, hearing it from the same voice that had once called her Mummy and asked for lullabies cut as sharply as a knife.

"You broke my father's heart, and I want nothing to do with you. None of us do," he added. "I know Daphne said as much when you arrived, but clearly, you refuse to listen. So, I will tell you one more time."

Clark stepped closer until he was all she could see, fury vibrating through him, his eyes burning with a fire that made Tessa clutch the gifts closer to her. He wouldn't strike her. She knew that. No matter her husband's faults, he hadn't been a violent man, nor would he abide his son treating a woman poorly.

Harlot or not. Yet no matter how much she tried to assure herself, her muscles strained as though bracing for a blow.

"We do not want you here. We disown you. Leave us be," he said through gritted teeth.

Spinning on his heel, Clark strode away, and only once he was out of sight could Tessa breathe once more.

Where had her sweet little boy gone?

Clinging to the gifts in her arms, Tessa lowered her head and prayed—not for the first time, and certainly not the last—for forgiveness. That she could receive pardon for the damage she and her husband had done to those dear little souls that had been given into their care. Though the action gave no concrete sense of peace or lightening of her spirits, Tessa prayed all the same. And she begged for wisdom.

Ignoring the stableboys and ostlers who pretended that they hadn't been eagerly listening to every morsel, Tessa moved through the yard and into the inn. No doubt this would only serve as more kindling for Mr. Vaughn's ire. Somehow, the blame would be laid on her doorstep. How long would she be made to bear the burden of her and Rodney's mistakes on her own?

That thought had her feet faltering as she climbed the stairs to her room. Only once she was safely tucked away from prying eyes did Tessa allow the tears to gather—yet they wouldn't fall.

Surely a broken heart was simply an idiom. Delicate though the organ may be, one couldn't truly destroy it. Yet as Clark's words echoed in her thoughts, Tessa felt detached from it all. Not apathetic, for the pain hovered just out of reach, and a prickle in the deepest recesses of her soul warned that she would feel this all the more later. But her heart felt wrapped in cotton. Muted.

For the first time since hearing of Rodney's passing, Tessa truly wondered if she'd made a mistake coming to Thornsby. Who was she to force herself upon her children? If they did not want her, she ought to respect their wishes. Yet so much of their enmity sprang from half-truths and twisted tales; surely if they knew all, they would welcome her back.

As she sank onto her bed, Tessa's arms sagged, dropping the bits and bobs onto her lap.

How could she make them understand without doing further damage? They already knew far too much of their parents' troubles. Must she tarnish their father's memory in the hopes of winning their compassion and forgiveness? Ought she to ignore their wishes and force her company upon them?

Would she cause them so much pain for her own benefit?

Lungs jerking, the tears broke free, and Tessa crumpled into the pillows.

# Chapter 19

A gentleman didn't debase himself with money. Never mind that every life was directly impacted by income; a gentleman of standing ought never to pursue it in any overt fashion. One must possess money, not earn the gauche stuff. Even the landed gentry preferred for a steward to manage the estate and, most especially, the collecting of rent. Then they needn't dirty themselves with receiving the few coins their tenants scraped together—lest the master be mistaken for someone in trade. Heaven forfend.

Thankfully, Gregory Vaughn was not a gentleman. Not in a traditional sense.

Of course, times were changing, and what was once a rigid definition of a man without profession (except a very few acceptable pursuits) now encompassed a far broader sense of the word. With each passing decade, the gentry's estates and tenant farmlands were being sold off as those families refused to economize and acknowledge the shifting winds.

As physicians were considered gentlemen whilst surgeons were denied that lofty title, the Vaughns had often skirted the line of acceptability, as country physicians often dabbled in both. But thankfully, being proper Doctors of Medicine gave

Edward and Father a cachet that allowed them to straddle the line of gentility. They were no mere "Mr.," which was more than most gentlemen could claim.

However, an apothecary was not acceptable in any fashion. Most especially one who dared to open a shop front and sell his wares like a common tradesman. Never mind that the work they performed wasn't any different than that of physicians, who were known to prepare their own remedies and sell them to their patients. But such was done behind closed doors, so everyone could ignore that glaring hypocrisy.

Thankfully, Violet Vaughn's love of medicine and her husband's disinterest in holding to social strictures led them to open this most beautiful of shops. The moment one stepped inside, it was clear that nothing had been placed by accident. Shelves rose in perfect lines along the walls, each one crowded with neatly labeled jars and bottles, bringing color and scent to the space with the bright bite of lemon balm, dried lavender, and hints of mint and camphor weaving through the richer notes of licorice root and myrrh. The counter gleamed, wiped down to a polish, and even the scales—brass and well-used—rested like showpieces upon a velvet mat.

For all its modest footprint, Vaughn & Co. stood as a quiet marvel of industry and precision. A childhood spent at his mother's side as she mixed and fashioned the medicines her husband prescribed had given Gregory a love of these herbs and spices, but his natural propensity for business had transformed the small shop into a well-oiled enterprise, with shipments reaching the apothecaries of Leeds and Manchester—and even drawing inquiries from London. And people across the county spoke of "Vaughn's" as if it were a long-standing institution.

Gregory had earned every inch of this success, one mortarful at a time.

And yet—blast it all—the shop was so very small.

"Vaughn's is the first place the villagers go for medical advice," said Mr. Sparks, motioning to the displays of ready-made powders and tablets. "As many cannot afford a physician's fees for minor illnesses, apothecaries are often called upon to diagnose coughs, headaches, and fevers."

Reed College wasn't a mighty institution, so Gregory hadn't anticipated Jackson's class to be so numerous. But perhaps it was merely that the room was far too tight for an additional dozen bodies. Most especially boys, with their utter lack of awareness of their surroundings.

"Mind your elbows," Gregory called as a lanky schoolboy nearly knocked over a trio of bottles resting on the countertop.

Mr. Sparks paused in his explanation and straightened it before Gregory did so, and then the fellow continued with his lecture about the shopfront. As grateful as he was for Mr. Sparks volunteering to lead the presentation, Gregory couldn't help wondering if the fellow was suited for the task as the boys grew more and more restless.

There was a difference between being skilled in a subject and teaching it, and it seemed Mr. Sparks was no better at the latter than Gregory.

"Boys," whispered Walter, dragging their attention back to the lecture.

Meeting his assistant's eyes, Gregory nodded toward the door at the back of the shop, and Mr. Sparks motioned the group toward it.

"Now, let's see the workshop," he said, guiding them into the corridor that divided the apprentices' space and Gregory's. "Do not touch anything unless you fancy a rash or a nasty burn."

At that, the boys' attention sharpened, their spines straightening as they craned to look into the room whilst Mr. Sparks led them to where Mr. Caney and Mr. Wolsey worked. The air in the workshop thickened with the tang of ground minerals and vinegar distillations. A large work table filled the room, leaving just enough space for the young men to walk around it, though with the added bodies, it was difficult.

Thankfully, the apprentices had cleared the table of its usual parchments, herbs, and pestles, leaving only that which was required for the demonstration. The students squeezed between them in a disorderly shuffle, each one trying to see everything at once while avoiding contact with the large glass alembics arrayed in the center.

Gregory resisted the urge to sigh. It was a beautiful little shop. His life's work. His pride and joy. But as the boys jostled and craned their necks, their heads nearly knocking into the low-hanging bunches of comfrey and meadowsweet, he could no longer deny the simple truth: the shop was simply not large enough. Not anymore.

As their wares grew more popular, they required more space to make them. And while Gregory was pleased to have such a healthy venture situated in Thornsby, the village simply did not boast the capacity to maintain the shop's growth. Even assuming he could find land on which to build, the cost of constructing a new shop would be astronomical compared to the many ready buildings in the cities.

For all that he had needed to meet with various suppliers and shops in Leeds, Gregory ought to have stayed at home. He hadn't intended to look at properties, but he hadn't been able to stop himself from noticing the building sitting vacant not far from his inn. No doubt it would be occupied before long, but it was such a perfect location with a nice storefront and close access to the railway station to transport their goods to every corner of the country.

And the space! Large enough for him to hire clerks and assistants or take on a dozen more apprentices. To say nothing of the vast selection of rooms to let nearby.

Mr. Wolsey lit the burner beneath the alembic, a bright burst of fire spiking up to lick the bottom of the rounded jar, and like moths, the boys drew closer with gasps of excitement.

"Careful," warned Walter, pulling back one of the boys who reached over to grab it.

Glass clinked as another lad backed into the shelves that held the ingredient bottles, and Walter steadied the objects before they fell. With another word of warning, they continued their demonstration of the distillation process, but Gregory glanced over the group and noticed Jackson wasn't among them.

Turning about, he searched through the group, but the lad was nowhere to be seen—then Gregory spied his workshop door open with Jackson standing just inside. Crossing into that room, he found Mother there, showing the lad how to roll out tablets. She guided his hands as he fashioned a long rope from the paste, and once it was the right thickness, Mother ran a metal paddle over the top to slice it into proper doses.

"See that?" she said, motioning for Jackson to try. His hand slipped as he moved the paddles, but she simply had him roll it out once more and try again. Mother smiled, and a knot in Gregory's chest loosened. There was a brightness in her expression that he hadn't seen in several days, and it only grew as the lad tried once more.

"You make medicines?" asked Jackson, glancing up at the lady.

"Like many physicians' wives, I assisted him in his work," said Mother. "My husband managed the diagnosis and the patient care whilst I did what I do best. Though I have turned the operation over to Gregory, I still assist when I can."

With an easy glide of her hand, she sliced the paste into small tablets and urged Jackson to lay them out on the sieve to dry. Mother looked so pleased with her work, and Gregory felt another pang in his heart. It wasn't as though he'd truly considered relocating to Leeds, yet he still felt he'd betrayed her by allowing the thought to pass through his mind.

Father was struggling with the transition into total blindness, and Mother adored helping in the shop, so not only would he be abandoning them, but he would be taking away something his mother dearly enjoyed doing. Gregory supposed he could keep the shop open in Thornsby as well (the villagers would require medicines, after all), but managing two stores on top of everything else was too much at present.

To say nothing of the eagerness with which Jackson worked alongside her as she helped him measure ingredients. The Stuarts were finding their place amongst his family, and to pull them away would be cruel.

"Afternoon," called Edward as he swept into the workshop like the dervish he was. Bussing mother on the cheek, he snatched a vial from Gregory's shelf and tucked it into his medical bag. "I restocked up front, but you are low on rhubarb powder."

"Edward," said Gregory with a scowl. "I've told you again and again, you are free to take what you require, as long as you—"

"Keep a list," said Edward, holding up a piece of paper with a smirk. "I included the measurements of each item as well."

The fellow looked so pleased with himself, and Mother didn't help matters when she chuckled.

"Little brothers are a bother," grumbled Gregory.

"Not true in the slightest," said Edward. Nodding at Jackson, he asked, "We aren't a bother, are we?"

"I'm not, though Wesley can be a pest," he replied in all seriousness. "He likes to take my things."

Gregory met his brother's eye and took the list. "I can imagine how trying that is."

Nodding at the trio, Edward swept from the room with the same burst of energy with which he had entered it, and Jackson's brows rose as he met his guardian's gaze.

"See, a pest," said Gregory.

But Jackson merely shrugged and turned back to Mother as she guided him through another set of tablets. Perhaps he ought to have encouraged the lad to rejoin his class, but both he and Mother seemed pleased with the arrangement, so Gregory wasn't going to disrupt their enjoyment.

Glancing through the doorway into the workshop opposite, it was clear that Walter and the other fellows had them in order. Adding another body to the room would only exacerbate the problem, so Gregory moved to his desk and sat down as the sound of Mother's instructions transported him back to when he was Jackson's age and eagerly assisted her in her work.

But then his gaze fell to the journal on his desk, and Gregory's heart sank. Rodney's marriage had lasted some eighteen years, and his friend had been an avid journaler, leaving countless pages to peruse. So much so that he'd taken to carrying them about to get a bit of reading done whenever he could.

The cover fell open to the sheet of paper Gregory had tucked into the journal, which held his personal notes (including a record of Mrs. Stuart's claims). Setting it beside the volume, he flipped to the bookmark and his stomach sank as he reread the words that he'd chanced across before the boys had arrived.

*Tessa is expecting again. She came to my study to tell me the news and had the gall to expect me to be pleased with the announcement. About a child who cannot be mine? The lady hardly deigns to do her wifely duty and believes I will ignore the fact that she climbs into bed with countless others?*

*The eagerness in her eyes was sickening. Tessa's acting abilities have grown tenfold during our marriage, for anyone who did not know her better might actually believe she was genuinely happy at the thought of our family increasing. No doubt she will explain away how the child has Gooding's nose or eyes.*

*I cannot do this any longer. I cannot ignore the fact that I live in a battlefield where every discussion ends with broken hearts and bloodied spirits. If she wants Trevor Gooding, she can have him. I will not raise another's byblow as my own, nor will I allow my children to be sullied by associating with a baseborn child.*

*Tessa's tears seemed so genuine when I turned her from the house. So much so that even my heart—which knows better—nearly softened toward her. But the child she carries is not mine, and I am done with turning a blind eye to my wife's infidelities.*

*Let Gooding deal with her now.*

Reading the passage a third and fourth time didn't alter the words one jot. Rodney had been the one to drive his wife from the house. Granted, it was a far sight better than what he could've done to an unfaithful wife, but it did prove one thing for certain: Rodney's letter and stories were inconsistent with the record he'd made at the time of the events.

That, in and of itself, did not throw everything his friend had said into question, but as of yet, nothing in the book contradicted Mrs. Stuart's claims. Except for the matter of her infidelities. Yet the more and more Gregory combed through the book, the less and less evidence Rodney presented. Surely there was something concrete. Something he'd witnessed. Something more than suspicions and hearsay.

"What has you pulling that terrible face?" asked Mother, glancing up from the powder Jackson was grinding with his mortar and pestle. "You look like you are going to worry yourself into an early grave."

Gregory didn't know what to say to that whilst in mixed company, so he shut the book and affixed a smile to his face.

"It is Mother," said Jackson as he worked the pestle.

Straightening, Gregory shook his head. "I am not worried about your mother. And you shouldn't be either."

But Jackson fixed his gaze on the book. "That's Father's journal."

Gregory's own mother glanced between the two, her eyes seeing far more than Jackson likely knew.

"I heard Mr. Wolsey is doing a very special demonstration in the apprentice's workshop," she said, setting a hand on the lad's shoulder. "I think we ought to join the rest of your class."

"But..." Jackson glanced at his work, which was only partly finished.

"Let us strike a bargain," she said. "If you will join the class, I will ask your headmaster if you mightn't stay behind to help me finish, and I will fetch you back to school after. Perhaps you can even have your supper with Grandpapa as well."

For all that it was a good bargain—one that favored him highly—Jackson didn't readily accept it. He glanced at the door and back at Mother, and she shifted so that she could loop her arm around his shoulders.

"Would you like it if I joined you?" she asked, seeming to sense what he wanted without the boy likely understanding it himself. Then and only then did Jackson nod, allowing himself to be led into the other room—though, like a lad of fourteen was bound to do, he pulled from her touch when his classmates were in sight.

Gregory settled into his chair and frowned at nothing in particular. Did Jackson yearn for parental guidance? Or did he seek a mother's company in particular? Regardless of the answer, a weight settled into Gregory's chest at the thought that he was failing both Jackson and Rodney. Not only was he questioning his friend's behavior, but the children didn't even look to him as a father figure.

Leaning forward, Gregory closed his eyes and massaged his forehead as a tempest swept into his sanctuary.

Again.

# Chapter 20

"I forgot some of Mother's wound balm," said Edward, followed by the sound of clinking glass as he opened and closed the drawers of the cabinet along the far side.

"Vaughn's Miracle Balm. There's a jar in the third drawer on the far right," said Gregory, not bothering to look at his brother.

Silence followed that. "Please say that is not its name."

Gregory finally cracked his eyes open, leveling an amused look at his younger brother. "No. But it rolls off the tongue better than balsam of meadowsweet and marshmallow."

"My brother has a sense of humor," muttered Edward with more than a hint of amazement, though there was a dash of jest threaded in his tone. "Will wonders never cease? Next, you will tell me that you're courting some young lady in the village and intend on joining in the Morris dancing at the Midsummer Festival."

"With ribbons and all," said Gregory.

"I look forward to your performance." Snatching up the jar, Edward turned to leave, but Gregory called to the fellow before he disappeared again.

"Have you heard anything about false allegations of grand larceny?" asked Gregory as he added the pilfered item to his brother's list.

Edward turned, tucking the jar into his medical bag. "As in, generally speaking? Or are you referring to something specific?"

Drawing in a breath, Gregory let it out. In for a penny. "Regarding ladies and their shopping. I was told the other day that a store clerk leveled false allegations of larceny against a patroness. Is there any possibility that it is true? The whole thing seems like bad business, which is certain to drive off customers."

Glancing back at the door, Edward shut it and took the seat beside his brother with a sigh. "It does seem illogical, but I assure you it happens, and more frequently than you might believe. Especially to ladies who are alone and unprotected."

"But the shopkeeper's standing would be destroyed, and he'd lose his clientele." Gregory frowned. "And grand larceny? That would require a fair bit of thievery."

"Again, that is the logical conclusion, but as the purpose is to extort ladies who are terrified of damaging their reputation, few are willing to speak of it. Thus, the shopkeeper's sins never come to light," said Edward, setting his bag on his brother's desk. "And a length of lace is expensive enough to venture into the realm of grand larceny whilst small enough to slip in amongst the lady's purchases. Once they leave the shop, they are 'caught' and threatened with legal charges. Most ladies would rather pay a bribe than risk a damaged reputation."

"That seems so ridiculous," said Gregory with a shake of his head, but Edward met that with a hard look.

"It happens."

"I am not doubting you," he replied with a shrug. "I am simply saying it sounds a touch far-fetched."

Edward's brows rose in challenge. "It happened to Sadie."

Gregory jerked upright as though leaping into action, his pulse quickening, though his brother's calm wave of the hand made it clear that the business was done and over with.

"She came for a visit when I was studying in London, and she dragged me to some marketplace, though I insisted on remaining outside whilst she dug through bolts of fabric." Edward shook his head as though chastising himself. "The moment Sadie emerged, the rat came scurrying out the door and accosted her, snatching back her purchases to reveal the 'stolen' item. She was beside herself, and had I not been there, Sadie would've handed over every last farthing she had and the clothes off her back to placate him."

It had been years since that had happened, yet Gregory felt a surge of fury ripple through him at the thought. Their little sister was just the sort of sweet soul that villains preyed upon, and he could well imagine how readily she would've paid.

"I was able to convince him to leave things be," said Edward, his lips twisting into a smile that was too satisfied to mean anything less than justice had been served. "And Uncle Franklin and I *paid a call* on the fellow later to discuss how terrible an idea it was for him to continue that business practice."

Gregory could hardly imagine Uncle Franklin doing anything of the sort (assuming the threat rife in his brother's tone conveyed just precisely what sort of visit it had been). Then again, Gregory wasn't one to resort to such brutish behavior either, yet the thought of Sadie falling prey to someone—even if it was only a threat to her reputation—sent a shudder of fury through him that proved he was quite willing to go to blows with the right incentive.

"But why are you asking? This doesn't have anything to do with a certain widow lurking about the village, does it, Gregory?"

"I heard she was arrested for grand larceny not long ago."

Brows rising, Edward huffed. "Mrs. Stuart is a bold woman. I don't know many who are willing to fight such injustice. It likely cost her a fortune compared to a bribe."

"I do not know for certain that it was false," said Gregory. "I assume she was found innocent, as she is walking free, but my informant did not specify the outcome of the trial beyond the fact that it occurred, and I am waiting for more details."

"I will wager everything I hold dear in this world—including my wife and children—that it was false," said Edward. "From what I have seen and heard of her, Mrs. Stuart doesn't seem the sort to steal in the first place. She's generous to the staff at the inn, has paid for most of her expenses in advance, and even donated to a charity fund that Joanna is collecting. Those actions aren't indicative of a woman who must resort to such underhanded deeds."

Gregory scratched his cheek and considered that. While Edward's logic was sound, Mrs. Stuart had confirmed that she was the sort to steal. At least from her husband.

Glancing at the journal, he wished he understood more about what had passed between the pair. In the good moments, Rodney's descriptions of his wife were glowing and tender. Clearly, they'd been in love once upon a time, yet those bright and beautiful feelings had devolved into thievery, broken promises, and lies.

Their accounts of what had occurred were so vastly different that one of them must be lying. And the more he read the journals, the less certain he was that it was Mrs. Stuart.

"Does this have anything to do with that tussle at the inn?" asked Edward.

"What tussle?"

Edward's brows rose. "Between Clark and his mother. The village has been buzzing about it for the past two days."

Frowning, Gregory shook his head. "No one tells me any gossip."

That drew up his brother's brows even further. "What? The ladies of Thornsby don't rush to your side to tell you all the latest *on dits*?"

With a grunt, Gregory pushed away from the desk, rising to his feet, but Edward grabbed his arm and pulled him back.

"Peace, Gregory. I was teasing. Between being the village physician, meaning I spend far too much of my time in parlors, and my wife being a veritable font of tittle-tattle, I hear far more than I wish to know about our neighbors."

Holding up his hands in placation, Edward waited for him to settle again before adding, "Clark accosted Mrs. Stuart in front of the inn. Though their discussion wasn't overheard, the lad threw something at her and looked liable to strike her down in the streets before he stormed away."

Gregory shifted in his seat. "No doubt the gossips are inflating what actually happened."

"Likely," said Edward with a nod. "But even taking that into account, it is worrying. I spoke with someone who witnessed it, and they were convinced he would lay hands on her."

Stomach sinking, Gregory considered that. Even if everything Rodney had said about Mrs. Stuart was true—which was seeming less and less likely—hearing that the lad treated any woman with such disdain was disconcerting. That behavior was unacceptable. And when paired with Walter's reports about Clark's performance at school of late, Gregory knew the lad's current state was devolving at a rapid pace.

And what was he to do about that?

"You are a father," said Gregory, rubbing his forehead. "Do you have any suggestions for how to manage an unruly young man?"

Edward jerked back, his hands up to ward off the question. "I may have children, but there is a world of difference between being the parent of little ones and those nearly grown. The older they become, the more my hair grays and the wrinkles deepen."

"Your children are dears."

Widening his eyes comically, he shook his head, "Marianne is an angel for now, but little Timothy looks to follow after Caro and Shirley's example and become a monster once he learns to say 'no.' And Oscar has always been a handful."

Edward gave a pained chuckle. "You, dear Uncle Gregory, see them at their best, for you are blessed to swoop in and spoil them when it suits you and leave Joanna and me to manage the rest."

Gregory's brows rose at that. "I am sorry if I have made your work more difficult."

His brother waved it off. "That is the purpose of aunts, uncles, and grandparents. I cannot describe how much joy it brings me to see my family dote on the children I love so dearly."

And a spark of that same warmth flickered in Gregory's heart at the thought of Mother working with Jackson and Joanna taking Daphne under her wing. In their own way, the family was reaching out to his own brood now.

"I fear, dear brother, that you have a difficult road ahead," said Edward with a sigh, "Being guardian to a child isn't an easy burden to bear, but at least natural guardians have the blessing of taking on one at a time as they slowly grow into more and more difficult issues. With most of my children, the greatest worry Joanna and I have is whether or not they will eat their supper or if they will have a difficult night's sleep. You have proper people to worry and fret over."

"And matters aren't helped by the fact that their mother is running about making trouble," muttered Gregory.

"Making trouble or attempting to set things to rights?" asked Edward.

But Gregory had no answer to give.

"Give yourself some grace, brother of mine," he said, rising to his feet. "You became guardian to six children all at once. You are going to make many mistakes, but you care too deeply to go too far afield."

Taking up his bag once more, Edward strode to the door and paused, his hand hovering over the handle. Turning back, the fellow considered Gregory for a long moment before speaking.

"I don't have much advice, but I will say that you ought to remember something Rodney never did: it isn't your place to decide what relationship the children have with their mother."

Edward paused, but there was far too much contemplation in that silence for Gregory to think he was finished, so he waited.

"As Joanna doesn't speak of her father, I doubt it will be a surprise if I say that she is not on good terms with him." Pausing again, Edward sorted through his words. "For reasons too complicated to enumerate here, my father-in-law does not love his daughter. Yet Joanna never stops hoping he will one day."

Setting the bag on the shelf beside him, Edward crossed his arms. "She wished him to meet the children, so we brought them to London as he cannot be bothered to visit. And though he dotes on them when they are underfoot, he doesn't give them another thought after we return home and never shows any interest in their mother. Her letters go mostly unanswered, and the scant responses she does receive show no interest in her whatsoever. And it pains her so much."

Edward's jaw clenched as he drew in a deep breath. "For a long time, I encouraged her to cut ties. To embrace the family she found with my kin. And though she has done the latter, she cannot seem to help herself with the former. I cannot bear to see the heartache it causes her, but forcing the issue merely placed a wedge between us. Eventually, I came to understand that my role as her husband is to reassure her that she is adored and valued—not to keep her locked away from anything that might harm her. It is her choice if she wishes to put her heart at risk, and it is my privilege to help her piece it back together."

Snatching up his bag once more, Edward nodded at Gregory. "Besides, from what I hear, Mrs. Stuart has purchased a seat on the stagecoach tomorrow. She is returning to Leeds, so I doubt she will be a bother in the future."

And with that, Edward took his leave, abandoning his brother to his thoughts.

## Chapter 21

News of Mrs. Stuart's impending departure ought to stir some sentiment within him, but Gregory couldn't say what he felt or thought about that development. A few days ago, he likely would have celebrated the victory, but a hollowness settled into his chest as he stared down at Rodney's journal.

Pulling open the cover, Gregory turned to the first section he'd bookmarked, his list of evidence poking up from the pages. Far too many passages left him feeling as though his clothes were made of homespun fabric, the fiber itching his skin.

Such vitriol. Animosity. Perhaps they were just the hyperbolic words of a man betrayed by the woman he loved, but Gregory couldn't imagine saying them to anyone, let alone wallowing in the sentiment for so many years—as was evidenced by Rodney's own pen.

And the list of contradictions grew with every page. Memories were flawed things, and a man's recollection was bound to alter over the years. So Rodney's fallibility was hardly a sign of guilt.

And yet…

Those two words kept bringing him back to the journal again and again, only to find more passages that sent shudders of dread running through him. The more Rodney wrote about his wife, the more it felt as though the fellow was trying to convince himself to despise everything about her. And the more Gregory searched for concrete evidence of Mrs. Stuart's wrongdoing, the more he questioned why Rodney believed so wholeheartedly in it.

Gregory couldn't help himself as he dove deeper into the journal, skimming over entries that had nothing to do with his quest.

*Tessa arrived on my doorstep today, demanding she be granted time with the children, claiming that she cared about their well-being—despite the fact that her very presence threatens to ruin them. If not their reputations, then their spirits. What sort of children would benefit from engaging with their jezebel of a mother?*

*We've lived apart for two years. Not amicably, to be certain, but we had reached a détente of sorts until I uncovered the truth about Eva. How can I trust her near my children when it is clear she is devoid of kindness and wishes to hurt their father?*

*But even with my plans to separate them from her influence, I have no guarantee that she shan't appear on my doorstep in Thornsby with demands, eager to spoil the haven I wish to build for my family.*

*As much as it pains me to write this, I do not regret the action I had to take. Tessa only desires control over the children because of the generous allowances I would grant them if we were parted. The only choice I had was to threaten to disinherit the children if she persisted in making a nuisance of herself.*

*Of course, no matter how much I despise their mother, I would never cut them off, but selfish creature that she is, Tessa readily accepted that a parent could be so cruel to his offspring.*

Gregory's stomach turned in a sharp twist, and he stared at the page, the words blurring, reforming, and blurring again as if his mind refused to believe his eyes. His breath came shallow, and a cold sweat broke across the back of his neck. His fingers curled around the edge of the desk, gripping hard enough to blanch the knuckles.

Disinherit the children? Threaten them to win an argument? Gregory could scarcely comprehend it. The same man who'd spoken so passionately about protecting his legacy and ensuring his children's future had wielded them like a weapon.

Gregory rose abruptly, the chair scraping behind him, and he paced in a tight circle, the journal still open in one trembling hand. It felt as though the walls were closing in, the familiar scent of licorice root and sage was suddenly cloying, and he needed air. He needed distance from the journal, from the office, from the growing certainty that he had been deceived in every possible way.

A hundred questions surged through his mind, but no answers accompanied them. How many other truths had Rodney twisted? His friend. His brother. The man Gregory had defended to others. And even to himself.

Rodney had lied. There was no way around it. His own words confirmed what Mrs. Stuart had said. His friend had forced her from his home and threatened their children to keep her away. Perhaps—just perhaps—that was warranted to protect the children, but Gregory couldn't say for certain that he believed anything Rodney had told him. Not anymore.

And he had to sort it out before Mrs. Stuart left Thornsby.

...

Curiosity killed the cat. The idiom may be truthful, but it provided not a shred of useful advice on how to avoid curiosity's all-too-alluring trap. After all, instinct usually warned of the danger to come, so adding an idiom was as useful as squeezing a bit of lemon into a papercut. Truthful it may be, but useful the phrase was not.

Staring at the paper, Tessa knew she ought to toss it into the fire and be done with it. Only someone whose faculties were greatly damaged would deign to read another word from Mr. Gregory Vaughn, let alone cling to the paper as though it were a lifeboat in a tempest. No matter how many times Tessa read it, the words remained the same.

*Please come to my shop. — G.V.*

There was no further explanation as to the purpose of the visit or what business he had with her, but Tessa didn't trust herself to be in the same room as that gentleman. Not without reverting into some twisted form of herself. And heaven help her, she didn't want that.

In her youth, Theresa Rush Stuart had believed herself a confident woman, avoiding both the dreaded pride and self-deprecation which led one to believe oneself better or lesser than others. She had achieved that beautiful balance between confidence and humility.

Then age and childbirth robbed her of her figure, leaving her without the strongest allure she possessed—the one that had secured her husband and the admiration of others. Without it, she was left to realize she hadn't been confident at all. Not when that trait had remained untested, for it crumpled as easily as tissue paper when the first hint of doubt stirred within her.

After years of effort, Tessa could finally say without hesitation that she admired the person she was. Imperfect and flawed though she may be, she accepted that work-in-progress and continued to improve with each passing day.

Yet Mr. Vaughn had a way of sapping that strength until she was the weak, vengeful creature she didn't wish to be. Clearly, the foundation Tessa had built over the past few years wasn't without its weaknesses, and the gentleman found each and every one.

Tessa shook that thought aside. It wasn't fair to lay the blame on him. She was the mistress of her thoughts and actions, and she had allowed them to pull free of her control.

But the question remained: did she wish to put herself in another situation in which she might fall to pieces? Ignoring crumbling mortar and stones only led to more deterioration, and now that Tessa knew that the strength she'd gained wasn't foolproof, would she cloak herself in self-delusion and pretend all was well? Or would she use the opportunity to shore up that weak foundation?

That thought rattled about in her heart, and before she knew it, Tessa stood before Vaughn & Co., its windows gleaming bright in the afternoon light. Her palms dampened her gloves, and she fought the impulse to rub them against her skirts. The paper was crumpled in one hand as she reached for the door handle with her other, her pulse quickening as she stepped into the shop.

She prayed that this time she would behave with more decorum. And that Mr. Vaughn hadn't summoned her for a tongue-lashing. Before her pulse quickened further, she reminded herself that his note had said "please." Though it may be simply a bit of ingrained politeness, that word was one of the reasons Tessa had allowed herself to be lured here.

"Good morning, Mrs. Stuart," called a fellow from behind the counter. "Mr. Vaughn said you would be stopping by for a consultation. Please follow me."

Tessa hid her initial surprise, but she supposed that ruse was true enough, and it allowed them to meet without drawing speculation.

Following the man into the corridor, she was ushered into the office in which their first true battle had been waged. Mr. Vaughn popped up from his seat behind the desk and motioned for her to sit before doing the same. Again, such politeness signified nothing—though he'd shown little of it in the past.

But when they settled into their chairs, Mr. Vaughn remained silent.

"Why am I here, sir?" she asked.

"Firstly, I wish to apologize for my behavior."

The statement was so wholly different from that which Tessa had expected to hear that she was certain her ears were playing tricks on her. She couldn't think of another man (let alone such a masculine specimen) willing to beg forgiveness of anyone. Especially a lady. And one who had been so vexing of late.

Mr. Vaughn's gaze didn't waver, meeting hers with determination, as though willing her to believe the sincerity of his words and tone.

"I am ashamed of what I said to you, madam, and I hope you understand that it was born of frustration and anxiety, though I do not want you to think that I am using that as an excuse for the inexcusable," he added with a frown. "No matter the troubles between you and your husband, I haven't the right to say what I did and treat you so poorly."

Again, Tessa sat there. Thankfully, her mouth was not agape, though it longed to hang open like the fool she was.

"I do not know what to say to that, Mr. Vaughn."

"You needn't say a thing," he said, easing back into his seat. "But it is high time for a frank discussion. One that doesn't devolve into an argument."

"Perhaps if we both do our best to hold onto our tempers, we might manage it," she said with the faintest of smiles.

But Mr. Vaughn's frown deepened. "I've never had a temper before."

That struck Tessa deep in her heart. Though he did not specify that it was meeting her that had brought out that hardness in his character, it was implicit in the statement, and a hollow ache opened in her chest, sudden and unwelcome. Glancing away from his eyes, which were too piercing and saw too much, Tessa tucked her hands in her lap with care, as if precision might make up for all the disorder she had caused. Her throat tightened, and the apologies she yearned to offer dissolved on her tongue.

"Mrs. Stuart, are you leaving Thornsby in hopes of drumming up sympathy?" Though the question was blunt, it lacked the sharpness of an accusation, and Mr. Vaughn watched her closely with a gaze that was wary but far gentler than before.

Tessa huffed. "I have no wish to playact, nor do I believe such deceptions would work. You have made your feelings clear. I am leaving to see to some business that requires my attention."

Forcing her tone to remain even, she added, "But in truth, I do not know if I shall return."

Mr. Vaughn gave a sharp hum that drew her gaze to him, only to find him watching her with raised brows. "After waging so many fierce battles, you are surrendering?"

Eyes fixed on her hands in her lap, Tessa fought against the blush that warmed her cheeks. Oh, how she longed to simply walk out the door and leave this conversation behind her. What good would it do?

Yet lying to herself was useless. If she were truly defeated, she wouldn't have answered Mr. Vaughn's summons. Whether or not victory felt far out of reach, that little glimmer of hope that sparked in her heart, which dreamed of healing the breach between her and the children, had brought her to this seat, and it wouldn't allow her to leave Mr. Vaughn's workshop any more than it would allow her to accept Clark's dismissal.

Mr. Vaughn had asked for frankness. And he'd done so politely. If her marriage had taught her nothing else, it was the importance of honest and calm dialogue. Even if she hadn't managed to do so with Rodney.

"I am not surrendering. I am acknowledging that it is unfair of me to force my company upon my children," she said, fighting against the quiver that threatened to take hold. "I love them with all my heart, but I will not allow my feelings to run roughshod over theirs—"

Tessa's voice stumbled, and she tamped down the pain that prickled through her heart.

Forcing her gaze to Mr. Vaughn, she asked once more with far too much desperation in her tone, "Why am I here, sir?"

Mr. Vaughn drummed his fingers against his desk for a long moment.

"You are here because I took your advice and read Rodney's journals," he said. "I've hardly done anything else for the past few days."

Giving him a closer look, Tessa spied the signs of sleepless nights. The dimness of his gaze. The darkness beneath his eyes. The disheveled quality to his coiffure. Even his cravat seemed deflated. She took it all in in a heartbeat, assessing the whole of it in the pause between Mr. Vaughn's words.

"I need more answers, Mrs. Stuart." His tone was cautious. Even a little resigned. "And I believe I am finally willing to hear what you have to say."

# Chapter 22

That flicker of hope in Tessa's heart—bright and sharp—burst into a bright ball of flames, and the heaviness in her limbs evaporated like the mist beneath the rays of the morning sun. It took every ounce of restraint to remain in her chair. Her fingers twitched with the urge to move, to do anything to match the sudden flare within her. Even her breath felt altered, lighter and fuller, as if the very air had changed.

But the warmth surging through her wavered as hope collided with doubt, muddling her thoughts until they no longer held shape, and her fingers clasped her skirts, gripping tight as though to anchor herself. Tessa had longed for this moment, but now that it had come, she didn't know quite what to do with it.

"That may well be, but I cannot ignore my children's wishes," she said, though she had to cut out a piece of her heart to speak the words.

Mr. Vaughn stared at her for a long moment before his own gaze fell away, dropping to the journal as his jaw clenched. He remained thusly for several excruciating moments before meeting her eyes once more.

"Might we not sort out this business first?" he asked, tapping the book. "My foremost concern is the children, and I am no longer certain it is in their best interest to separate you."

Once more, that hope expanded until it filled the whole of her and threatened to seize control, but just as it was unwise to allow her temper free rein, giving into even a joyful emotion could cause great harm. Self-control was key, and though tamping one's emotions entirely was damaging, surrendering to them was just as unwise.

Caution was best.

"I have questions, and I want honest answers," he continued. "I give you my word that I will not rush to judgment, but I insist you do not prevaricate. I am not asking these questions to condemn you but to better understand the situation and what it might mean to the children."

"I swear to speak truthfully," said Tessa, her head bobbing fast as she nodded. "Ask me anything, and I will answer."

Mr. Vaughn drew in a breath, his dark eyes boring into hers as he asked, "Did you break your marriage vows?"

The question struck like a church bell—sharp, booming, and impossible to ignore. Given the history between her and Rodney, it was hardly unexpected, yet those blunt words knocked the breath from her lungs. Tessa's lips parted, but no sound emerged, and her body stilled as though the world itself had gone motionless. Heat flared in her chest, pulsing up her neck, but still she said nothing, caught between the sting of indignation and the sobering gravity of the moment.

"I understand that you have heard much from Rodney's perspective..." she began, the words rushing out before she stumbled. "No doubt it is shocking that... I struggled to..."

Pausing, Tessa drew in a breath. Honesty. No one could predict what the future held for her, but she knew without a doubt that nothing but the unvarnished truth would set things to rights.

"According to the letter of the law, no," she said, forcing herself to hold Mr. Vaughn's gaze. "But I broke the spirit of it. I opened my heart to other men, and had things continued as they were, I would have broken my vows fully."

Tessa's gaze grew unfocused, drifting away from Mr. Vaughn as her thoughts sifted through the past. Where to begin? How to explain it all? Even though she had lived through the whole of it, she couldn't believe how things had altered over the years, twisting what had been a happy beginning into something unrecognizable.

"My husband and I were a love match," she said, a smile gracing her lips as she contemplated those early months when they had enjoyed spending every moment together. "But all those similarities of thought and feeling that we had believed were the sign of a good match led to it becoming that dead and desiccated thing you knew. Like so many courting couples, we valued a similarity of opinions and interests, completely ignoring the fact that our sameness meant we bore the same flaws and shortcomings."

Tessa couldn't help the bitter chuckle that escaped. "It wasn't until I was much older that I realized that differences tempered with understanding and compassion make for stronger relationships than a sameness of opinions. We were both short-tempered, quick to find fault, and slow to forgive—all of which led to the chasm in our marriage. Every difficulty we faced only forced us further apart and added to the resentment brewing on both sides."

Straightening, she smoothed her skirts and forced herself to face Mr. Vaughn again. "Like far too many ladies, my sense of self was contingent on my appearance, which altered greatly with each child I bore. And that pain grew as my husband's attraction faded. But other men flirted with me. Complimented me. They thought me beautiful whilst my husband did his best to hide his apathy."

Tessa's cheeks burned, but she refused to shy away. "Now, I see that it was just a game to them, but at the time, it mattered not one jot. I thought myself disgusting and worthless, and garnering their attention allowed that pain to ease, though only as long as they were smiling at me. So I sought them out more and more."

Mr. Vaughn said nothing. His expression gave no hint as to his thoughts as she confessed her sins, and Tessa refused to consider how his opinion of her was shifting with each one.

"I wish I could say it started innocently, but my broken heart knew what it was doing," she said with a shake of her head. "I set my feet on a path that led to ruin, justifying my shameful actions because my cold-hearted husband no longer loved me. I convinced myself that the true betrayals were Rodney's doing, not mine."

They say the truth shall set you free. Tessa prayed it was true.

"Our separation happened before I crossed the line into true infidelity, and thankfully, it shocked me enough to draw me back from the edge, but I am ashamed of the way I conducted myself, and I do not blame Rodney for believing the worst of my behavior."

Mrs. Stuart's words didn't shock him, not exactly. They simply fit too well into the gaps left by Rodney's narrative, giving weight to the half-formed theories that had taken shape in Gregory's mind. What had once been fleeting discomfort while reading his friend's account now became something far heavier, anchored in his heart by the lady's quiet, matter-of-fact admissions.

Simplicity had been easier. Cleaner. But now, every line of that journal felt suspect, and nothing about this situation could be called simple.

"But to answer your question in full: yes, I broke our marriage vows." Mrs. Stuart's dark eyes held his, shining with a sorrow too sincere to be cast aside. "I did not share my bed with another, but that is the very least required of a marriage. Fidelity is not the only vow we make, and I did not remain true to my promise to love, honor, and cherish the man I had chosen to be my husband."

With a shake of her head, Mrs. Stuart's eyes fell away once more as she examined her hands in her lap. "That was the trouble with our marriage, Mr. Vaughn. Neither of us held true to those vows. And rather than examine our own behavior, we fixated on the other's. For every action Rodney took against me, I returned it in spades, convinced that I was right to defend myself from the brute that was my husband. Just as Rodney felt justified in retaliating against me. And the ones who paid the most for our behavior were our children."

Brows raising, Mrs. Stuart paused for a long moment before rising to her feet, and with a voice tinged with worry, she murmured, "I shouldn't be here. I have already done enough damage to my children, and I have seen enough to know you are a fit guardian. Forcing myself upon them would only serve my pride and damage them further. I cannot do it."

"Peace, Mrs. Stuart," said Gregory as he stood.

"No. For their good, I ought to leave things be. I shouldn't have come in the first place. It was selfish of me, and I am done placing my own desires above what is best for my family. Rodney and I caused all this trouble because of our selfishness, and I will not repeat the mistakes of the past."

With that, the lady moved to the door, shaking her head back and forth as though chastising herself, and Gregory found himself hurrying over to block the way.

"I shan't lie and say I haven't wanted this from the moment I discovered your identity," he said, warding her off. "But your leaving doesn't feel right."

"You do not strike me as a man governed by his feelings, Mr. Vaughn."

"Any man of sense knows there are times when one must embrace instincts, and mine are shouting that this is a mistake. I beg you to wait a moment."

Leading her back to her seat, Gregory perched on the edge of the desk and crossed his arms as he considered the problem before him. "I cannot promise that remaining will be easy on you or the children, but they need their mother."

"They despise me." Mrs. Stuart's voice was filled with abject sorrow, as though speaking those words ripped free a bit of her soul, and her chin trembled as she met Gregory's gaze, pleading with him to deny it whilst expecting him to agree.

"They are hurting and confused, and unfortunately, Rodney has filled their heads with half-truths," he said in a low voice, hoping his tone might soothe her troubled spirits as much as the words. "However, I do not think they would be so angry if they did not care very deeply."

Mrs. Stuart looked away from him, her shoulders slumping.

"I am speaking from experience." Gregory cleared his throat, attempting to find the words to explain the situation without wandering into territory that was best left alone—for all their sakes. "I am not always comfortable around others, yet I enjoyed your company so very much during our journey to Thornsby. Only to discover you were the monster I had been warned about."

Tilting his head to the side, he added, "Then our interactions cast doubts on the honor of the man whom I considered a brother, which pained me all the more. And rather than investigate, I badgered and berated you, hoping you would leave so I wouldn't have to question my loyalty to your husband. Unfortunately, confusion and fear can often emerge as anger."

Gregory sighed and shook his head. "Yet leaving will not save the children from those feelings. They will only fester. The best hope for them is if you remain and sort this out. Please. For their sake."

Pressing her fingers to her mouth, Tessa willed herself to breathe, to think, to remain composed, but the swell of emotion rose faster than she could brace against it. Each thought crashed into the next, too loud, too fast. She blinked hard, but her vision blurred, and her throat closed tight around the breath she tried to take.

Tessa clutched her skirts as though they might anchor her, but they didn't. Nothing could. She had spent years building herself into something strong and steady, and it was all undone in one conversation. She covered her face, half hiding, half trying to gather herself, but it was no use. It was too much.

The tears broke free in great heaving sobs.

Then a hand rested on her shoulder, and Tessa forced her eyes open enough to see Mr. Vaughn through the haze of tears. He had moved to the seat beside her and was staring at her with wide eyes as though she were a lit cannon ready to fire, and the sight drew forth a frenzied chuckle from her lips.

"I apologize," she managed between shuddering breaths. "I am a mess. I know it. But after so many years of being told I am unfit... To hear someone say... My own son calls me a jezebel, but you..."

It was no use. The words crumbled, leaving her a sniffling, hiccuping mess.

"Clark said that?" Mr. Vaughn's tone was sharp, and Tessa took the handkerchief he offered, wiping at her cheeks.

"Do not be angry with him," she managed as she made a proper mess of the linen. "He has always idolized his father, and he was only repeating—"

"Something his father ought never to have said to him in the first place," said Mr. Vaughn, his tone even sharper. Letting out a sigh, the fellow added, "Clark will be the hardest to sway, and I do not know how we should go about this, but I do believe it is for their good, Mrs. Stuart."

Tears threatened to redouble, but Tessa breathed deeply, forcing the air into her chest to loosen the tightening muscles. "My thanks, Mr. Vaughn."

His brows rose at that.

"For putting their well-being first," she explained, though she couldn't keep the tears from wobbling her voice. "I am grateful they have someone who cares so deeply about them. Rodney chose well."

Straightening, though his hand remained on her shoulder, Mr. Vaughn studied her for a long, quiet moment. His gaze possessed such strength that Tessa felt like she might wilt beneath it, so she steadied herself by cleaning the last of her tears from her eyes.

"After how I have treated you, I do not feel I deserve any thanks," said Mr. Vaughn with brows pulled low.

Tessa dabbed at her face. "We all make mistakes. The important thing is whether you are willing to recognize it and set it to rights once you do."

Giving that a nod, the gentleman gave her a half-smile. "Then I suppose it is time we discuss how to do so with your children."

## Chapter 23

The rain had done its worst the day before, leaving the village damp and glistening; though the roads and fields held the memory of yesterday's storm, the worst of it had passed. Now, sunlight filtered through the clouds in fitful gleams, dappling the landscape with hesitant cheer, and though the air was brisk enough to button one's coat a bit higher, the chill made the warmth of the sun feel like a reward.

Thank the heavens. Today was going to be difficult enough on its own. Fair weather was the very least they could ask for, though Gregory found himself petitioning heavenward for more than clear skies. History was littered with greater miracles, so surely they might be graced with this little one today.

Eden Place didn't boast the sort of expansive grounds one might expect of a grand estate, as the past owners had sold off the bulk of the property to supplement the very income that was destroyed by parcelling off the land that provided it. However, there remained a large enough portion of parkland around the building to lend it a feeling of vastness.

Lawn surrounded the building itself with smatterings of forest in the distance to give the view the necessary visual interest the wealthy thought nature lacked. The copse around them stretched wide, with oak, hazel, and ash forming a patchwork canopy above, their leaves fluttering in a breeze that carried the cool scent of damp soil. Here and there, the undergrowth thickened with brambles, heavy with the promise of fruit to come, and ferns unfurled like peacock plumes along the base of the trees.

The storm had washed everything clean, making the green of the moss and the brown of the bark all the more vivid, deepening the tones until it felt as though an artist had painted over the world, and everything smelled alive. Fresh.

A pair of wood pigeons startled overhead, wings flapping as they took flight, and the usual chorus of songbirds fell silent as the Stuart horde invaded their sanctuary.

Of course, Daphne walked calmly like the young lady she was becoming, and Faith was as quiet as ever as she walked hand in hand with Gregory, but the rest of the children more than made up for that display of decorum. The boys, freed from school for their half day, dashed to and fro, tromping through the undergrowth to examine the trees and greenery whilst Eva chased after them.

Gregory reviewed what he needed to say, though he still hadn't found the right combination of words. They had a few minutes before they reached the picnic site, but he needed to reveal their purpose before they arrived, as springing Mrs. Stuart on them would hardly be an auspicious beginning. Yet all explanations slipped from his grasp.

Praying with all his heart that this was the right way forward, Gregory begged for assistance—that they might heal the breach between mother and children, and the latter would not begrudge their guardian for his role in it.

The path sloped slightly downward, and in the distance, the trees thinned, revealing an open meadow bathed in sunlight. And before he could say a word, the boys and Eva sprinted ahead, darting into the open grass.

"Wait!" he called, moving to follow, though Faith would not release his hand or walk quicker.

"What is she doing here?" shouted Clark, and as Gregory broke free of the forest with Faith and Daphne in tow, he spied the lad standing just beyond the edge of the copse, his finger pointed toward Mrs. Stuart, his muscles tightening with that movement like some furious spellcaster, desperate to curse the lady.

"Clark," she said in a soothing voice, stepping around the blankets and pillows that had been arranged by the servants. With hands raised to calm the lad, Mrs. Stuart tried to smile, though it was strained. "I know this is a shock, but might we speak?"

"You said she left the village," said Daphne, her wide eyes burning into her brother's back, and the lad turned as though to face her but stopped halfway, refusing to give his mother his back but determined to keep both sister and mother in sight.

"She did," he said, scowling at her.

"I had business to attend to in Leeds, but then I returned," said Mrs. Stuart with a note of pleading in her tone.

Reaching for Daphne, Gregory pressed a gentle hand to her back, but she refused to move. The boys and Eva all stood in the field like statues, facing their mother, though the youngest's gaze darted between them all. Stepping forward, Gregory moved closer to Mrs. Stuart, and Faith walked with him, her hand tightening around his; her eyes sparked with surprise and more than a hint of fear, yet Faith did not release him, following along with a trust that Gregory hoped he wasn't betraying.

"It is time that we all had a conversation," he said, giving each of the children a measured look, though Clark wouldn't remove his eyes from his mother. "There have been some misunderstandings in the past, and I think it is time to clear the air."

Clark scoffed. "There is nothing to clear with *her*. How can you even suggest such a thing!"

"Peace," said Gregory, holding up his free hand in placation (though the other remained firmly in Faith's hold, as she refused to release him).

"I know you are angry with me," said Mrs. Stuart. "And you have a right to be. I have made many mistakes, but not the ones you believe."

"And you think that simply exchanging one set of mistakes for another will make us forgive you? Listen to you? Welcome you back?" asked Clark, his hard tone at war with the peaceful setting around them. "You have nothing to say that I wish to hear."

"I am not here to offer excuses," she hurried to add. "I am simply hoping for an opportunity to mend—"

"There is nothing to mend," said Clark, stepping backward. "We want nothing from you, except to be left alone."

Spinning on his heel, he leveled a glare at Gregory and motioned for his siblings, but they remained rooted to the ground, their attention fixed on their mother. Mrs. Stuart stepped forward, drawing closer to Eva, and that jerked Daphne from her stupor. Darting forward, the young lady rushed to her youngest sister, snatching up the girl's hand and dragging her away from the lady.

"Are you coming?" called Clark, his glare boring into his younger brother, and Jackson glanced between him and his guardian.

"It is your decision," said Gregory, holding the lad's gaze for a moment before looking at the rest of the children. "This is an opportunity for you to speak to your mother if you wish."

"I will not force my presence on you," added Mrs. Stuart. "But I would like to know you—"

"*We* do not wish to know *you*." Then, going over to his brother, Clark yanked on the lad's arm, trying to drag him away. "Come on!"

But Jackson remained firm and shook him off, earning him a glare from his elder brother.

"You cannot mean to remain here," Clark said, scowling. "You know what she did to Father. What she's done to us."

"But she's our mother," said Jackson, his brows furrowing as he glanced between her and his brother.

"Don't be a fool. She is the woman who abandoned us so she could *whore* herself out—"

"Watch your tongue." Gregory managed to speak evenly, though a flare of temper made it difficult to do so. "You do not speak that way—"

"Don't call her that!" shouted Jackson, launching himself at his brother. Clark cocked his arm, slamming it into Jackson's nose, and then the elder boy was on the younger like a tiger, tearing and swiping, though with the two of them grappling so close, neither was able to land decent blows.

Their mother rushed over whilst Gregory tugged at his hand, trying to extricate himself from Faith's hold as he shouted for them to stop. Just as Mrs. Stuart drew close, Clark aimed another blow at his brother, but it swung wide, almost striking the lady. Giving the child at his side a promise to return, Gregory yanked free and ran over, grabbing Clark by the collar and dragging him away from the others.

"Don't you dare lay a hand on your mother—" but Clark swung about, and his fist flew at his guardian next, though Gregory caught it. "You have every right to be angry, but you do not have the right to sling insults or fists."

Turning his gaze to Jackson, Gregory added, "Either of you."

"Traitor!" Jerking free of his hold, Clark shoved at Gregory's chest. "You were Father's friend. He trusted you to keep her away, and now you're protecting her?"

"It is complicated—"

"No, it isn't!" shouted Clark. "I am old enough to remember her leaving, and I won't be taken in by her lies."

"If you do not wish to remain, that is your choice, but I will not allow you to choose for the rest. They may stay here if they so desire," said Gregory, meeting the lad's gaze with an unspoken challenge. Though he couldn't say he knew much about children, he understood battles for dominance quite well, and to show even a shred of weakness in this moment would be to grant the lad the freedom to continue on this cruel path he'd chosen.

Gregory remained there a long moment before Clark finally broke eye contact, tugging at his frock coat as he set himself to rights once more. Turning a burning glare to Jackson, the lad studied his younger brother, and though it was clear a slew of words flitted through his mind with every fractious beat of his heart, Clark remained silent and turned away.

Daphne followed after, towing Eva along, though the child's brow furrowed as she stared back at her mother. Gregory considered what to do about the situation, for he refused to allow Eva to be dragged off if she wished to stay, but before he could say a word, the child drew into her elder sister's side, giving her mother her back as well.

But the rest remained where they were.

Faith hadn't moved, and when Gregory returned, she snatched up his hand and burrowed into his side as Eva had done with Daphne. Jackson dusted himself off, glancing warily at their mother, and Wesley stood alone; neither his position nor expression had altered from the moment that they'd spied Mrs. Stuart, so there was no telling what the lad was thinking.

Turning to Mrs. Stuart, Gregory wasn't entirely certain where to go from here; the entire situation was fraught with difficulties that were nigh on impossible to anticipate. But then he glanced down at Faith, whose attention was fixed on her mother.

"We brought a picnic," he said, nodding toward the hampers, which were overflowing with far more food than a group of five could eat. But Gregory had thought it better to plan for the best outcome, which would've required enough for eight.

Faith allowed herself to be led to the blanket, and Jackson followed suit, though Wesley remained where he was, standing amongst the grass and wildflowers. Helping the child to sit, Gregory joined her, though she leaned into him close enough that she was nearly in his lap; had she not been too grown for such a thing, he would've happily obliged, but he contented them both by settling an arm around her.

"Are you only here because Father's gone?" asked Jackson, his expression and tone hard as he dropped onto the blanket on the other side of his sister.

Mrs. Stuart knelt before them, her eyes bright with emotion as she folded her hands in her lap. Her gaze flicked to Gregory, and he gave her a nod in support. This was not a simple discussion to have, and he prayed the children would accept what they had decided to share.

## Chapter 24

"I always wanted to be with you." Clearing her throat, Mrs. Stuart clenched her hands in her lap and glanced toward Wesley, who remained close enough to hear. "Your father and I did not suit, and we didn't try hard enough to be peaceable with one another. My leaving was due to troubles between us, not because I wished to leave you, and I remained away because I believed it was better for you if I did."

Gregory prayed that this was the right thing to share. No falsehoods or condemnations, but not the whole truth, either. A smidgen of it. The children required an explanation, but having been dragged into too much of their parents' troubles already, they didn't need more details.

"But know that I love you. I have always loved you." Mrs. Stuart's eyes brightened with clear signs of the emotion of which she spoke. "I hope you can forgive me for being absent for so long, and that you will allow me the opportunity to know you once more."

No one spoke, and the silence stretched thin like taffy, lengthening with every heartbeat.

Gregory's gaze flicked between the children, searching for the smallest shift that signalled their thoughts. The silence pressed against his ears, loud in its stillness, and he held his breath without realizing it. Every second that passed strained his nerves further, the question unspoken yet pounding in his mind: would they accept or turn away?

Then Wesley stepped closer. Slowly, he wound his way to the blanket and sat, crossing his legs, and Gregory felt Faith's muscles relax as Jackson's posture softened, though neither moved closer to Mrs. Stuart. None of their reactions was an obvious acceptance, but they signified a beginning. And with the joy shining in the lady's eyes, it was clear that she thought this a victory of great proportions.

Turning to one of the hampers, Mrs. Stuart set out the dishes that the kitchen staff had prepared, which featured more than a few sweets and treats (likely far more than was good for the children, but after so many difficulties, it was precisely what was required).

But then she pulled out three parcels wrapped in brown paper and handed one to each of the children. Faith's was a large, thin rectangle, and when she didn't take it, Gregory retrieved it for her, setting it in the girl's lap. Wesley accepted his, though his elder brother stared at it a long moment before coming close enough to do the same.

"Another bribe?" asked Jackson, a sharpness to his tone that sounded too much like Clark for Gregory's liking.

Mrs. Stuart met that with a hesitant smile. "I know you did not want your other presents—"

Wesley's eyes darted to his brother, and Jackson shook his head. At his side, Faith tensed, and Gregory tightened his arm around her shoulders. She needn't worry; she wouldn't be forced to surrender her precious book.

"—but it feels wrong to approach you without a peace offering. Think of it as a belated Christmas."

The boys stared at the parcels without moving, and it was Faith who first reached for the twine and pulled it free. The brown paper unfurled to reveal a portfolio, which she opened to find several sheets of music.

"I heard you are studying the pianoforte and are quite skilled," said Mrs. Stuart, her eyes flitting to Gregory's for a heartbeat with a blaze of gratitude shining in those depths.

Faith straightened with a gasp, her hands hurriedly sifting through the pages. Then, snapping the cover closed, she drew it into her arms, holding it fast as though expecting someone to snatch it from her. And like that, the boys turned their attention to their own offerings.

"Amazing," gasped Jackson as he pulled out an apothecary's encyclopedia and immediately began flipping through the pages, examining the diagrams of alembics at work. And Wesley was no less effusive as he held his sketchbook and drawing pencils aloft, showing them to Faith, who still held her music clutched to her chest.

"And I still have the others, if you wish them," said Mrs. Stuart, holding out the bag of marbles and penknife. "I don't know if you play marbles, Wesley, but I do not know a lad who doesn't. And a young man of learning ought to have a proper penknife."

Though they paused, it was only a fraction of a heartbeat before the boys accepted them as well and set them alongside their treasures.

Clearing his throat, Gregory drew their attention and nodded toward Mrs. Stuart. The trio glanced at one another before offering up quiet words of thanks. Gregory wondered if he ought to encourage more, but Edward's counsel returned to his thoughts, reminding him that it wasn't his right to prod. And with Mrs. Stuart beaming, he didn't think this moment required it.

This was a beginning. That was enough.

...

The clouds passed lazily through the sky, casting fleeting shadows over the field in slow, dappled waves as the sunlight gilded the tall grasses and wildflowers in gold. Blankets lay spread across the uneven ground, their edges fluttering in the breeze, while open hampers slumped contentedly beside them—pillaged yet still brimming with food—and the scent of trampled clover and crushed grass lingered in the air, mingling with the sweet trace of summer fruit and flaky pastry.

With three children missing, the afternoon wasn't perfect, but as Tessa had feared none would accept her olive branch, the day was far better than she had anticipated. This was simply the first step. There was time to win over the others.

And now, her daughter was snuggled into her side as Tessa wove wildflowers together.

"Daphne makes those, too," whispered Faith.

"I taught her how to make them when she was Eva's age," replied Tessa, giving the girl a conspiratorial smile.

Tugging one final knot into place, Tessa completed the crown, and she settled it atop Faith's head. Then the girl was stuck in that most difficult of predicaments—wishing to see what she looked like with the adornment but without a looking glass on hand. There wasn't even a pond surface to serve that purpose.

"If you are careful, it should last until you arrive home," said Tessa, and Faith perked.

Turning her gaze to Mr. Vaughn, the child waited, and before Tessa could nudge him toward the proper response, the gentleman's brows rose as he graced Faith with a warm smile.

"You look lovely," he said with far more sweetness than Tessa would've anticipated from Sir Stoneface. "Quite becoming."

Faith's pink cheeks and the smile on her lips betrayed her feelings on the matter, though she tried so very hard to hide them. Then Wesley lifted his sketchbook, shoving it toward Mr. Vaughn.

"What do you think?" he asked, and the gentleman took hold of it, turning the sketch this way and that.

"I don't know how you managed to capture a cockchafer so well while it was squirming around like that," said Mr. Vaughn.

Tessa couldn't help staring at the fellow. For all his hard edges and stony exterior, Mr. Vaughn was as kind and tender to the children as if he were their own father. More so than many, in fact. For she knew plenty who wouldn't bother bestowing that much attention on anything but their newspapers, sports, and bank accounts. Her own father found more interest in his vices than in his daughter's accomplishments.

Turning it about so that Tessa could see, Mr. Vaughn displayed the sketch. Though it was certainly a rough job from someone who was only beginning to dabble in such things, it showed great promise.

"I love the way you capture the beetle's legs," said Tessa, pointing to one particular area. "That is a difficult angle to draw properly, especially with a live subject."

Wesley didn't blush or smile as Faith had done, choosing instead to stare at her for a long moment before taking back the sketchbook and settling it into his lap. The lad didn't say much to her, but he'd accepted her gifts and remained. That was something.

Meanwhile, Jackson wasn't aware of anything going on around him, as he was deep into his book, poring over the instructions, though he occasionally pulled free long enough to ask Mr. Vaughn about some detail.

Such a beautiful day. Near perfection. The sort that Tessa had dreamt of for years yet never dared to hope that it would come to pass. Then her eyes fell to Mr. Vaughn, and she tried to convey the gratitude bubbling up inside her. Pressing against her ribs, the sentiment squeezed her heart, but Tessa forced herself to keep control. This was not a time for tears. Even the happy sort.

"I hate to be the bearer of bad news, but the hour is growing late," said Mr. Vaughn.

Tessa's joy redoubled when the children voiced their disapproval. Of course, she knew it was just as likely a byproduct of a child's wish never to accept an order without a great deal of wailing and gnashing of teeth, but Tessa held tight to the hope that it meant they did not wish to leave her.

Mr. Vaughn rose to his feet, offering her a hand, and Tessa stared at it only a moment before accepting the assistance. Being married but alone, she'd learned not to expect gallantry. For all that many claimed such decorum was common amongst all men, Tessa knew too well that most manners were more often trotted out for mothers, wives, sisters, and sweethearts and overlooked in any other circumstances.

Leaving the blankets and hampers for the servants to fetch home, the children took their presents in hand as the group wound their way through the meadow. Mr. Vaughn kept pace with Tessa, and though Faith remained at their side for a little while, the opportunity to try her new music was too great a pull, and the girl chased after her brothers.

And once they were alone, Tessa glanced at the gentleman at her side. "Thank you, Mr. Vaughn. This has been a wonderful day."

Nodding, he turned a pleased grin in her direction. "And the others will come around."

Tessa nodded. "I have waited years to see them again, and I will happily wait years more as long as there is hope."

And as much as the older pair's reactions pained her, Tessa felt the rightness of her words. She knew them to be true. If Mr. Vaughn thought it possible, she would trust in the man who cared only about their well-being.

They walked beneath the shelter of the trees, the branches arching overhead like a vaulted ceiling, green and shifting with the breeze. The path was narrow, winding gently through thickets of hazel and hawthorn, and somewhere in the distance, a bird called out, answered by another deeper in the wood, their voices lilting above the rustle of the canopy. And as their footsteps moved in tandem, a hush fell between them, not uncomfortable but contemplative, like the quiet that followed honest conversation.

Yet as she considered the gentleman at her side, Tessa wondered if she ought to mention something that had been pricking at her all afternoon.

## Chapter 25

"Please do not think me forward..." began Tessa, though she immediately realized that statement in and of itself was a touch forward, for it implied that something problematic was forthcoming. She hesitated.

"Speak freely, Mrs. Stuart," he said, slanting her a hint of a smile. "After the prying I've done into your life, I do not think there is anything forward you could say."

"I was looking for a gentle manner in which to broach the subject, but I don't suppose there is a need, is there?" she said with a responding half-smile, though it fell away as she considered what Faith had said to her that afternoon. "May I make a suggestion concerning the children?"

"Certainly, though whether or not I accept it will depend on the suggestion," Mr. Vaughn replied in his usual brusque manner.

Tessa drew a sharp breath and forged ahead. "The girls need a proper nursemaid. Though they have Mrs. Todd to manage their education, and maids to attend to some of their needs, far too much of the work falls to Daphne."

Mr. Vaughn halted in place, lifting his head as he gazed out at the forest with raised brows. "I assumed they didn't have one because the girls were too old for such things."

"True, but Eva is only eight years of age and exuberant." Tessa paused beside him, her nose wrinkling as she considered that. "As much as I still wish to think of Daphne as a child, she is a young lady now, and ought to be spending her time out in company."

"She is only seventeen," said Mr. Vaughn, continuing on his way with a shake of the head.

"And many girls her age are already out. I made my debut at sixteen."

That drew him to a stop again, his complexion growing ashen. "Sixteen is far too young to be in the company of men."

Tessa's brows rose. "That it is, but their company is not the only reason a girl makes her debut. My older sisters were enjoying themselves at balls and parties, and I did not wish to be left alone in the nursery. I wager Daphne is eager to join her friends in their merriment, and one's coming out does not signify that one must accept a gentleman's suit. I, myself, did not marry Rodney until I was two and twenty, despite having ventured into society at the *shocking* age of sixteen."

Pleading eyes turned to her, and for all that Mr. Vaughn was quite a composed gentleman, the fatherly fear of daughters drained his face of its color.

"Daphne has already received an invitation to a small card party, but she isn't out yet," he said.

Tessa grinned, a flutter of excitement skittering along her skin as she recalled the first invitation she had ever received (or rather, the first her parents had received that included her name on it). Mrs. Pettit's penmanship was unparalleled, and the card she had sent round was of the finest quality. With it being her first dinner party, Tessa had thought it the height of fashion, though with more mature eyes, she realized it was quite a simple affair.

"Is Daphne getting a new frock for the occasion?" asked Tessa, lapping up every detail she could scour.

"I haven't said she could attend."

"Are the hosts unsuitable?" Tessa asked with a frown.

"No, they are good people. Their daughter and Daphne are thick as thieves. And my brother and his wife will be in attendance."

Tessa straightened. "Then why not? It sounds as though it is to be an intimate evening. There is nothing untoward about a young lady her age attending small affairs, even if she is not fully out in society yet." Pausing, she reconsidered. "Unless you do not trust your sister-in-law to serve as a suitable chaperone."

"Not at all. But she is a child still... It is... I cannot..." Poor Sir Stoneface began to crumble before her, his pallor increasing as he stumbled for an explanation. "I know little of young ladies, but I know young men, and I do not trust them anywhere near her."

The gentleman spoke with such terror, as though the very hounds of hell would surge up from the depths to steal her away. And though the thought of her little girl facing mercenary menfolk sent an echoing shiver down Tessa's spine, seeing the care and concern etched into Mr. Vaughn's face helped to calm her own nerves: Daphne had a guardian to fend off the pirates that may try to come alongside, and hopefully soon, a mother to help her navigate the stormy seas. The girl was not alone.

"I know it is frightening, Mr. Vaughn, but locking her away isn't the solution," said Tessa. "Daphne is a young lady and ought to be allowed more freedom, else she shan't be prepared to step into the world on her own—unless you wish her never to leave your side."

Mr. Vaughn shook his head, and Tessa gave him a commiserating smile.

"Let her attend, and purchase her a new frock for the occasion," she said as years of anticipation bubbled up in that sentence.

From the moment Tessa had learned she was expecting, she had imagined the child's life. Being a mother. Raising this little one. And when Daphne was delivered, those imaginings sharpened into something more concrete. Visions of gowns and ribbons. Balls and parties. Shopping excursions and gossiping into the wee hours of the morning.

So much of that had been lost.

"If I agree to it, would you help her choose a gown?" asked Mr. Vaughn.

It was as though he had reached into her head, plucked out her dream, and presented it to her. Yet that same imagination that had built up such castles in the sky insisted on showing her the truth as well, and Tessa knew how Daphne would react.

Shaking her head, she forced a fragile smile. "If I attend, the outing would become about me when it ought to be all about her. There will be more shopping in the future. Hopefully, she will allow me to be part of it."

Tessa clung to those words. This wasn't Daphne's first gown, and even if it held significance, there would be many more to come.

"But ask that sister-in-law of yours to take her. And the other ladies in your family," said Tessa. "Daphne will require assistance, and I've seen how sweetly your family has accepted the children into their ranks."

"That is an excellent idea, Mrs. Stuart," he said with a nod, reaching over to shove aside a branch that hung in her path.

"I am glad to be of service," she replied, and before she could think better of it, Tessa forced out the words that had been festering in her thoughts since their previous conversation. "And I wish to apologize for the poor influence I've had on you. I swear my behavior at the picnic is more indicative than what you have seen of late."

"Poor influence?" Mr. Vaughn jerked to a stop again, forcing Tessa to face him. "What do you mean? You haven't been, else I would've been far more concerned about reintroducing you to the children."

Clasping her skirts, she turned down the path, lifting them as she stepped over a fallen log. "I do believe you said you never had a temper before meeting me. It appears I have a habit of enraging the men in my life."

But before she could cross the barrier, a hand darted forward, grabbing her and pulling her to a stop before him.

"That was not what I meant, Mrs. Stuart," he said with a frown. "I hadn't thought I possessed a temper until this situation. The strain of all the upheaval of late, combined with my confusion and pain surrounding the revelations about Rodney's behavior, was at fault. You, unfortunately, were merely the recipient of that fury, and I am sorry for that."

Though it hurt to say those words aloud, Gregory's heart lightened at the admission. Hiding from the truth only added to one's troubles, and denying facts didn't make them any less true. Whether or not he had been acting on the knowledge he had at the time, it still pained him to think of how he had treated her.

Mrs. Stuart nodded and continued down the path, though when her ankle wobbled, Gregory chastised himself for not having offered his arm sooner. With a smile of gratitude, she took it now, and the pair wound their way through the forest.

"That may be true, Mr. Vaughn, but I did not help matters by allowing my temper to slip from my grasp."

Gregory huffed at that. "The more I come to understand the history between you and your husband, the more I am in awe of your self-control, Mrs. Stuart."

Despite having forced himself to stop many times, Gregory found himself back in Rodney's journals again and again, turning through the past as he uncovered the earliest days of their marriage. Reading through it was like witnessing Rodney's accident. Gregory had seen the signs of the coming trouble—the dancing hooves, the horse's shrieks—yet knowing hadn't stopped that fatal injury.

"I cannot believe I did not see what sort of person he was. I thought I knew him, and to discover it was all a lie..." said Gregory, the words struggling to get loose. The heaviness in his middle sank further, weighing him down with all the questions he would never have the answers to. "I believed him to be honorable and kind, and I fear it took me too long to realize the truth—"

Mrs. Stuart pulled on his arm, drawing him to a halt, and when Gregory faced her, a furrow marred her brow.

"Rodney had many good qualities, Mr. Vaughn. That he was fallible doesn't discount how kind and honorable he was in most circumstances or that he was a good friend to you and a loving father to our children."

"You are defending him?" asked Gregory, his brows rising. "After everything he did to you and your family?"

The faintest of smiles flitted across her face, all confusion with a dash of wry humor.

"Believe me, sir, I never thought I would say such things," said Mrs. Stuart, a whisper of a laugh weaving through her tone. But her expression sobered as she reached over to rest a hand on his forearm. "No one is without sin, and I would hate for people to judge me based on my worst behaviors, so please do not judge Rodney because of his."

"True," he said with a nod. "However misguided his actions, Rodney believed himself the victim of your marriage, and he acted accordingly. Had his version of the past been true, I wouldn't fault him for much of what he did."

Drawing in a breath, Gregory peered into Mrs. Stuart's eyes, hoping she would understand his meaning. "What troubles me is that even after years of separation and maturing, Rodney was so convinced of his goodness and your wickedness that he was more concerned about you gaining control of the children than the fact that they were about to lose their father. You stand here, advocating for compassion and understanding, but he went to his grave cursing your name."

And though Gregory didn't know what he had expected to see in her expression, it certainly wasn't the sorrow that dimmed her eyes and drew her brow low.

"I am sorry for that," she said, her gaze turning to the forest around them. "Though I cannot say that I am surprised. I would like to say I would've come to my senses on my own, but I am fairly certain I would've ended as bitter and angry had I not lost everything."

With a pained smile, Mrs. Stuart took his arm once more and nudged him down the path, their steps moving in time.

"You say I am compassionate, but that is only because you know me now. Had you met me just before Rodney left Leeds six years ago, you would've despised me as much as I despised myself," she said in a hollow voice. "It took losing everything for my heart to soften. I couldn't accept responsibility in our mutual destruction until I had nothing left and was forced to ask myself why."

Mrs. Stuart snatched a leaf from a branch and twirled it in her free hand. "When Rodney cast me out, my parents refused to drag the family into it. My friends took pity on me for a time, but after almost two years, they soon grew tired of their charity case and asked me to leave. Just about that time, Rodney accepted Eva's parentage and moved the family out of my reach."

Letting out a huff of self-deprecating laughter, she glanced at him. "I considered kidnapping them and escaping to the Continent or America, but thankfully, I didn't have the money to do so. Else I wouldn't have reached that terrible moment where I had nothing and no one, and I realized I had to choose between wallowing in misery or changing."

"And you chose the latter." Though he didn't need to say the words, Gregory voiced them all the same, unable to mute the awe that he felt.

For all that the lady spoke as though making that choice had been a foregone conclusion, facing his demise and the Judgement to follow hadn't inspired such a change of heart in her husband. That moment had been the perfect time to see his life with new clarity, yet Rodney had wasted his final moments scaring his children's guardian away from the one parent they had left in the world.

"Do you regret your marriage?" he asked.

# Chapter 26

Gregory wasn't certain what had possessed him to ask such an intrusive question, but Mrs. Stuart merely gazed out at the forest, her eyes scouring the foliage and greenery as though they might supply the answer.

"I regret not being mature enough to learn my lesson before I lost everything, but I will never regret marrying Rodney," she said with a wistful twist of her lips. "I married him because I loved him, and together, we created six beautiful children, and our marriage made me the woman I am today. So, I cannot regret him."

Looking at him from the corner of her eye, Mrs. Stuart added, "If I may offer another piece of advice, Mr. Vaughn. It does no good to hate. I spent far too much of my life allowing my anger to poison my life. No matter what my husband cost me, I refuse to allow those feelings to fester any longer."

Pausing, she wrinkled her nose. "Of course, that may not be clear based on how I have behaved over the past few weeks. I feel as though I ought to apologize again."

"Peace, Mrs. Stuart," said Gregory. "I think we can both agree that neither of us is pleased with how that unfolded. Rather than castigating ourselves again and again, we ought to move forward."

"Perhaps," she said, slanting him a sly look. "If you promise to give me a tour of your shop the next time you are in the village. I cannot claim that I paid any attention to it when I visited." She paused and added with a slight wince, "Twice. I have been there twice, and yet I cannot say that I recall anything about the place. Beyond it being very neat and orderly—which is no great surprise, given what I know of you."

Gregory's brows rose at that. "You wish to tour the shop?"

"You spoke of your business with such passion when we were driving to Thornsby. I would like to see it."

And just like that, they slipped into conversation. It was as though the past few weeks had not occurred, and they were transported back to that stagecoach once more.

Except it wasn't the same as before. Not precisely. That had been a conversation between two strangers. Two people tossed together with no true understanding of their backgrounds and the lives that had led them to that moment. Now, Gregory knew far more about the lady than he ought, and though much of it was shocking and more than a tad embarrassing, when one looked at the whole of it, he couldn't help but be impressed by the lady at his side.

The past informed the present, but no one was held captive by it. One may struggle with the consequences of decisions, but one was still the lord and master over the direction of one's life. Unfortunately, far too many chose Rodney's path, preferring to view themselves as slaves to the past and victims of the present with no hope for the future.

Yet this lady had changed. Even if Mrs. Stuart wished to dismiss it as being the byproduct of her terrible circumstances, the truth was that far too many people chose to wallow in that unending misery she'd rejected.

The journey from the picnic to the house was not far, though Gregory was quite happy for his steps to slow. He didn't bother lying to himself that it was solely to ensure that Mrs. Stuart was afforded a comfortable pace. The truth was that he enjoyed speaking with the lady.

Mrs. Chatterbox was out in force once more, speaking of everything and anything, leading the conversation on a path that was more twisty and winding than the one at their feet. They spoke of business ventures and the children, and Gregory was surprised at how easily she prodded him into speaking, though he was quite content to hear her expound on a good many subjects.

The forest opened before them, petering out into the lawn that surrounded Eden Place. The children were long gone, and through one of the open windows, the sound of the piano rang out in the afternoon air, proving that Faith was enjoying the gift. In the distance, clouds gathered, promising that today's gloriousness was soon to be replaced by more rain. But for now, the world was still perfect.

Despite the ground being far more even than their forest path, Mrs. Stuart did not release his arm, and Gregory was all too happy to have her hold fast to it as long as she wished.

Spying the house just ahead, he knew he was not ready for their time to end. After so many years of terrifying the ladies of Thornsby and Danthorpe with his stony facade and dull conversation, Gregory had found a lady who not only dubbed him Sir Stoneface and laughed at the appellation but found his company enjoyable in a way that no one else did.

And the more he came to know Mrs. Stuart, the more Gregory desired her. He had never imagined that such a thing could strike so quickly, but it had, and with Rodney's lies sorted, was there any reason he couldn't pursue her?

They drew ever nearer to the house, and there was only so much slowing Gregory could do before they were simply standing in place. He hoped it was a good sign that Mrs. Stuart seemed not to notice their crawling pace. Then they arrived at the drive, the gravel crunching beneath their shoes as he led her toward the gate that stood at the entrance to the property.

"I can call you a carriage," he said.

"That is kind of you, but I am very used to walking. And it is not far to the village," she said, motioning down the road.

Gregory considered that and wondered if it would be too presumptuous to accompany her home. That was gentlemanly, wasn't it? And did it matter if it was forward of him? A fellow didn't want his overtures to be overlooked.

But when he asked, she shook her head.

"Again, you are kind to offer, but I am very used to walking alone," said Mrs. Stuart with a smile. "I shan't come to harm."

Gregory could well imagine that a lady would have to be resourceful when she was so very alone in the world. Thornsby was safe enough for her to walk about, but Leeds boasted footpads and ruffians, and the thought of her managing such dangers stoked the heat in his heart. Curse Rodney. How could he abandon his wife in such a fashion and leave her to fend for herself?

"Then perhaps we might try this again in a few days?" asked Gregory. "You can come for dinner with the children. Or even spend the whole day here."

"I need to return to Leeds on Thursday, but I would love to do so before then," she said, that brightness in her eyes blazing all the more. "Though I suppose if we wait until after I arrive home on Saturday, the boys will be back from school."

"You are visiting Leeds again?"

Mrs. Stuart sighed. "Yes, unfortunately, there are several matters that I must attend to. But thankfully, with travel improving, it is easy enough to make the journey in half a day, so I can leave in the afternoon, have a day in Leeds, and then return the next. If only they would finish the rail line to Brackenfell sooner, then I could make the journey in half the time."

Gregory straightened, considering that. "It shan't cause trouble, going back and forth like that?"

"I cannot see why it would," she said with a considering frown. "Mail allows me to correspond with those who manage the daily operations, and though it isn't ideal, I can travel to Leeds for anything important."

Could it be possible? For so long, Gregory had thought expansion was a question of either-or. Either his family or Leeds. Either uproot the children from their home or abandon thoughts of building up his business. Of course, there was no question as to which side he would choose, for his family and the children were his priority. But could he have both?

"I see I have given you much to think about," said Mrs. Stuart, studying him.

"That you have."

"Well then, this afternoon has been quite successful all around," she said, giving him a broad smile as she finally released his arm. "But I ought to be on my way. Send word when you wish me to visit next."

Gregory bowed and watched as the lady strode down the lane. It wasn't until she disappeared around a bend that he turned on his heel and marched across the drive, taking the front steps two at a time. Opening the door, he divested himself of his outside clothes and abandoned them on the side table for the servants to see to.

But when he turned to move past the entry, Gregory spied a lone figure sitting on the steps of the grand staircase, hands tucked in her lap as Daphne's eyes bored into him.

"Are you courting her?" she demanded, her tone as warm as a winter's night.

"No." The answer was truthful enough, but Gregory paused and considered that. In all actuality, he wasn't courting Mrs. Stuart. But that didn't mean he didn't wish to. Did he owe the children that clarification?

Before he could consider what they deserved to know about him and his intentions, Daphne rose to her feet, a hard glint in her eye that wasn't as vengeful or violent as her brother's but was still sharp and unyielding. Standing on the stairs as she was, Daphne towered over him, and she lifted her chin as she stared him down before turning around to climb up to the next floor.

"Would you care to go shopping for a new frock?" asked Gregory.

Daphne paused and peered over her shoulder, her eyes narrowed as she quietly asked, "Why?"

"I heard that every young lady ought to have a new frock for her first party."

The ice in her expression melted away as she spun in place, her mouth agape as his meaning struck. "The party?"

Drawing in a deep breath, Gregory forced himself to answer. "Assuming my sister-in-law is willing to play chaperone, I see no reason you cannot attend the Billings' card party. And I thought I could ask my mother and my sisters if they would take you shopping for a new gown for the event."

Daphne gasped. "Truly?"

"Truly."

Though she was dignified enough not to squeal and dance up on her toes with delight as Eva was prone to do, light filled her being, making Daphne shine in a manner that had her guardian worrying all the more. All it would take was one of those smiles and every unmarried man in Yorkshire would be clamoring to court her.

Throwing her arms around him, Daphne embraced him before he knew what she was about. Though clearly, she hadn't expected it either, for she jerked back with a blush on her cheeks. Then, spinning about, she hurried up the stairs as she rambled about needing to review the latest fashion plates.

"It was your mother's idea," called Gregory.

Daphne halted, her hand on the railing as she peered over her shoulder at him with brows pulled low and confusion gleaming in her eyes. Then, leaving the girl to her thoughts, Gregory turned away and strode toward the parlor.

# Chapter 27

The green at the heart of Thornsby had been transformed from the tranquil stretch of lawn into a blur of color and motion. Stalls lined the edges of the grass, their awnings casting patchy shade over tables piled with goods and wares, with a rainbow of bunting that wound from vendor to vendor, drawing the customers deeper into the merriment.

The scent of warm pies, buttery toffee, and roasted meat drifted on the air in a heady mix. And beneath the shade of a sycamore, an old fiddler sawed out a lively tune while a line of Morris dancers hopped and stamped in time, the bright ribbons tied to their legs and hats fluttering with each movement. A small crowd had gathered to clap along, their faces alight with mirth, as children darted around the edges in their own chaotic imitation.

It was enchanting. As though the world was suspended in a blur of brightness and motion and filled with joy and laughter. Or as much as it could be whilst accompanied by a fifteen-year-old boy who was doing his utmost to try everyone's patience.

More than a month had passed since reintroducing the children to their mother, and though Clark was as determined as ever to growl and hiss whenever she was about, Eva and Faith followed the lady as she wandered over to a stall that was particularly packed with knick-knacks. Even Joanna looked eager to see Mrs. Stuart at work, accompanying them with Timothy in her arms and Shirley on her heels.

"Oh, this is a lovely piece," said Mrs. Stuart, holding up an old cup fashioned from brass for her audience to inspect. "It needs a bit of polishing, but people are always in need of more dishes. And though a utilitarian piece like this shan't fetch a handsome price at market, a stall that sells lower-priced but sturdy quality can earn just as much as those who offer the finest china."

"Ah," said the woman manning the booth, "I see I have a customer of discerning tastes."

Straightening, Mrs. Stuart gave her opponent a narrowed-eyed assessment. "I know something of market stalls."

"Is that so?" came the reply with a knowing smile. And with that, the seller rattled off the price of the piece, and the two began haggling with all the talent of those who knew their business well. The audience's eyes darted between the two, and though Mrs. Stuart drove a hard bargain, she settled on a reasonable price, and the two shook on it.

Clark scoffed and crossed his arms, kicking at the ground as he turned his gaze away from the sight. "I do not want to be here."

"As you've made abundantly clear," murmured Gregory in a low tone. "As I said before, you do not have to speak to her if you do not wish to, but you will join your family for the festival and you will be civil—as you should be to all people."

Gregory glanced over to where Daphne stood; the young lady managed an air of disinterest as though her mother did not exist, which bothered him no less, but at least it did not have the unfortunate tendency to annoy everyone around. Though that changed when Faith grabbed her mother's hand and tugged her toward another stall. Daphne's posture tightened at the sight, and redoubled when Eva hurried after the pair, jabbering furiously at their mother.

With a sharp huff, Daphne turned and stomped away.

"If she's leaving, so am I," said Clark.

"You are free to explore as you wish," said Gregory, projecting his voice for both of them to hear. "But do not leave the festival, and meet back here in an hour."

The two refused to acknowledge him, and Gregory's feet yearned to follow after them, though he didn't know if this was a battle worth waging or if that bit of insolence ought to be ignored.

Mrs. Stuart glanced over her shoulder at him and pulled a mocking scowl. "Oh, is Sir Stoneface attending the festival today?"

"Sir Stoneface?" asked Shirley, her expression scrunching. "That's Uncle Gregory."

"I hate to disagree, my dear lady," she said, crouching before the girl. "But I assure you that is a gentleman I met on the road to Thornsby. He looked so stern that I couldn't help but dub him Sir Stoneface, for his expression was so very somber."

That drew a giggle from Gregory's niece, and Eva's hands flew to her mouth as she stifled her own. Traitors. For all that his family claimed to love him, the group began tittering and guffawing as Mrs. Stuart did an impression of Sir Stoneface—their mirth doubling when they glanced at him. Apparently, her imitation wasn't far from the mark.

"Come now, Sir Stoneface. You cannot be dour at a festival." Stepping closer, Mrs. Stuart added in a low voice, "Do not take their behavior to heart, Mr. Vaughn. Clark and Daphne are at difficult ages and are struggling with so much of late. They are going to be ill-tempered. It is only natural. It feels like a victory that they attended at all."

The warmth in her voice settled into Gregory's chest, coating the frustration like a balm. No matter that the pair's ire had been directed more at her than him, Mrs. Stuart accepted their behavior and sought to comfort him.

Stepping back, she raised her voice again. "What say you, Sir Stoneface?"

The children all watched him closely, and when Gregory looked down at them, he twisted his features into a maniacal grin and crossed his eyes. They burst into giggles before skittering this way and that as the festival seized their attention once more.

Which was when he noticed Edward and Joanna watching him, their brows raised with equal expressions of surprise and amusement. And though he hadn't done anything wrong, Gregory felt his face heat, and he hoped that it didn't show (though judging by the gleeful glint in his brother's eye, he suspected it had).

Clearing his throat, Gregory nodded toward a stand that was selling fruit buns. "I think it is time for sweets."

That earned him a bellowing chorus of support, and the children charged the stall en masse as the parents followed after.

"Is Sir Stoneface joining us?" asked Edward with a singsong lilt to his tone, but he was silenced when Joanna elbowed him in the ribs and deposited their babe into his arms so she could herd the children into a semblance of a queue.

Coming to her father's side, Caro took his hand and said with utter reverence, "No one should be dour at Queen Bess's Festival."

"Ah, yes, the festival commemorating Queen Elizabeth's red hair," said Mrs. Stuart in a serious tone.

Eva made a face as she took her mother's hand. "No, it isn't."

"Or is it her birthday?" asked Mrs. Stuart, tapping her chin with a finger.

"It is the day she visited Thornsby," said Caro with the sort of exasperation usually reserved for parents attempting to dress their wriggling children in layers of winter flannel. "Her carriage stopped at the Silver Lion, and she sat in their chair!"

"Yes, I was ever so blessed to see the article myself," said Mrs. Stuart, turning her laughing eyes to meet Gregory's. "Though the proprietor wouldn't allow me to sit in it."

"Of course, you cannot!" gasped Caro. "It was Queen Bess's chair!"

...

The children tugged her this way and that, and though Tessa desperately longed for a seat (even Queen Bess's), the fact that they were eager for her presence made her wish that this moment would last forever. Faith and Eva held fast to her hands, though the latter held still for only moments before darting this way and that, and of course, the boys were far too grown-up to hang on their mama, but they did not wander far from her side.

Music filled the air, and Tessa pulled the others to a stop beside a makeshift dance floor. Poles marked the edges, with bunting strung from top to top, forming a ceiling of sorts, and to one side sat the musicians. Though each bore a sprig of flowers adorning their person, they looked like they had just emerged from the pub and were enjoying the "fortifying" drinks on hand more than the music ringing from their instruments.

The lively tune wound to a close, and as the dancers took their leave, the leader of the band raised a mug and called out, "To Queen Bess!" The others echoed it, downing enough ale that she doubted they would remain upright for much longer.

Caro hopped up on her toes, clapping as she turned to Tessa. "A Queen Bess dance. All the unmarried ladies must dance with the partner of their choosing. You must. It's tradition!"

"Do it, Mama," added Eva, threading her arm through Caro's. "It's tradition."

"That is well and good, but I am not unmarried," said Tessa with a wince. "I am widowed—"

But the girls waved away the concern.

"And I am newly widowed. It wouldn't be appropriate," added Tessa, glancing out at the others as though the crowd might rise up against her for the dishonor to her late husband. Mourning rituals were a personal matter, and though the family hadn't adopted the more rigid strictures that some chose to follow, even the loosest of guidelines would find it shocking to see a widow dancing at a festival less than three months after her husband's passing.

"Yes, do," said Mrs. Joanna Vaughn, coming up beside Tessa with her babe on her hip. "It is a festival, and you ought to enjoy it." Then, with a sly little smile, she added in a conspiratorial tone, "Lest you dishonor that very great and regal Queen Elizabeth by not participating in a dance meant to honor her."

For all that Mrs. Vaughn spoke quietly, Caro gasped like a heroine on the stage as though it was an affront to her own honor.

Leaning close, Mrs. Vaughn lowered her voice so it only carried to Tessa's ears. "Caro is mad about Queen Elizabeth at present, so do not let her sway you. But you should dance if you wish. It's a bit of fun. That is all."

Tessa glanced about for a possible partner, but Clark was nowhere to be seen (not that he would allow himself to be conscripted into dancing with her, tradition or not). When Jackson met her gaze, he must've realized her intention, for he blanched before blushing red, his eyes scouring the crowd as though fearful that his school chums were lurking there, ready to witness this most mortifying of moments. And though the dear lad would likely accept, Wesley was both too short to stand up with her and too large for her to heft into her arms.

There was no one to dance with her, so the issue was moot.

But then Mr. Gregory Vaughn and his brother strode into view, with the rest of the children waddling around them like ducklings, rushing to and fro but never straying far from the adults. Mrs. Joanna Vaughn met Tessa's gaze and nodded toward her brother-in-law.

And Tessa found herself mimicking Jackson, glancing about as though someone might notice just how warm her cheeks were growing.

# Chapter 28

Asking a gentleman to dance wasn't an easy thing. Though Tessa doubted he would refuse her, she also found it difficult to imagine Mr. Vaughn dancing—yet when the musicians struck the first notes of the tune, she found herself standing before him.

"Would you do me the honor?" she asked, nodding toward the congregating dancers.

"A Queen Bess dance, is it?" he replied with the slightest twist of a smile.

"Yes, and your sister-in-law and niece are emphatic that I must stand up," said Tessa, nodding toward the others. With a wince, she added in a whisper, "Please save me."

"I would be honored, madam," he said, raising his voice so the others would hear.

With a sigh, Tessa placed her hand in his as he led her onto the dance floor. The strains of a slow polka were struck, and Mr. Vaughn settled his hand at the small of her back whilst clasping her other. She stood there a moment, his arm wrapped about her, and with a silent count of four, he swept her into the fray.

A flush of heat stole through her as they settled close together. It was nothing improper, though she couldn't keep her gaze from turning to his, staring at him in a manner that was not entirely decorous. One shouldn't meet their partner's gaze whilst so intimately tucked together, yet Tessa couldn't help herself.

But when his eyes narrowed on something over her shoulder, she glanced to see Daphne in the arms of a young man, which was a tad surprising as she ought not to be dancing publicly until she was properly out. Though it was harmless enough and not wholly outside the bounds of propriety.

Tessa was about to reassure Daphne's anxious guardian when she spied the fellow's hand drifting low on his partner's back. And when he leaned closer to whisper into her ear (which elicited a giggle!), the bounder didn't return to his previous position, remaining far too close to the young lady. Tessa's expression shifted, mimicking that which she'd seen on Mr. Vaughn's face, and she studied the man who was far too old to qualify as a "young" one.

"Who is that?" she asked.

"I do not know, but I will soon," said Mr. Vaughn in a low tone that helped to chase away the frisson of unease. His gaze remained locked on the pair, taking in every detail with all the firmness that Sir Stoneface could muster. Yet there was something buried beneath that hard exterior.

Standing so close whilst his attention was elsewhere, Tessa was free to study him, and it took only a moment for clarity to strike.

"You are a good guardian, Mr. Gregory Vaughn," she said, drawing his attention back to her. For all that he appeared as firm as ever, Tessa spied the fear shuddering beneath the surface.

"How am I to protect her when she is beginning to venture out on her own?" he whispered. "I cannot follow her about, ensuring that she only mixes with the best company every hour of the day."

"You cannot," said Tessa with a sad smile. "Pain and difficulties will meet her no matter what you do. But with your stalwart support and comfort, Daphne will weather it."

"How can you say that, given your history?" Despite the sharpness of the question, Mr. Vaughn's tone wasn't accusatory but contemplative.

"I say that *because* of my history. You are a good man, and you care dearly for those children," she whispered as a hint of tears blurred her vision. Tessa blinked them away, refusing to allow them to fall. "It is one of the things I admire most about you. Despite that stern exterior, I know you will do your best to aid and protect them."

Mr. Vaughn turned his gaze toward Daphne again, his brows pulling tight together, and Tessa lifted one of her hands to nudge his chin toward her again.

"It is only a flirtation at present, but press the issue too hard, and it will force her into his arms. Nothing makes a man more appealing than having one's parents forbid the match."

Mr. Vaughn's lips curled into a smile, the strain in his eyes fading as he held her gaze. "My thanks, Mrs. Stuart."

"For meddling in your affairs and foisting my opinions on you?" she asked with a hint of a laugh.

"For being unafraid to speak your mind. Your opinions are insightful and often help me to see things in a new light," he said in a tone that was far too serious for her good. "You are a bold and intelligent woman, and I am grateful when you 'foist' your opinions on me."

Those dark eyes held hers with a gentleness that one didn't expect from such a hard-looking man. The music drew them along the floor, their feet moving in time together, and Mr. Vaughn's gaze studied her as though memorizing every line of her face, his eyes caressing her cheek.

Tessa wanted to ignore it. Dismiss it as a trick of the light. But standing out of doors in broad daylight, it was difficult to dismiss what was standing right before her. It didn't seem possible, yet she felt the warmth of his attention seeping into her.

It was like drinking a hot cup of tea on a cold winter's night, heating her from the inside out.

Clearing her throat, she forced herself to break his gaze and seized onto the first subject she could think of. "I am afraid I must return to Leeds in a few days."

---

"Again?" Gregory managed to keep the whine from his tone, but the thought of her leaving had his shoulders slumping.

For the past few weeks, Mrs. Stuart had woven herself into his days—as much a part of his life as the children and his work—and her absence left him feeling out of sorts. Like missing his breakfast and morning perusal of the newspaper. Or putting on a frock coat that was a touch too tight. He was a grown adult with responsibilities, which meant such upsets did not keep him from completing his work, but it left him off-kilter.

Incomplete.

Mrs. Stuart gave him a wan smile. "I fear I may have been a bit too optimistic about my ability to manage my business from afar."

Heart sinking, Gregory listened as she detailed the troubles that were arising from living in this limbo. Clearly, she could not remain in Thornsby indefinitely, and a choice needed to be made.

Perhaps relocating to Leeds was the proper thing to do; with things mending in the Stuart family, it was only right that they ought to be nearby. Now that he knew her character, Gregory couldn't deny Mrs. Stuart access to her little ones, nor could she surrender her income, which was dependent on Leeds.

But Thornsby was the children's home.

Regardless, it didn't absolve him of his own responsibility to his parents and siblings. Gregory was the eldest son. The next head of the family. It was his duty to watch over the Vaughns. They needed him.

Just as the Stuarts needed their mother.

Gregory felt caught in a current, putting all his might into moving forward, yet the stream continued to pull him back. Going nowhere, and only succeeding in exhausting himself.

Forcing that thought from his mind, Gregory turned his attention to his partner. Mrs. Stuart spoke about the goings-on in her business and the children; it was as if everything she said was filled with her whole heart.

Gregory had never met such a passionate person before, who cared so much about everything within her sphere. Mrs. Stuart met his gaze without flinching, able to meet his every question and comment with her own insight. Her eyes gleamed, sharing their light with him and filling him with a brightness that he never knew existed in the world, and his hand itched to brush her cheek.

Was it as soft as it appeared?

Applause erupted around them, jerking Gregory's attention away from Mrs. Stuart—only to discover that somehow their steps had slowed, leaving them standing in the center of the dancers, with her clutched so close that it bore no semblance to any recognized dance position. Gregory was simply embracing her in the midst of the dancers, his arms holding her flush to him.

Mrs. Stuart stiffened, her eyes widening at the precise moment that he realized the impropriety of their situation. Giving a tiny squeak of surprise, she jerked backward at the same time he did, his face heating as he glanced about to see if anyone had noticed.

Only to see the whole Stuart clan watching them with wide eyes.

Pressing her hands to her cheeks, Tessa tried to calm the burning flush that had taken hold of her, but there was nothing to be done about it. Especially with Clark's eyes burning holes into her. She crossed the dance floor in a flash, but he spun on his heel, striding in the opposite direction.

"Clark, please," she said, though she didn't know what more to say. Tessa didn't know how they'd ended in such a shocking embrace, but that mattered not a jot, as her son refused to listen to her apologies.

Turning to face her, Clark's whole being sneered at her, the strength of the emotion vibrating through him. "It wasn't enough to ruin our father? Now, you are going to ruin our guardian as well?"

Clark lobbed the words at her, and his aim struck true; each sank deep into the fragile places of her heart. Spinning about, he gave her his back and marched away, but Tessa stood frozen in place, her limbs as heavy as stone. Her chest tightened as her mouth opened uselessly, as if to call him back, to plead, to explain.

But no sound came.

Mr. Vaughn drew up beside her, his hand resting at her back for a brief moment before he jerked it away. "Allow me to speak to him."

And with that, the gentleman gathered the children and followed after the lad.

# Chapter 29

Despite having most of the seat to himself, the carriage felt cramped. Confined. As though the very air squeezed him tight as six pairs of eyes stared at him. Except for Wesley (who had pressed himself into the corner as far from Gregory as he could manage), the children were piled together on the seat opposite, and their gazes bore into him.

Gregory cleared his throat. "I know that might've been a bit surprising—"

"No." Clark's response was sharp and final.

Silence fell once more, and Gregory prayed for insight. No doubt Mrs. Stuart would know how to manage the issue, but as she was not on hand and bringing her into the discussion was only bound to enrage the children further, he was on his own to sort this out. Besides, this was his doing.

For the life of him, Gregory didn't know how they'd ended up in such a shocking embrace. The only saving grace was that the vast majority of people had been too preoccupied with the festival or their partners to notice them, but that was of little comfort when the only ones who had witnessed the incident were those who were most angered by the display. No doubt the rest of the village would cheer that the Vaughn bachelor had finally found a lady.

The carriage pulled to a stop, and Clark shoved past the rest and strode out the door before the groom could reach the handle. But Gregory was on his heels.

"A moment, Clark," he called.

The lad refused to listen, his feet carrying him around the side of the house. No doubt, he was looking to escape into the nearby woods, and though Gregory considered letting things lie for now, he shook off the idea and gave chase.

"Clark, stop!" he ordered. And despite everything that had happened today, the lad obeyed—though he looked as surprised as Gregory that the command had worked. Leveling his surliest of expressions on his guardian, Clark remained where he was, his arms folded.

"Come," said Gregory, nodding around to the back side of the house.

Tucked behind a stone wall beside the kitchen door sat a pile of logs and an axe. Slinging off his frock coat, Gregory hung it over the wall and snatched up the axe, standing up a log before bringing the blade down in a mighty strike that split the piece in two. Clark gave a start and stared at the pieces.

Handing the axe to the lad, Gregory set another log in place and nodded at him. "Have at it."

But Clark stared at him, unmoving.

"You are angry. Take it out on the wood," prodded Gregory.

Hands tightening around the handle, Clark swung it high and brought it down, though he missed the log completely, striking the stump below. Growling, the lad glared at it, but Gregory stepped forward, repositioned everything, and gave a few pointers before moving out of the way.

Clark swung again. And missed.

Another few words of instruction and encouragement, and the lad continued for a quarter of an hour before he managed to strike the log, and another quarter until he was able to get the axe in deep enough to do any good. But with each attempt, the axe flew truer.

Soon, the lad's coat was abandoned, his sleeves rolled up to the elbow as he struck the logs again and again, reducing them to kindling. It was some time before Clark's fury was spent, his lungs heaving as sweat dripped down his temples and neck.

Lowering onto the ground, Gregory leaned against the wall and stared at the lad.

"Whenever I am angry or frustrated, I split kindling," said Gregory, nodding toward the large pile that was prepared and ready to be used by the servants. "I find it helps to clear my head."

Clark sat as well, his lungs still heaving and his jaw clenched.

"Why are you so angry?" asked Gregory.

Everything inside the lad tensed at the question, and the fury drove him to his feet as a flurry of words spewed from his mouth. "You were pawing that harlot—"

"Go split some more." Gregory pointed toward the logs.

Clark's fists clenched, and his arms shook with the strain as he stared down the gentleman. Gregory could see the thoughts flitting through his mind as the lad considered whether or not he could win a round of fisticuffs, and Gregory let him. Meeting the lad's gaze, he held firm.

"You are allowed to be angry, Clark, but don't stop splitting until you can explain why you are so overwrought."

"But I was!" he shouted, and Gregory nodded to the wood again.

Clark scowled and snatched up the axe. Gregory watched as the lad grew more familiar with the tool, the movement helping him to work through the insensible rage. When the lad paused, Gregory met his gaze, an eyebrow raised in question.

Clark spoke more clearly this time, his voice even as he said, "She ruined everything—"

"Continue splitting. Don't stop until you can explain to me *your* behavior."

The thud of the axe sounded again, and the minutes ticked by as Clark swung it over and over.

As coal was the preferred fuel for heating and cooking, wood wasn't required in large quantities, but the kitchen used kindling to help along the coal fires, so chopping wood was still a task that needed completing.

As a lad, Gregory had kept Hawthorne Cottage stocked, and that hadn't changed when he'd taken up his own rooms above the apothecary shop; a bachelor hardly required any, and his household alone couldn't keep him occupied enough. Of course, Eden Place required a vast amount, but coincidentally, Gregory had also found himself at odds so much of late that keeping them in kindling was no trouble at all. Thus, the pile was already quite large, but Clark was doing his best to grow it.

Quite some time passed before the young man lowered the axe once more. Clark's face was flushed, and as he dropped onto the ground before Gregory, the sag of his shoulders testified that his fury was spent. And Gregory made note to send word to Walter; no doubt the headmaster would eagerly grant Clark use of the school's woodpile when the school term began.

Gregory leveled another questioning look, and Clark drew in a steady breath.

"Father hated her," he began, but when Gregory motioned for him to return to his work, Clark held up a staying hand. As the lad was speaking calmly, he nodded for him to continue.

Letting out a sharp huff, Clark shifted, his hands picking at the blades of grass. "He was my father, and she made him miserable. She hurt him. I don't want to forgive her, and I am angry that the rest of you are falling under her spell. If Father hated her, how can any of us treat her kindly?"

Clark's eyes held Gregory's for a long moment, and with his emotions spent, all that remained was a genuine question burning in his gaze. And perhaps he was ready to hear the answer.

"You know that I loved your father like a brother," said Gregory, and he waited until the young man acknowledged that with a nod. "Then you should know that I struggled greatly when your mother arrived in town. As you were at school, I doubt you saw the majority of it, but I assure you that I did not take kindly to her being here. I held onto my anger for your father's sake."

Gregory sighed. "And then I came to know her and realized that the past is far more complicated than your mother being wrong and your father being right—"

"Are you saying Father lied?" asked Clark with such a disbelieving frown that Gregory considered that for a long moment before he answered. Heaven knew he'd thought Rodney a liar on more than one occasion, yet that aspersion was incorrect. Incomplete.

"No." Pausing, Gregory cleared his throat and tried again. "But their history is far more nuanced than one side being good and the other bad, and when I was willing to accept that, I was able to make up my own mind about your mother. I urge you to do the same."

Leaning forward, Gregory hoped what he was saying was the right thing. "Believing differently isn't a betrayal. True unconditional love is recognizing differences of opinion and loving the other still."

"But she was unfaithful to him," said Clark, though the faintest hint of a question lay in his tone. "That is abhorrent."

Gregory considered how to explain matters (for Mrs. Stuart's complicated past with her marriage vows was something her son didn't need to know at this juncture), but before he could, the young man began describing the things his father had revealed. And with each, cold seeped into Gregory's heart.

How could Rodney have told his son such details? There were things you shared with children, and others you revealed only when they were old enough to understand, but Mrs. Stuart's indiscretions fell into neither category—even if the accusations were true. It wasn't as though the lady had filled their heads with lies that Rodney needed to refute. No good came from sharing the intimate details of one's marriage with one's children.

It was little wonder the lad hated her so. Though Gregory did his best to explain away the past.

"If you like her, do you hate him for what he did?" asked Clark.

The question struck Gregory to the core. That was a complicated question with a complex answer, and he took a moment to consider it.

"I do not believe it is an either-or decision," he finally said with a frown. "I am sorry for what has happened, but no one is insisting we must choose one over the other."

Or there wasn't any longer, for Rodney could not voice his objections.

"And I do like your mother. Very much so. If you open yourself to the possibility, I believe you will find many reasons to adore her." Rising to his feet, Gregory brushed off his trousers. "It is your choice what you wish to do, but know that your parents and I care deeply for you. All of us—both your father and mother included—wish you to be happy."

That was truth eternal. It was the one thing that both Rodney and Tessa agreed upon, and though their father had opinions on what the children's happiness entailed, Gregory was determined to see that vision fulfilled.

In his own way.

# Chapter 30

As much as the weather had been cooperating of late, one could not depend on it being kind for long, yet anyone with sense knew there were ways to enjoy the world despite its fickle behavior. Thankfully, Edward and Joanna were quite sensible. At times.

With little work, canopies were hung from the side of the house, ensuring that if any rain fell, the revelers remained dry. Then mounds of blankets were produced for the older generation, who were more apt to enjoy the food and conversation than run about like little wildlings, who paid the weather no mind.

Another Sunday, another family gathering.

Edward and Joanna sat side by side, watching the mayhem unfold as the children flitted about, quickly dividing into teams and games, some choosing to playact whilst others insisted on some entertainment with winners and losers. Tessa occupied a chair near them, and she and Joanna spoke of the goings-on of the village.

Though Walter and Sadie were conspicuously absent (having chosen to attend their parish), those children in attendance did their utmost to ensure that the noise and chaos made up for their cousins' absences. Shirley snuck a slice of cake from a tray, hurrying out of reach before her mama could stop her and dividing the treat between Caro, Eva, and herself, though their fits of giggles made it difficult for them to eat properly.

And Mother and Father had chosen not to attend. Once again.

As much as Gregory enjoyed watching the Stuarts and Vaughns blending, the thought of his parents being alone settled uneasily in his stomach, and with a nod at the adults, he left the children in their care and made his way down the road to their home.

Rehearsing in his mind how he might convince them to join in the revelries, Gregory wondered what he would find. With both of them absent, Father must be in a truly dour mood.

Yet when he climbed the stairs to their rooms and found his way into their parlor, he discovered the pair curled up on the sofa together. Father's frock coat was cast aside, his arm wrapped around his bride as she reclined into him, her feet upon the cushion as she read aloud.

"'Thunder cracked overhead as the great doors flung open,'" she read, her voice coming quicker as she sped through the sentences. "'Dripping with rain and cloaked in shadows, his eyes blazed with fury and some darker purpose not yet known. The count had arrived at last—'"

"Dearest," said Father, brushing a hand along her arm. "We must stop. Your voice needs a rest."

Mother gaped as she glanced at him. "Nonsense, I can read for some hours more, and the count is at the castle—"

"Our son has come to pay a call," he added with a smile.

Turning her head, Mother lowered the book and straightened as she stared at Gregory as though he had appeared from the ether, rather than the front door. Perhaps he ought to have flung it open in the pouring rain as the thunder crashed overhead.

"You knew it was me?" asked Gregory. He strode across the room to the chair beside them as his mother rested her head against her husband's shoulder.

"Only family arrives unannounced. Sadie and Joanna are always accompanied by at least one of the grandchildren, and Edward seems to rush everywhere he goes," said Father. "Your footsteps are far too purposeful for that. And Walter makes no noise at all. It startles me every time."

Gregory didn't know what to say to that, for he didn't know how a footstep could be "purposeful" nor how that would sound, but it was unimportant at any rate.

"And how are you this afternoon?" he asked, glancing between his parents.

"Oh, that is such a serious tone," said Father with a sly grin.

Leaning closer, Mother whispered *sotto voce*, "And his expression is equally grim."

Gregory frowned. "You needn't laugh at me. I was concerned because you did not attend Edward's luncheon today."

The laughter fled his parents' expressions, and Mother settled her feet on the ground as Father straightened.

"We didn't mean to upset you, dearest," she said.

"It is kind of you to be concerned, but we are doing well," added Father. "We didn't come because your mother is too impatient to wait to see what happens in our book. I was afraid she might perish on the spot if I required her to put it aside until tonight."

"Then I shall leave you to it," said Gregory, shifting his weight to rise, but Mother leaned forward and caught his arm.

"Please do not leave yet. With all that has happened of late, we hardly see you," she said with a frown. "Having six children in your care is difficult, yet you rarely ask for assistance. To say nothing of having lost your friend. We worry for you, dearheart."

Ignoring the oddity of her saying that when Gregory had arrived on her doorstep for that very same reason, he considered the whole of his situation. As was true in most instances, his life boasted both sunshine and rain, being difficult in many facets yet simple in others. Regardless, his parents had enough difficulties of their own without his adding to their burdens.

"I am managing," he said.

But Mother's brows rose at that. "Something is amiss. I can tell, and it isn't like you to beat about the bush. Out with it, Gregory."

"There is one reason a man 'beats about the bush,'" said Father in a dry tone, his sightless eyes turning toward his son without focusing on him. "Does this have anything to do with that sweet widow you are spending so much time with of late?"

Gregory huffed at that, though he couldn't look directly at the gentleman (even though his father couldn't meet his eyes). "She is the mother of my wards. Of course, we spend time together."

"That was a palpable hit, my love," whispered Mother as she leaned into her husband. "He is avoiding looking at you, and I do detect a hint of a blush in his cheeks."

Despite Gregory forcing his gaze to them once more, he couldn't erase the telltale pink in his cheeks, and he cursed both it and his parents. Murmuring a curt farewell, he rose to his feet, but Mother once more snatched him by the arm and forced him back into his seat.

"Peace, son," she said with an apologetic wince that was almost genuine. "You must forgive your parents for a little teasing, but you look so stern. You need a bit of twitting from time to time."

Rodney's words rose to his thoughts: *"You need Stuarts in your life to pull you from that solitary rut you enjoy far too much. Without us, you are bound to grow so dour that even the maid's lotion shan't be able to save your face."*

And heaven help him, Gregory couldn't help but think of Mrs. Stuart's knack for doing just that. Of course, Rodney hadn't meant *that* Stuart, but it was true nonetheless. Whenever his troubles weighed him down, she nudged him into a brighter mood with a lighthearted comment and the proper amount of jesting—and she managed to do so without irritating, as his family were wont to do.

"Please talk to us," said Father, giving him a warm smile. "We are a troublesome old pair, but every young man needs a bit of help when it comes to courting."

Gregory held up his hands. "I have said nothing about courting."

"You ought to," replied Mother in a dry tone. "I cannot say I know her well, but I like Mrs. Stuart more each time I speak to her. She is good for you."

"That well may be, but it isn't as simple as me deciding to court her," he murmured.

"The good ladies always require a bit more effort," said Father, lifting his wife's hand to his lips.

Shifting in his seat, Gregory cleared his throat. "Effort isn't the issue. I do not fear hard work, but it isn't my feelings alone that I must consider."

And with that, he unwound the tale of Rodney and Mrs. Stuart, passing over many of the details of their past together; it was not his tale to tell, nor were the details relevant to this conversation. But his parents were familiar enough with Rodney's feelings for his wife that they didn't require much explanation as Gregory detailed his struggles with accepting Mrs. Stuart's presence and the mounting contention amongst the older children.

"Daphne and the Spooner boy?" asked Father with a grimace.

"He is hardly a boy any longer," said Gregory. "It matters not that such age differences are common enough with courting couples; he is far too old to be sniffing around a young lady who isn't out yet. To say nothing of the rumors circulating about his behavior."

"Daphne is aching from the loss of her father and struggling with her mother's reappearance," said Mother. "But she's a sensible girl and will see through his artifice soon enough. Clark is more concerning."

Gregory sighed and considered the massive pile of kindling at Eden Place. "Matters have improved over the past sennight in regards to his temper. I am more concerned about the fact that I could destroy the tenuous hold I have on their affections if I actively pursue their mother."

Closing his eyes, he rubbed his forehead. "And not just with Clark and Daphne. All the children have been distant since the festival, and I cannot consider anything with Mrs. Stuart if it risks their happiness. My first responsibility is to them, and I will not shirk it."

The silence stretched, and each second passed with excruciating slowness, drawing out each breath and heartbeat until the quiet became a living thing. Its presence settled into every corner, watching and waiting for someone to break it. Daring them to.

What was the good to be had in discussing this? There was no altering the facts. The children may be accepting her more and more, but they would not welcome their guardian courting her. And Gregory would not hurt those children. He could not. Whatever his feelings for Mrs. Stuart, there was no good to be had in placing his desires above theirs. They had suffered so much already—

Father cleared his throat. "Son, do you believe it is detrimental if their mother is more fully ingrained in their lives?"

"Absolutely not," said Gregory, straightening. "Mrs. Stuart is a good mother. An excellent one, in fact. She is patient and insightful, and the children are blessed to have her example."

With a sharp nod, Father concluded, "Then what else do you need to consider?"

Gregory's brows pulled low. "I am their guardian, and I must put their needs first—"

Holding up a staying hand, Mother gave him a wan smile. "Raising children means sacrifice, and it is good that they are foremost in your thoughts, but that does not mean you must ignore your needs entirely. Even if you are a lesser priority, you are still important. And dearest, I fear you are allowing the responsibility you feel for those children to keep you from what could be a good match."

"By all means, tread carefully," added Father. "However, it is your decision who you marry. Not theirs. This will impact the rest of your life. Not theirs. They will grow and build lives of their own. Be their own people. For goodness' sake, the youngest could be stepping into society in ten years, but your wife will remain at your side for decades more."

Mother nodded, her brow furrowing as her voice grew heavy. "Do not sacrifice all that simply to appease them for a few short years. The children are your responsibility—your family—but that does not mean you must surrender the whole of your happiness for their sake."

Lifting Mother's hand once more, Father pressed a kiss to it, his sightless eyes gleaming with such tenderness that Gregory felt he was intruding on a private moment. Dropping his gaze, he considered their advice; there was wisdom in their words, though he couldn't say if he wanted to accept it simply because it gave him what he wanted or because it was the right choice.

Clearing his throat, Father added, "And Mrs. Stuart lives in Leeds."

Gregory sighed and rubbed his forehead once more. "Yet another hurdle to face. Even if I wished to pursue her, she cannot remain in Thornsby indefinitely and see to her business. Mrs. Stuart depends on that income."

Father chuffed, and Mother struggled against a smile.

"Like father, like son," she murmured.

"Like mother, like son, you mean," he whispered back. "You eagerly threw yourself on the metaphorical altar as a sacrifice for your family. And I wasn't this clueless."

Mother brushed her thumb against his cheek. "You were going to abandon me and return to London."

"In my defense, I didn't realize you fancied me."

"If you had said the word 'courtship' even once, I wouldn't have assumed you thought of me only as a friend," she replied with an arched brow.

Father bowed his head in acknowledgement. "Touché."

Apparently done twitting one another, they turned their attention back to their son.

"I wasn't meaning that she ought to move here," said Father, the corner of his lips pulling into a wry smile, though there was a tinge of sorrow to it. "We know you wish to live in Leeds."

# Chapter 31

"We've wanted to speak with you about it for some time," added Father, "but you are a grown man, and we haven't wanted to stick our noses where they don't belong."

"You are my parents," said Gregory, frowning. "Your noses belong wherever they wish to be."

"No, they do not," said Mother with a shake of her head. "A parent's role is to teach and guide you through childhood, and then step into the background—supporting when needed—as you venture into adulthood. We are doing you no kindness if we continue to treat you like you are a child under our care."

Father waved away his son's concerns with a flick of his hand. "Regardless, we have long suspected that you wanted to leave Thornsby but that you feel like you must stay for our sake."

Though the gentleman couldn't punctuate that with a knowing gaze that bore right into Gregory's heart, Mother managed it well enough for the both of them, her eyes demanding answers.

"I know you are struggling of late," said Gregory with a sigh. "Father's blindness has been difficult on you both, and as the eldest, it is my role to step in and aid the family however I can. I cannot do so in Leeds."

"Oh, dearest," said Mother, giving him a sad smile. "Firstly, it is no one person's responsibility to manage the entire family. You are all helping in your own manner, and you needn't sacrifice your future for our sake. Because secondly, these struggles are ours to bear. Not yours. We will manage."

Reaching over, she wrapped her hands around Father's, looking into his face. "Yes, it has been difficult for us to adjust to this change, but life is full of trying moments. Your father and I have weathered them before, and we will do so again. Together."

A tender smile softened the gentleman's expression as he held fast to his wife. "And in truth, I do have my moments where I am frustrated or downcast, but in general, I am hopeful. I am still strong. Still contributing. This new life is an adjustment, but it continues on."

As both turned their attention to him, the two looked like a matching set. Pieces that fit together perfectly. The sort of pairing that Gregory had always dreamed of finding. One that strengthened both, blessing each.

"So, Gregory dear," said Mother, a challenge in her tone. "The one question that you need to sort out is, what do you wish to do? If there were no 'hurdles' or barriers to your desires, what path would you choose?"

"Court Mrs. Stuart, and settle in Leeds." Gregory didn't need to consider his answer, for his thoughts had mulled over that question for some time now.

"Then do it," said Father, smiling. "Or try, at the very least."

"Just uproot the children and move them to another city when so much of their lives has already been upended?" he said, shoulders slumping.

"Children are far more adaptable than we give them credit for," said Mother. "And, speaking as someone who once uprooted my whole life for the chance of something better, I can tell you that remaining in the same place may be the safe choice, but it is rarely the wise one. It is far too easy to be trapped in the past, and I think the children may benefit from a change."

"I never thought I would have to say this to you, Gregory, but it seems I must," said Father with a hint of a laugh in his tone. "It is time to be bold, son."

...

The garden hummed with life. Chatter carried on the air like birdsong, blending with the clink of china and rustle of skirts as the family wandered between blankets and chairs. A breeze stirred the canopy overhead, tugging at its corners, but the rain that had threatened to make an appearance had yet to arrive.

Laughter rang out, small feet pounded against the turf, and the occasional shriek of playful outrage rose from the younger children as they tumbled in and out of games. Tessa sat with her hands folded neatly in her lap, nodding along to Joanna's musings, but her gaze strayed to the children darting across the lawn without care or caution.

It was chaos, certainly, but it was a domestic sort of chaos. Familiar. Inviting. The sounds, the scents, and the cheerful disorder washed over Tessa like a balm. This was not a moment she would have dared hope for weeks ago, and yet here she was, tucked into a chair as though she belonged.

And perhaps, for now, she did.

Her gaze drifted toward the front gate; from her current position, Tessa could see if someone were to open it, whilst still being free to maintain a conversation with her newfound friends. She was not spying for Mr. Vaughn. That would be foolish. No, it was simply wise for someone to keep watch, lest one of the little ones slip away.

But as Tessa's gaze swept over the gathering, she was struck by another realization.

"Have you seen Daphne?" she asked, turning to Joanna.

With a frown, the lady straightened and cast her gaze this way and that, but it was her daughter who answered.

"She went to greet her fellow," said Shirley, pointing a jam-covered hand down the lane.

"Her fellow?" Tessa lurched up from her seat and strode across the lawn. It couldn't be. She had been watching the gate and would've noticed Daphne sneaking away. But it wasn't as though she could see the entrance that well, and if someone had opened it only partly to slip through—

No.

Waving for Joanna to remain, Tessa hurried through the gate and gazed this way and that, though there was no sign of the young lady. Turning toward the section of road that did not cross in front of the gathering (which she most certainly would've seen), Tessa sped down the lane.

Tucked up beside a cottage two houses down, Daphne was just out of sight of the passersby, though not her mother's scouring glance. And she wasn't alone. Mr. Spooner's arms were locked around her, and that bounder had his hands all over her daughter, drifting into places he had no right to touch as his lips devoured hers—and Daphne matched his passion, meeting each with eager noises as she pressed deeper into him.

"What do you think you are doing?" Had Tessa been in her right mind, she would've spoken quietly, but her voice snapped like the crack of a pistol, ringing out for anyone in the streets to hear. Stiffening, Tessa threw a startled look over her shoulder, but there was no one about on this quiet Sunday afternoon. Hurrying forward, she grabbed Daphne, but the girl pulled out of reach and draped herself over that bounder's chest.

"Leave me alone," said Daphne, clinging to him as though he were the very source of life itself. "This is none of your concern."

Mr. Spooner rubbed the girl's back, and triumph glinted in his gaze as he glanced out at the street. Then, raising his head and his voice, he drew in a breath.

"I—"

Tessa lunged forward, her hand swinging with all her strength. It cracked against his cheek with such force that her palm stung, and his mouth snapped closed before he could draw attention to them.

"How dare you!" cried Daphne, and Tessa pressed a hand over her mouth, latching the other around her daughter's arm and pulling her away from the bounder.

"Keep your voice down," said Tessa in a low hiss.

"I do not care who sees us." Though Daphne did not match her mother's volume, she at least had the good sense not to raise it again, either.

Mr. Spooner moved, but Tessa leveled a hard look at him, promising him far more pain should he dare take another step, and he must have sensed just how eager she was to inflict it, for he held up his hands in placation. Not that it mattered, as Daphne was spouting nonsense that proved he had his hooks in her far deeper than Tessa had realized.

"I love him!"

For all that she had warned Mr. Vaughn about drawing hard lines with Daphne's actions, no amount of wisdom could overcome the panic surging through Tessa. Had anyone witnessed that embrace, Daphne would be ruined. Mr. Vaughn didn't seem the type to force her into such a terrible marriage, but her daughter's life would be forever altered regardless. Indelibly marred by a poor choice when she was but seventeen.

To say nothing of how far such behavior might've gone had Tessa not interrupted—and how many other lives might've been trampled under Mr. Spooner's heel. So many fears and concerns flooded through her, and Tessa grasped for anything to say or do to pull her daughter from this path.

"You hardly know the man, Daphne. And even if he was your one true love and this was everything you had wished for, you do not allow anyone—*anyone*—to treat you with so little regard. To paw you in public as though you are unworthy of being treated with respect and dignity."

Turning her burning gaze on Mr. Spooner, Tessa scowled. "Have you no shame?"

Daphne sneered. "That is rich. You have no right to chastise me for my behavior. Not when yours destroyed our family!"

"Do not speak to your mother like that."

Mr. Vaughn's voice cut through the afternoon air just as he came around the corner, his eyes darting over the trio, taking in the whole of it in one heartbeat. With his gaze narrowing on Mr. Spooner, Mr. Vaughn's entire demeanor shifted. It was as though his features were chiseled from granite, and his eyes were flaming coals as he stared down the cad.

"I will pay a call on you later today, Mr. Spooner," said Mr. Vaughn, his voice slicing through the air with deadly finality.

And for the first time since stepping into this mess, the blackguard appeared properly cowed. Blanching, his arms fell away from Daphne as his mouth opened to say something, but Mr. Vaughn's expression darkened, and Mr. Spooner stepped away without another word.

Daphne watched his retreat, wide-eyed and gaping, and the moment he was out of sight, she rounded on her mother, her hands clenched and shaking as she glared at the lady.

"You have no right to interfere with my life!" Daphne's fury burned bright, and Tessa's heart sank at the sight of yet another of their children who had been cursed with the Stuart temper.

Nodding toward the lane, Mr. Vaughn said, "Return to my brother's house, and wait there for me, Daphne."

As bright as her anger had burned, the firmness in his tone snuffed it out, and her complexion paled almost as much as Mr. Spooner's had. Lowering her eyes to the ground, Daphne nodded and turned away, but she lifted her gaze just enough to meet Tessa's, flashing once more with fury before she hurried to obey.

"But Mr. Spooner might be waiting for her," said Tessa, motioning toward the lane, her feet desperate to follow after. "We have to speak to her. Make her understand—"

"Believe me when I say that Mr. Spooner is already locked in his home, hiding under his bed," replied Mr. Vaughn. "And before we do anything else, we need to calm ourselves."

Tessa scowled at him, knowing full well that there was no "we" in that, for he looked plenty calm and relaxed as he stood there, his arms folded.

"You didn't see what I saw!" she said, pointing at the place in which Daphne and Mr. Spooner had been embracing. "Had I not come along when I did, she might've given him everything right there and then!"

Panic clawed its way up Tessa's throat, tightening with every breath until it felt as though air refused to enter her lungs. She wrapped her arms around herself, fingers gripping her elbows so tightly she half expected bruises to bloom, but the image of Daphne in that man's arms replayed over and over, a cruel loop that refused to release her.

What had Daphne been thinking? Tessa didn't know—she couldn't know—because the girl barely looked at her, let alone spoke to her.

And if she *hadn't* come along when she had? The thought was too much to bear. Even if the indiscretion had remained secret, with no outward sign to harm Daphne's standing, giving herself in such a fashion to such a man would leave a mark on the poor girl. A bruise upon her heart and soul. The act of a desperate, unhappy person, seeking validation from someone who could never love her.

Taking such a step was setting her on a dangerous path, and Tessa's pounding heart drowned out the world around her as her mind spun with all the worst-case outcomes she could not prevent. She was losing her again. No—she had already lost her.

What power did she have? What claim? Daphne wouldn't listen. None of them would.

"Breathe, Mrs. Stuart," said the gentleman, settling his hands on her shoulders, rubbing them as though soothing a fractious child.

And though the comparison was unflattering, Tessa clung to his touch all the same. Forcing air into her lungs as Mr. Vaughn continued to caress her arms and speak in that calm manner of his, Tessa felt her pulse slow and reason settle back into place.

# Chapter 32

"This is startling, but we will manage it," said Mr. Vaughn in an even tone. "And I will speak to my family about the situation, and they shall help keep watch. Between us all, we will ensure Daphne won't be cornered by him again."

"It isn't just Mr. Spooner," said Tessa, shaking her head. "Daphne is making choices that might do serious harm, and she doesn't seem to understand—"

"Breathe," he repeated, and it was only then that she realized how lightheaded she was.

Tessa peered into his eyes with a frown. "How are you so calm?"

Tilting his head as though to consider that, Mr. Vaughn frowned. "I don't know. Seeing you so distraught allowed me to keep my wits about me, just as you were able to remain calm at the festival when all I wished to do was bludgeon the fellow. I suppose we are a good pair."

Pressing a hand to her hot cheeks, Tessa shook her head. "I reacted poorly. After all my lecturing you about not forcing her into his arms, I've done just that."

Mr. Vaughn's brows rose. "We cannot know that. Not yet. But I know that had I been the one to discover them, Mr. Spooner would've needed to be carried home on a stretcher."

Tears brimmed in Tessa's eyes. "Daphne is so angry. I do not know if she will ever forgive me."

"She is a brokenhearted young lady who has been struggling with her father's passing. That alone would cause anyone trouble. But you are a good woman and a loving mother," he said in a low voice. Those hands continued to massage her arms, each touch helping her heart to settle a little more. "Daphne will come to see that. She may not thank you for your interference now, but I am certain she will one day."

Mr. Vaughn stood so close to her, his presence seeming to envelop her. It was like a crisp breeze on a hot summer's day, sweeping through her and settling the unease in her heart.

Tessa's breath caught. She felt the heat of him—so near, so steady—and his voice seemed to rumble through her bones, stirring something inside her. A hum beneath her skin that sent ripples of awareness through her. The world narrowed as she held his gaze, erasing all her worries and fears and healing the ache in her chest. There was only Mr. Vaughn and her standing there together, looking into each other's eyes.

"Should—" Tessa's voice wobbled, and she cleared her throat. "Should we speak with her?"

Mr. Vaughn considered that for a moment, and she awaited his opinion. Tessa wasn't certain she could trust her own thoughts at present.

"We ought to allow tempers to cool," he said, his voice quiet and soothing. "But we will find a way to help her."

And when he said that, Tessa couldn't help but believe him. Mr. Vaughn may find his guardianship daunting, but the certainty with which he said "we" settled into her bones. Together, they would find a way to help her lost child.

Nodding to him, Tessa took another deep breath. "I think I ought to return to the inn. I fear Daphne will grow agitated again if I rejoin the party."

Turning toward the road, Mr. Vaughn offered his arm. "Then may I escort you home, madam?"

"I do not want to be a bother."

But the gentleman held her gaze and said in a voice so low that it was nearly a whisper, "It is no bother."

Tessa hesitated for the briefest of moments before placing her hand on his arm, her fingers curling against the fabric of his coat. It was foolish to feel this flutter in her chest. Nonsense, really. They were only friends. Nothing more.

But the memory of their dance returned to her with startling clarity: the warmth of his hand at her waist, the way their steps had fallen into rhythm so easily, how her heart had leapt when his gaze had held hers just a little too long. That was only a dance. A moment. And yet, walking beside him now, her thoughts tangled in knots, leaving her unsettled and far too aware of the quiet man at her side.

Together, they wove through the streets of Thornsby. With the shops closed for the Sabbath, there were few people about today. There were couples in gigs, enjoying an afternoon out and about, and the odd farmer's cart rumbling along the road, going about its business, as cattle and grains did not understand the importance of this day of rest, but Thornsby was mostly quiet.

Compared to her home in Leeds, this village was little more than a hamlet. A speck in the English countryside. Yet there was a beauty and grandeur to the place that a city could not recreate. Though coal smoke pumped from the chimneys, it wasn't enough to cast its black pall upon the brown and grey stonework. The shutters were brightly painted, accented by the flowers that crept and climbed along the buildings and walls.

It was a perfect sort of place. And though neither she nor Mr. Vaughn spoke a word, it was a perfect sort of silence. Not filled with discomfort or the fretful need to fill it. Just two people enjoying the world together.

They arrived at the inn too soon, and Tessa found herself reluctant to release her hold on him.

"My thanks, Mr. Vaughn," she said, patting his arm before stepping away.

But the gentleman reached forward, taking her hand in his as his eyes seized hold of her as readily as his fingers. "I wish to court you, Mrs. Stuart."

Tessa's mouth opened, and though she tried to keep from looking a fool, she couldn't help gaping. "Pardon?"

"We may have been at odds after arriving in Thornsby, but I do not think I am speaking out of turn when I say that before that moment, we looked upon one another favorably. And since settling our differences, that feeling has grown."

The gentleman spoke with the sort of directness that would've startled another lady, but Tessa took in the words, appreciating the honesty of his declaration. Having spent the last several years of her life wading through the business world, she found she preferred it to the delicate prevarications of society.

Yet they were not speaking of a financial transaction.

This connection she shared with Mr. Vaughn was nothing like her first marriage—even in the early days, when she and Rodney had been happy. Their lives had blended with an ease that only those with matching personalities could manage. Never arguing. Not once. Not when all was good and right in the world.

Only once the road had grown rocky had the arguments begun. And they were far larger and more important than disagreeing on what books to read or which horse was the better mount.

But she and Mr. Vaughn? They often sat on opposing sides of a discussion. He challenged her. Pressed back. Even infuriated her at times. Their views and opinions were often vastly different, yet their values and goals were the same, and as a whole, it was far more appealing than even the best of days with Rodney.

Yet in one way, both men were the same: the law gave them power over her children.

A tremor began in her fingertips and spread upward, tightening her arms and shoulders until she held herself stiff as stone, and a cold sweat broke across her back despite the warm evening air. Her breaths came too fast, shallow and useless, catching in her throat with each sharp inhale as her pulse pounded in her ears like a drumbeat driving her toward some unseen danger.

Every part of her body screamed retreat, but her feet remained frozen in place.

"Peace, Mrs. Stuart," said Mr. Vaughn, his brows rising as he watched her. "Please tell me what you are thinking. You know I value your honesty."

Though her throat felt like it was coated in sand, Tessa faced him and spoke. "The children. They are angry with me as it is, and their reaction at the festival—"

"They will come around," said Mr. Vaughn, studying her. "But that is not what has you looking as though you might faint dead away."

Fear held her fast, but Tessa considered it and the man before her. "Do you not see the impossibility of my situation? If I reject your suit or if things sour between us, what will happen then? You could cut me off from my children, and there is nothing I can do about it."

Mr. Vaughn's brows rose at that. "I hadn't thought of it from that perspective, and I apologize for making you anxious. Whatever your decision, you are their mother, and I will not stand between you and them. I am not Rodney. Surely, you know that."

No, he was not. Tessa felt it in her bones that this man couldn't be more different from her late husband. Enough so that she couldn't imagine how the pair had been friends. Then again, Tessa was coming to think of Mr. Vaughn as one of her dearest, and as she and Rodney were so similar, she supposed it made sense.

The quiet, calm tenor of his voice wove through her as his hands held hers gently. It was such a strange juxtaposition—

this seemingly hard and unyielding man who was so tender and kind beneath.

"Setting the children aside, what do you want?" asked Mr. Vaughn.

"I cannot set them aside—"

"Just pretend for a moment, Mrs. Stuart," he said with a faint smile that held just a touch of a rueful edge. "If it were just me standing before you, offering you my heart. What would you say?"

Tears blurred her vision as her heart fluttered in her chest, picking up its pace until she could hardly breathe. Another pulse of panic reverberated through her, echoing from deep within her bones. A part of her that she had ignored for so very long surged to the forefront, making her hands tremble anew, and she fought to keep her voice steady as she tried to put the feeling into words.

"I would say that my history with love is abysmal, Mr. Vaughn. I may trust you in many aspects, but I do not know if I can trust myself," she whispered. "The thought of marrying is terrifying to say the least, especially as I doubt my ability to choose my husband wisely."

Mr. Vaughn gave a vague hum of consideration. His expression did not alter one jot, but Tessa could see his thoughts sifting through his head.

"Then you are afraid that it will not only affect the children adversely, but you do not know if you ever wish to accept any man's suit, let alone mine?" he said in that succinct manner of his. "But you are not set against it, either."

Just hearing that set her pulse racing again, yet Tessa couldn't deny the truth of those words. Some small part of her heart still hoped. Despite everything, that starry-eyed young lady she'd buried long ago still recalled the good moments in her marriage and yearned for more.

But that sort of thinking was the very thing that had driven her into Rodney's arms in the first place.

"I can accept that," he said with a sharp nod as a glint of determination shone in his eyes. "If you want a friend and companion, I can be that, Mrs. Stuart. Anything you wish, as long as it means you are near."

Tessa straightened, and everything stilled inside her as his thumb brushed against the back of her hand, sending gooseflesh up her arms. Mr. Vaughn stepped closer, his gaze holding her captive as he lowered his voice until it sounded like warm honey.

"But the moment you wish for something more, you need only say the word." Mr. Vaughn's gaze bored into hers as he lifted her hand to his lips, pressing a kiss to her knuckles.

Tessa couldn't breathe. Or blink. Or move. Her hand remained in his, the ghost of his kiss lingering against her skin. His words felt like a vow, and it wrapped around them, locking them together as the world hushed and time paused between heartbeats.

For a heady moment, neither of them moved, and then, with a nod that felt far too formal for what had just passed between them, Tessa slipped her hand from his and turned toward the inn door.

"Good afternoon, Mr. Vaughn," she said, her voice steadier than she felt.

"Good afternoon, Mrs. Stuart."

With that, Tessa hurried through the public room and up into her bedchamber, not pausing until the door latched behind her. Sinking onto the bed, she willed her pulse to slow, but it refused, thumping against her ribs with a determined beat as though she were standing on a precipice.

And she couldn't help wondering if she had already stepped over the edge.

# Chapter 33

Evening settled gently over Eden Place, drawing long shadows across the study and casting the room in a hush that felt deeper than mere silence. A single lamp burned on the desk, its light pooling over the scattered correspondence and ledgers, while the rest of the room remained cloaked in dusky stillness.

Outside the tall windows, the lawns were swallowed by darkness, save for a sliver of moonlight that broke through the parting clouds and cast a silver glow across the tops of the hedgerows. There was a bite to the air—autumn's first nibble—which warned that the seasons were shifting, and somewhere in the corridor, a grandfather clock ticked its steady rhythm, counting the seconds of a day as they slipped away unnoticed.

Gregory had spent the better part of the evening here, retreating into the study after the house had quieted for the evening. His nightly ritual. Or so it had been for the past month. Availing himself of the tea that the maid had set on the corner of the desk, he pored over the latest letter from his solicitor in Leeds.

Another property. Another set of details to comb through. No matter that he had yet to give the fellow permission to pursue a particular property, Mr. Castle was sending a steady stream of recommendations as he scoured the city; Gregory reviewed every possibility, weighing each with the same careful deliberation he applied to everything else in his life. Relocation wasn't a decision he could make quickly, not with so many lives now tangled with his own.

Storefronts and workshops were easy enough to sift through, as any building Gregory chose would require extensive reworking to suit the needs of his business, so he had few requirements and found many possibilities.

But a home? That decision was far more daunting.

Mr. Castle described three separate properties, each of which would suit but for different reasons. There were homes aplenty outside the city, which would grant them grounds and stables. Plenty of space indoors and out. All in all, it wouldn't be much different from what they had in Thornsby. Familiar. Comfortable.

But it required significantly more travel; not only for him, as his business would require daily drives into the city, but anytime they wished to visit Thornsby, as the house was far from any railway station. To say nothing of the limited society outside the city proper, which would be a hindrance to the girls as they came out.

Considering that, Gregory wondered if it was prudent to find a copy of Eden Place; sometimes a complete change was better than a slight shift. Which led him to reconsider the terraced houses in the heart of town.

They boasted garden squares to allow the children a dash of nature, though it would be shared with the neighbors. And with livery stables, they could still keep horses, though without any proper places to ride, that was of little use. Yet there was the benefit of society and proximity to his business and Mrs. Stuart's home, which would allow the lady to visit the children more frequently.

All in all, it boasted the exact opposite blessings and drawbacks of settling outside of town.

Then there were the villas that sat somewhere between the country estates and terraced houses. It might seem as though it was a beautiful compromise between the blessings of the country and the heart of the city, but being on the outskirts only brought the troubles of both with few benefits to balance them out—less nature and society with greater distances to travel.

At least that made it easy to cross those off the list. And if it were left solely to him, Gregory thought the city boasted far more benefits than the country, especially as they wouldn't surrender their home in Thornsby. It would be easy enough to take the children to Eden Place whenever they had need of fields and forests.

And Mr. Castle's descriptions were intriguing. Tall windows and tidy brick façades. Orderly rows that edged the garden squares, where children played beneath the watchful eyes of nursemaids. Shops lining the neighboring roads, close enough for the older children to run errands or fetch sweets on special occasions.

The interiors were well maintained, with high ceilings and ample light. Large public rooms that were cozy enough for a family to enjoy on a quiet evening and large enough to entertain, should the desire strike him. It hadn't ever before, but then, he'd never had reason to do so.

Gregory could picture them there: the thrum and vitality of the city with jaunts to the country whenever it suited. Though he was not ready to commit to this change, something inside him had begun to shift since speaking to his parents last month—a quiet, persistent awareness that life in Thornsby, for all its familiarity, might not be the final chapter after all.

Yet as he sat there, eyes scanning the delicate loops of his solicitor's handwriting, Gregory felt the weight of uncertainty settle heavily across his shoulders, and he rubbed a hand across his brow, easing back into the chair as the scent of old leather and drying ink wrapped around him like a memory. There was still time to decide, but he would need to do so soon.

The echo of a closing door snapped him from his thoughts, though he paid little heed to the sound. The servants were still occupied with their work for the day, after all. But when it was accompanied by hurried footsteps, Gregory straightened and looked at the door just as a knock sounded.

"I am sorry to bother you, sir," said Fanny as the maid swept into the room with a bob. "But Mr. Reed just arrived from school with Master Clark."

Gregory tossed aside the letter. The devil take the boy! The Michaelmas term had only just begun, and the lad had seemed to settle of late, but if Clark had behaved badly enough for them to bring him home in the middle of the night—

"He's terribly sick," she added.

Leaping out of his seat, Gregory was down the corridor in a flash, arriving at the front door to find his brother-in-law giving orders to the staff. Walter turned to meet him, his hat clutched in his hand.

"We do not know how he caught it," he said, his brows twisting. "One of the benefits of a country boarding school is the isolation from illnesses. We watch over the children so closely—"

"Peace, Walter. It happens, and you hold no blame. Where is he?"

"In the carriage," he said, nodding toward the door, but when Gregory moved in that direction, Walter grabbed his arm and pulled him to a stop. "We need to approach this carefully. Sadie is certain it's scarlet fever."

Those two words struck Gregory dumb, his feet anchored in place as he stared at Walter.

"We don't know how he was exposed—"

"Edward warned me there was a case of scarlet fever in Danthorpe," said Gregory, running a hand through his hair as he considered the situation. "I spent the last few days preparing the shop for what might come and kept the girls away from the village to be safe."

Walter nodded. "Sadie recognized the signs right away, and since Eden Place isn't far from the school, we thought he would rest easier in his own bed. We do not have the means of keeping him properly quarantined, and we cannot risk it spreading."

"Of course not," said Gregory. "You did the right thing."

Shoulders straightening, Walter seemed to calm at that reassurance. "Sadie remained home to ready the school if it spreads." Pulling a slip of paper from his pocket, Walter reported, "But she administered willow bark tea and a small amount of laudanum before we left, and I bathed his head with vinegar during the drive."

He handed the note to Gregory, who glanced at it, but Walter had conveyed Sadie's instructions well enough. Tucking it away, he dove into action.

Mrs. Ferrell stood at the ready, awaiting her master's orders.

"Send for my brother and Mrs. Stuart, but warn her not to come if she hasn't had it before. This may affect children more than adults, but it strikes far worse for the latter, and we cannot risk it. And prepare Master Clark's room and the guest bedroom beside it," he began, and the housekeeper immediately set to work, snapping off more orders as the staff scurried to obey.

Stopping her, Gregory added, "And once that is complete, send the servants home. We need to keep him quarantined, or this will spread through the village like wildfire."

"Clark has scarlet fever?" Daphne's voice trembled, and Gregory spun around and spied her on the stairs, wrapped in a dressing gown with her plait slung over her shoulder.

"Come no closer," he ordered.

"I've had it," she said, taking the last few steps, but she stopped when Gregory raised a staying hand.

"But your sisters haven't, and they need to be relocated immediately. I do not want them within a mile of this. I cannot leave Clark, and they need someone to watch over them." Pausing, he considered where to send them. Walter's home wasn't safe, and Edward's was filled to the rafters and could be equally dangerous during this ordeal as he worked to heal the village.

"Your parents would welcome them," suggested Walter. "And I cannot think of better protectors. Even without his sight, your father is a brilliant physician, and your mother knows more about medicine than either you or Edward."

Gregory nodded. "The girls can sleep together in the spare room."

But when he turned his attention back to Daphne, her chin was jutted out in that Stuart manner. "I do not want to run away and hide with my sisters. Clark needs me. I must stay and assist."

Before Gregory could insist that she was more helpful watching over her sisters, he made the mistake of meeting her gaze. Those eyes were so like her mother's, and they were filled with unshed tears. They shone with the heartbreak of one having watched her father pass only a few months ago, and Gregory's heart cracked as he faced the thought that he had been determinedly ignoring.

Clark would survive this. He would.

"Please let me stay," she whispered. "You cannot nurse him on your own. I can be helpful. I promise."

It took only a heartbeat for him to decide, but he held up a finger. "But first, I need you to prepare the girls. Pack whatever they will require for the next fortnight. Do not scare them. We do not know how serious his case is, and there is no need to fret at this juncture. He will likely be right as rain in a few days, and we are being overly cautious."

Daphne nodded, taking his orders with all the seriousness of a soldier, and she swiftly climbed the steps, calling out for one of the maids to follow her.

Glancing at Walter, Gregory said, "My clothes will be too large on you, but you'd best change. Wrap yours in canvas and have Sadie boil or burn them when you arrive home." Gregory paused and amended, "Or I can have my servants handle it before they leave. Either way, we do not want any noxious vapors to remain."

Not waiting for Walter to make his decision (he could discuss that with the servants), Gregory strode through the front door and peered into the waiting carriage.

"Good evening to you, Clark," he said, adopting a jovial tone and leveling a smile on the young man. But only the sound of heavy breaths answered. Lifting the rag from Clark's forehead, Gregory held fast to his composure as he inspected the ruddy complexion, tell-tale rash, and unfocused eyes. "I understand you are feeling poorly."

"Mr. Gregory?" Clark's voice was distant, as though struggling to comprehend the world around him.

Gregory considered how to move the lad, though he was large enough that he was no mere lad any longer. A finger to Clark's neck confirmed the rapid heartbeat. Thank heavens Sadie and Walter had moved quickly; scarlet fever set in fast, and before long, he would've been too ill to move.

"Here," said Walter, pulling away the ropes that were strapped across the boot. "Your brilliant sister insisted the school needed a stretcher on hand, and with those rambunctious boys, it's come in handy on more than one occasion."

Together, they laid the stretcher on the ground and carefully pulled Clark through the carriage door, laying him atop the canvas. Then, taking the positions at the poles, the two men hoisted Clark and carried him into the house.

Maids scurried away, giving them a wide berth as they arrived on the second story, and with a few prods, Gregory guided Walter into the bedchamber and deposited Clark onto the mattress. Mrs. Ferrell shooed away the remaining servants and strode to where the medicine chest sat, opening the main compartment.

"You should be on your way, Walter. I have it from here," said Gregory, nodding toward the door. Turning his gaze to Mrs. Ferrell, he instructed her concerning the fellow's clothing and added, "I need rags, a teakettle, and as much vinegar as you can bring me."

Though Walter looked as though he wanted to stay, Gregory shooed him away with more reminders about cleansing his clothes of any vapors. Once the door was closed on his brother-in-law, Gregory strode to the window, throwing it open to let the breeze clear out the stagnant air.

Sifting through the medicine chest, Gregory sent a prayer of gratitude that the Vaughns were a prepared lot. Just as Sadie had her stretcher, he had a veritable apothecary shop before him, and pulling out a few vials and bottles, he drew them over to the table beside the bed.

The cloth Walter had used had slipped free, and Gregory repositioned it, mopping the young man's brow. "You're home now, Clark. All will be well."

# Chapter 34

Tessa surged up the stairs, her skirt tangling at her ankles, and she gripped the banister hard enough that her fingers ached; each step felt both too slow and far too fast, her mind racing ahead to the worst possibilities even as her feet fought to carry her faster. A sick, rising dread lodged in her throat and burned behind her eyes, but she pushed it down.

Not now. The moment she let fear take hold, it would paralyze her.

Despite her making enough noise to raise the dead, there was no movement in the house, and that silence pressed in around her, cruel and absolute. With every breath drawn sharply through her nose, the shadows at the top of the stairs seemed to stretch longer, darker, and more threatening.

"Mr. Vaughn?"

"Here," he called as she arrived at the landing.

Tessa rushed forward, and the gentleman appeared in the doorway, the concern in his eyes clear to see, even in the dim candlelight. She peered around him, but before she could move closer, he stopped her.

"I had scarlet fever as a child," she said, hardly sparing him a look, for her eyes were riveted to the listless figure in the bed.

Mr. Vaughn stepped aside and led her to the bed. A breeze carried through the room, flavored with the scent of vinegar from the soaked rags that hung before the window. Eyes fixed on her son, Tessa removed her cloak, and the gentleman took it without a word, tucking it away as she sat in the chair he had vacated.

The lad lay in the bed, his eyes open but unfocused. They turned to her, though he made no sign that he recognized her at all. Reaching for his forehead, Tessa brushed a touch across the skin, which felt fevered even to her uneducated touch.

"Oh, my little Clark," she whispered. On the bedside table sat a bowl with a rag, and Tessa took it, pressing the cool cloth against his skin as Clark turned toward the touch. "How is he?"

"It is too early to tell. I sent for Edward, but he is seeing to another patient in Danthorpe, and it will be some time before he can arrive. I am quite capable of managing without him, but I would feel more at ease with a second opinion."

"I am certain he is in good hands," said Tessa, though her voice caught, and Mr. Vaughn drew his arm around her shoulders.

"He is going to heal quickly. He is a Stuart," said Daphne with a sharp tone as she appeared beside the bed, standing opposite Tessa. Her eyes drifted from her guardian to the hand he rested on her mother's shoulder, and Tessa straightened, easing it away. "Jackson, Wesley, and I all had it some years ago, and it was nothing at all. A minor inconvenience."

For all that the young lady's eyes burned as she looked at her mother, the words had an edge of desperation to them, as though willing her belief into existence, and Tessa longed to pull her daughter into her arms.

"Daphne has been an excellent assistant," said Mr. Vaughn, clearing his throat as he began expounding on the various treatments they'd enacted already, from the medicines administered to the rag baths with vinegar and alcohol, and including the food they were able to feed him. And though Tessa tried to take note of it all, her attention was fixed on her son's face.

Her Clark.

The years faded away until all she could see was the tiny, squalling babe the physician had placed in her arms. With his strong set of lungs, Clark had been determined to show all and sundry just how loud he could be, but the babe had settled the moment she'd spoken to him. As though he'd been waiting to hear her voice.

"I am here now," she whispered, carefully mopping his brow with the rag. "I will watch over you."

"We do not require your assistance," said Daphne. "Clark will be right as rain in a few hours, and he has Mr. Gregory and me to watch over him."

"Another set of hands will be a blessing," said Mr. Vaughn. "With the three of us, it will allow us to sleep in shifts, else we risk making ourselves ill as well."

"I can take this first one," said Tessa, glancing up at him. "You two can rest. I do not think I could sleep."

"Clark wouldn't want you here," said Daphne, her tone growing harder with each interjection.

"Then it is doubly good that I take the nighttime hours, for he will be asleep and not know I am here," said Tessa, meeting her daughter's burning gaze.

The young lady pointed to her chest. "But *I* know you are here."

Shooting to her feet, Tessa held her daughter's gaze with steely determination. "It is time you and I had a discussion."

"I have nothing to discuss with you," said Daphne, crossing her arms.

Mr. Vaughn opened his mouth to speak, but Tessa held up a staying hand.

"Oh, I believe you have plenty you wish to say to me," she said, motioning toward the door. But Daphne didn't move until her guardian gave a direct order, and then the young lady stormed into the corridor, not looking at her mother.

Tessa led her into the adjacent bedchamber, closing the door behind them.

"I know you are furious with me, and with how your father and I behaved. You have every right to be," she said, holding up placating hands. "But Clark needs all the assistance we can render. Whether he wishes me there or not, I am his mother, and I am not going to leave until he is well again."

Daphne's arms tightened around her chest, and she glared. "Do not dare to claim that you care about any of us besides Eva."

Straightening, Tessa frowned. "What do you mean? I do not love Eva more than the rest of you."

"Do not try to lie your way out of this," scoffed Daphne. "She is the only one you took with you when you left our home in Leeds. You didn't care about abandoning the rest of us."

Tessa's eyes widened. "That isn't what happened—"

"Do not tell me what happened!" shouted Daphne, her hands falling to her sides, clenched tight. "I may have been a child, but I was old enough to remember. You ran off with Eva, not caring one jot that the rest of us wanted you. None of us mattered at all."

Though Tessa tried to defend herself, it was as though a valve had opened within her daughter, and she continued pouring out her heart, sharing every secret pain she felt. The nights when all she had wanted was her mother to rock her to sleep. The milestones Tessa had missed. The holidays and celebrations for which she'd been absent. Daphne unleashed them all, heaping them upon her mother with abandon.

And Tessa remained silent.

Standing there, she felt the anguish radiating from every sharp word and the betrayal vibrating through her clenched muscles. Though Daphne showed none of the signs of violence Clark had demonstrated, it was clear that the fury she'd felt was just as powerful—and far more repressed. So, Tessa kept her own counsel, allowing her daughter to unearth all that pain.

It took quite a length of time before Daphne's words slowed, and she stood there, lungs heaving as though she had run a race as she stared down her mother.

Allowing the silence to linger for a moment, Tessa prayed with all her heart that she would know what to say. After all the mistakes she had made in her life, she yearned for wisdom and clarity so that she could heal the wounds she'd left on these poor, innocent children. And though she tried searching for grand and eloquent explanations, three small words rose to her thoughts.

"I am sorry," whispered Tessa.

Daphne stilled, her eyes unblinking as she watched her.

"I am sorry," Tessa repeated, shaking her head. "I should've been a better mother to you. I am sorry that my weaknesses and flaws caused you so much pain. I wish I could undo it all, but I cannot. And I am sorry for that as well."

The silence dragged on for several long moments, and though the tension in the air did not evaporate, it eased the slightest bit.

"But I do not love Eva more than any of the rest of you," said Tessa. Daphne's hands clenched at that, but Tessa held up a staying hand and spoke in a calm tone. "I know you remember much about what happened in our home, but you were a child, and I fear you did not understand. I only took Eva with me because I was expecting her when your father and I parted ways."

Crossing her arms tight across her chest, Daphne's eyes narrowed. "I do not believe your lies. Father wouldn't have allowed you to separate him from his children because he loved us too much. And even after you took Eva, you couldn't be bothered to keep her."

What did one say to that? To tell her daughter the whole truth would be to drag her into more of the troubles that ought to remain between man and wife. Yet to remain silent would leave the wedge between mother and daughter.

"I love you, my darling girl," whispered Tessa. "I did not want to be parted from you. Any of you. But your father believed I had been unfaithful and that Eva was another man's child. When she was old enough that even he couldn't deny her parentage, he took her to live with him."

Drawing in a breath, Tessa added, "He loved you dearly, but I did as well. I simply did not have the power to keep you with me. The courts rarely grant mothers custody, and you older three were beyond the age where I could even petition for it. I couldn't bear to drag the lot of you into a scandal."

Daphne turned away, giving her mother her back as the silence enveloped the room once more. Tessa longed to reach out for her daughter. To take her in her arms. But there was a gulf between them. A chasm that stretched out over the years.

"You are my firstborn, and I loved you from the moment I discovered I was to be a mother. So deeply. So dearly," whispered Tessa. "I am sorry I gave you reason to doubt that, but you are constantly in my thoughts and in my heart. And I promise that the fracture in our family had everything to do with the troubles between your father and me and naught to do with how much we love you children."

Now that the conversation had begun, Tessa yearned to press the issue until everything was settled to her liking. It was an itch that dug into her skin, burrowing deep inside her. But her heart knew that forcing the issue would only make matters worse.

Daphne had spoken her piece. Tessa had spoken hers. And only time would tell if these wounds would now heal.

So Tessa slipped silently from the room, closing the door behind her. And when she stepped back into the sickroom, Mr. Vaughn was waiting, his eyes full of such warmth and understanding that she yearned to throw herself into his arms.

*"You need only say the word..."*

His voice echoed from her memory with promises of protection and safety. Of a stalwart friend and ally. In her youth, she hadn't prized those qualities, choosing to chase after beaus blessed with wittiness and easy manners. But in those days, comfort and support had been in abundant supply. Now, nothing was more appealing than a safe harbor in which to rest.

Forcing her eyes to Clark, she returned to the seat at his bedside, and Mr. Vaughn dragged over another, setting it at her side. Silent and calm. Tessa felt herself leaning into him—and stopped.

The bedchamber door creaked open, and Daphne slipped inside without a word and took a seat at the end of her brother's bed. She didn't look at her mother or her guardian. Her entire attention was fixed on the young man in the bed, his breath coming quick and shallow.

"I will sit with him first," said Tessa. "You both need to rest so that you can take over in the morning. If Dr. Vaughn arrives, I will make note of everything he says."

The two sat there, watching as Tessa took up the rag once more and bathed Clark's flushed skin. Then, without a word, Daphne nodded and slipped from the room as silently as she'd come. Reaching over, Mr. Vaughn settled his hand atop Tessa's; the weight of it was as welcome as a proper embrace. It grounded her and filled her with his quiet strength.

And then, he was gone, though the feel of his hand on hers remained with her well into the night.

# Chapter 35

The candlelight flickered across the edge of the coverlet, throwing long shadows over the curve of Clark's cheek. He lay motionless, his features far too still, his breath shallow and uneven. Tessa reached out, brushing her fingers along his forehead in the faint hope that her touch might comfort him. But he gave no sign.

Her voice was barely more than a whisper as she sang, the tune uneven with fatigue. It was an old song, one she used to hum while rocking him as an infant, and though the words caught in her throat, she pressed on.

Pausing between verses, Tessa babbled to him. As she'd done this for days now, the words came without thought, repeating the same pleas again and again—hoping that he knew how loved he was, how proud she was of him, and how strong he was.

And that she was here. That she would stay. His mother was nearby.

Body aching, Tessa didn't bother shifting positions. The chair was as comfortable as it could be whilst allowing her a proper angle to bathe his fevered face. Her spine throbbed and her eyes stung, but she couldn't bring herself to move. Not when every part of her screamed that her place was here, watching over her boy.

The door opened, and she looked over her shoulder to see Daphne there.

"Is it morning already?" Tessa asked, stretching her back.

Not answering, the young lady strode to the windows and pulled back the curtains, and Tessa winced against the light streaming through. That was answer enough, she supposed. As was Daphne's continued silence. Four days. Four mornings. And still, she had yet to speak a word after their last conversation.

A yawn filled Tessa's chest and twisted her face, but something tickled her lungs, and she let out a cough instead. Pausing, Daphne finally looked at her mother, but Tessa waved it away. It was nothing.

"He woke for a few minutes," said Tessa, drawing Daphne's attention to her brother, and the young lady perked as she hurried to his bedside.

"He wasn't lucid, but he spoke a touch. I think the fever is finally breaking," said Tessa, reaching forward to test Clark's forehead once more. Daphne may refuse to speak to her, but as his nurse needed to know the present state of things, Tessa relayed all the medicines she'd administered, the various changes wrought in the patient, and anything else Daphne ought to know.

With a silent prayer of gratitude, Tessa leaned down to press a kiss to his clammy forehead. Rising to her feet, she surrendered her seat to her daughter but perched on the edge of his bed.

"Do you mind if I remain a little longer, Daphne?" That drew her daughter's gaze, and Tessa rose to her feet once more. Motioning toward the door, she added, "I do not need to, if you do not wish."

"You ought to rest."

The words were quiet. Hardly audible. But Daphne had spoken. Tessa paused and tried not to stare at the girl, who had done her level best to pretend her mother did not exist.

"I will in a bit," said Tessa, settling back into her seat. "But I do not know if I could sleep. With the sun up, my body is determined to keep me awake. Besides, Mrs. Ferrell requires assistance with the laundry, as we were only able to finish half of what needed doing yesterday, and Clark has gone through so many linens."

Turning toward her son, she hummed a few more bars of her song and straightened the bedclothes. In truth, she couldn't bear to be away from his side. Not simply because of the illness, but because this was the most she had been near him since he was a little boy, and Tessa couldn't bring herself to waste a single minute of it.

Who knew what was to come when he awoke.

"I know that song," said Daphne, though there was a hint of a question in her tone.

"I sang it to you children just as my mother sang it to me," she said, settling her hand over Clark's.

"I remember."

Daphne straightened, her brow furrowing as though she was uncertain what to do with that revelation—though she still did not look at her mother. As Tessa refused to infer meaning in that quiet tone, she chose instead to revel in the joy of having her daughter speak to her in any fashion.

Rising to her feet, Tessa turned to the door. "I will go fetch the breakfast tray."

"Mrs. Ferrell hasn't prepared it yet," said Daphne.

"Then I shall simply have to prepare one. Poor Mrs. Ferrell has enough to do with the staff gone." Yet Tessa lingered at the threshold, looking back at her children. Returning to the bed, she leaned over her son and pressed another kiss to his forehead before whispering, "I will be but a moment."

Straightening, Tessa looked at her daughter, but Daphne wasn't meeting her gaze, and she abandoned the instinct that prodded her to kiss her daughter's forehead as well. Then, turning on her heel, Tessa went in search of breakfast. Clark needed to keep up his strength, and to do so, the weak broths and teas that Mr. Vaughn allowed the lad needed to be administered far more often.

Tessa slipped down the stairs and swept into the kitchen. Mrs. Ferrell was there, readying the tea and buns and filling the tray until it was laden with food for the patient and caregivers.

"I was just about to bring it up," said Mrs. Ferrell, but Tessa took it in hand.

"I have it," she said, stepping backward through the door to push it open before retracing her steps.

Clark was on the mend. Thank the heavens. Scarlet fever was such a frightening thing, for there were so many wretched outcomes possible. But with the disease running its course without any surprises, it seemed that Clark would likely be spared the lifelong damage it could wreak.

Thoughts of that blessing brightened Tessa's mood, and she felt like flying up the stairs—though her feet refused to do so. Her muscles shook as she passed the halfway mark to the first landing, and the tray rattled as she fought to keep it upright. It felt as though the stairs were coated in tar, her shoes sticking to each one, and her lungs began to burn as she strained against the load she carried.

"Mother?" Daphne appeared at the top of the stairs, and Tessa felt like sagging in relief as the young lady hurried down, relieving her of the tray.

But even without the burden, the rest of the trek felt like a mighty summit, and her lungs struggled for air. Sitting down on the top step, Tessa struggled to catch her breath. When a cough shook through her, Tessa tried to brush it aside, but her lungs refused to clear, and she fought for air.

"Mr. Gregory!" Daphne's voice rang through the silent house, and she abandoned the tray on the top step and disappeared as Tessa fought through the coughing fit.

Her eyelids felt so heavy, and when she forced them open again, Mr. Vaughn was suddenly there in his trousers, his shirt billowing around him, and despite the strength sapping from her limbs, Tessa couldn't help but notice the way the collar gaped open, displaying his bare neck and a flash of his chest.

Smiling to herself, she slipped into oblivion.

...

The sunlight had softened with the passing afternoon, pooling like amber on the floor and in the folds of the curtains. Gregory sat motionless beside the bed, a book balanced on his knee, but the words swam before his eyes, their meaning slipping away each time he tried to focus. Despite being one of his favorites, Gregory's attention stumbled at every creak of the floorboards in the corridor; he'd read the same sentence three times and still couldn't recall how it began.

Yet a smile graced his lips as he shut the cover and glimpsed the authoress's name, recalling the conversation he'd had with Mrs. Stuart about the great Helen Gardiner.

The arm of the chair dug into his elbow, but he made no move to readjust. Outside, the muffled sound of birdsong drifted through the glass, and somewhere downstairs, the faint clatter of crockery reminded him that the world still turned, but in this room, time slowed. Each minute stretched long and thin, and Gregory sat with the book in his lap, his posture stiff, as though any movement might break the fragile peace holding everything together.

Gaze falling to the bed, he straightened when he spied Clark's eyes open.

Reaching for a cup of tea on the bedside, Gregory gave the lad something to drink, and Clark accepted it without comment, his eyes focusing with far more clarity than they'd seen in the past few days.

"How are you feeling?" asked Gregory.

Clark stared at him, as though studying every feature in his guardian's face.

"Do you know who I am?" he asked.

The lad gave a faint nod, and Gregory relaxed, breathing deeply once more.

"I thought someone else was here," croaked Clark.

Just hearing the lad's voice was enough to lighten Gregory's spirits, though there was a rasp to it that testified that the boy needed more to drink. He reached over to help Clark, and the lad lifted a hand as though to take the cup himself.

"Allow me. You'll be pretty weak for a few days at least, but you've made it through the worst of it," said Gregory. "Who were you expecting to see?"

Clark turned his gaze away, glancing at the far wall. "I thought I heard *her*."

"If by 'her' you mean your mother, she was here," said Gregory, trying (and failing) to keep the strain from his tone. "She's hardly left your side since you arrived home."

The only answer he received was a sharp huff as though Clark was dismissing that claim altogether, and for all that he wanted to be patient with the lad's struggle, the sight of Mrs. Stuart collapsed on the stairs still burned bright in his mind.

"Your mother was here," repeated Gregory with more emphasis. "She spent more time watching over you than anyone else in this house. The only reason she is absent now is that she worked herself into such a state of exhaustion that she fell ill herself. It isn't scarlet fever—thank the heavens, as the effects on adults are far more brutal and long-lasting—but she hasn't been lucid in a day or two."

For all that Clark's gaze jerked back to his guardian, Gregory spied sleep tugging at his lids.

"Is it serious?" he asked, his voice growing foggy as his body slipped back into unconsciousness.

Such a little question. And with his tone such a mumble, Gregory couldn't say what inflection the lad meant to use, but he hoped it was a good sign.

"I do not believe she is in danger," replied Gregory, though he didn't know if Clark heard him or if it was the whole truth.

# Chapter 36

The sky stretched above her—vast and rippling like someone had thrown a stone into a pond. Bright puffs of white hung in the unending blue, but when she looked at them closer, they weren't clouds but billowing smoke. Inching forward like a worm, it swallowed the sky and then the ground at her feet. Soon, the miasma enveloped her, but when she screamed, dried rose petals fell from her lips, floating in the air around her.

Then the world shifted, and she found herself in a boat, the water pouring over the lip and filling the bottom no matter how hard she bailed. A distant voice called her name, but it came from the white-capped waves, the mists in the air, and the very wood beneath her feet. It echoed beneath her skin.

Tessa's eyes opened. The world was cloaked in darkness, though candles and lamps did their best to stave off the black, and she felt like a pudding left to steam for too long.

"Mama?" A young lady appeared before her, and a smile tugged at Tessa's lips.

She knew that face. Knew that voice. Joy sparked in her chest, adding to the flush of heat burning through her, but when she tried to reply, her mouth was so dry, and her tongue refused to work. A cup was pressed to her lips, and though it helped some, Tessa couldn't form the words she needed to speak.

"Hush, Mama," whispered Daphne. "Rest."

And with that, Tessa's eyes slid closed, and the bed beneath her crumbled into ash, the world flaking away until there was nothing but sky once more. As she stepped into the blue, her skirts brushed the edges of clouds, and somewhere in the distance, a bell tolled. The deep, mournful sound echoed in her chest.

Looking down, she found herself wrapped in lengths of black crepe, the fabric crinkling as she tried to free herself of it. The more she pulled, the tighter it clung, winding about her arms and waist like mourning ribbons come to life. The sky around her dimmed, the colors leeching out, and with them, her strength.

She called out, but no sound came. Then a child's cry reached her ears, faint and familiar, but she couldn't place it. Couldn't move toward it. Her feet sank into the air like mud, and behind her, the tolling bell rang again. Closer this time.

The sky twisted, and in the distance, she spied a shape. A small boy, perhaps? But when she blinked, he was gone, and all that remained was the sound of dripping water and the scent of lavender.

Sunlight peeked through her eyelids. Tessa strained to block it out, but when Clark's face came into view, she ignored the burning and forced her eyes open. But it couldn't be.

"Clark?" she whispered, reaching up for him.

But darkness filled Tessa's vision once more, and when it cleared, she found herself in a garden she almost recognized. As though she had visited once before, though she couldn't say when or where. The plants were in full bloom, the flowers garishly bright with petals as wide as dinner plates, and their sickly-sweet scent coated her nose like tar.

She tried to move toward the shade, but the path twisted into a maze, the hedges growing taller with each turn as it doubled back on itself. A laugh—mocking and sharp—echoed from the greenery, and the rustle of paper filled her ears. Then the world tilted, and she fell through the sky, the wind slicing past her as books flapped through the air like birds.

Tessa woke with a gasp, the ceiling swaying above her, her skin damp and leaden. The world felt too loud, too close, too bright. Holding up a hand, she tried to shield her eyes from the afternoon glow.

"Mrs. Stuart?"

Cracking her eyes open, Tessa turned to see Mr. Vaughn seated at her bedside. The gentleman reached forward, taking her hand in his, but just as she was about to revel in the feel of his fingers, they shifted, reaching for her pulse in her wrist. And Tessa groaned—though she couldn't say if she was mourning the loss or bemoaning her silliness.

"Clark?" she asked, though the word grinded in her throat like the rusted gears of a steam locomotive. Tessa tried to swallow, but the skin was so rough and dry, and she hadn't a drop of moisture in her mouth.

Mr. Vaughn drew near, lifting her for a drink, but he didn't answer the question. Surely Clark hadn't grown worse. Tessa's pulse quickened, her hands reaching for the gentleman, though she didn't know what she intended to do.

"How is he?" she croaked. "Tell me. Please say he is well."

Just the thought that matters had worsened for him brought tears to Tessa's eyes. Her chest ached as her ribs constricted around her heart.

And just as she was about to demand an answer, Mr. Vaughn pointed to the foot of her bed.

Blinking heavily, Tessa turned her gaze in that direction. Wrapped in blankets, Clark was seated in one of the library's armchairs with Daphne beside him, their gazes fixed on her. A smile drew up the corner of her lips as she met their gazes, and she tried to speak, but no words came forth.

Tessa shifted to rise, but gravity's pull was too strong, and she fought against the darkness as it stole away her strength, forcing her eyelids to close once more.

It was a nothing sort of day. The sort of afternoon that begged one to slough off the work to be done and escape to a meadow for a picnic. The weather was an impossibly perfect combination of warm and cool, suitable for lounging about or active sport. Food was abundant. Conversation, even more so. All her beautiful children were present, seated alongside her and Mr. Vaughn. Enjoying one another as they hadn't in so very long.

A hand wrapped around hers. So real and tangible that Tessa swore it wasn't just a manifestation of the dream—for, though she wished to believe this perfect moment was true, her consciousness now recognized the vision for what it was.

Yet as the image faded to gray, she swore she felt the fingers wrapped around hers. Tessa didn't open her eyes, but she considered its owner, certain it wasn't Mr. Vaughn's. It was much smaller than his.

Reveling in the contact, Tessa feigned sleep until curiosity got the better of her, and she forced her eyes open. The hand jerked away, slipping out of reach as though it had never been there. Turning her head in that direction, she spied Clark seated at her bedside, picking at the peeling skin on his palms—a sign that he was truly out of danger and the disease had run its course.

"You should be in bed," she whispered.

Clark shrugged. "Mr. Gregory said I could leave my bedchamber, but this is as far as I can manage."

The dismissive tone stung, but with the memory of his touch still fresh in her mind, Tessa brushed aside his excuse. Whether he was ready to accept it or not, she spied the glimmer of concern in his gaze.

"How long have I been in bed?" she asked, struggling to sit upright, and Clark snapped up from his seat, helping to settle her more comfortably. Though Tessa refused to be undone by that act of kindness, tears tingled in the corners of her eyes. Now was not the time for that!

"Four days. Mr. Gregory said you were worn out and needed the rest." Clark's throat bobbed as he swallowed.

"I am sorry if I frightened you," she whispered.

With the sort of feigned disinterest that only a lad of fifteen could manage, Clark shrugged it away, though his eyes held his heart. Whatever he may say, the boy had been worried. About her.

The realization settled over her with a weight both tender and unbearable. It caught in her throat, made her vision blur, and for a moment, she could do nothing but stare at him. Perhaps it was foolish to hope, but if there was a morsel of affection still lingering in his heart, was it so terrible to try?

Swallowing hard, Tessa steadied herself. Maybe, just maybe, it was worth pressing her luck. "Would you please do me a favor?"

Again, Clark shrugged the question away, which she supposed was the best answer she would receive.

"I had a reticule with me. Can you fetch it?"

Casting off his blankets, Clark strode to where her gown sat neatly folded, her shoes standing beside it, and he grasped the small pouch from atop and brought it to her. Tessa could feel her weary body yearning for more sleep (though she didn't know how it could require more after so much), but she tugged open the strings and reached inside.

"This belongs to you," she said, handing him the pocket watch.

Clark's brows rose as he turned it about in his hand. "But...I..."

With a sad smile, Tessa nodded. "Yes, that one was broken beyond repair. However, I spoke with a watchmaker, and he was able to salvage the case and put new working parts inside it. So, it is a bit of your grandfather, and a bit of you."

Staring at the watch in his hands, Clark pinched his lips together, his shoulders tensing.

"I've been carrying it about in hopes that I might be able to return it to its proper owner," she added.

His left leg, perched on the ball of his foot, bounced as his gaze fixed on the watch, but otherwise, Clark sat there like a statue for several long moments. He coughed, though it sounded strained, as though covering for something else, and then he sniffed, turning his face out of view.

Another cough, and another sniff. And Clark's leg bounced all the faster.

Tessa yearned to tell him to let out the tears but remained silent, choosing instead to reach for his arm, tugging him toward her. The move was impulsive. Careless. Had Tessa been in her proper mind, she wouldn't have been so bold as to attempt it. But Clark leaned into her, accepting her embrace as he shook.

"I am sorry," he whispered.

"As am I," she replied. "I love you so very much, and I am sorry to have caused you pain. And I am sorry if I frightened you."

Clark's arms tightened around her, and Tessa held him close. Together, they sat there for an age, simply existing in that moment, and Tessa was quite happy to hold him forever.

Giving another discreet cough and a sniff, Clark straightened and pulled back, turning his face away as he rose, muttering something about needing to be in bed so he could rest and return to school and his friends. For all that he blustered about, feigning that nothing was amiss, Tessa spied the redness in his eyes.

And he still held the pocket watch.

When he reached the doorway, Tessa spied Mr. Vaughn standing there. He clapped the lad on the shoulder and moved to let him pass before coming over to sit in Clark's abandoned seat.

"He is like his father," whispered Tessa with a slight smile. "Doesn't care to be emotional in front of others."

"True, but he is a good deal like his mother," said Mr. Vaughn, settling into the chair. "The moment he was allowed to leave his bed, he came here."

The gentleman watched her with that intensity that was so synonymous with Gregory Vaughn. As though he saw right into the heart of her, knowing her as no one else ever had, and that slight smile on his lips made her feel as though he liked every bit of it.

But that was when Tessa realized he was seeing her exterior as well. Her cheeks were clammy, and she could well imagine her skin was ruddy. To say nothing of the wisps of hair that were cemented to her neck and temple from the sweat that had gathered there.

Patting at her hair, she didn't need a looking glass to know that her plait was in disarray—which was also the moment she realized that she was clad in a nightgown, not the dress she'd been wearing. Despite having seen her clothes neatly stacked on the other side of the room, the implications hadn't struck until now.

Good heavens! Praying with all her might, she hoped Daphne and Mrs. Ferrell had dressed her.

"Don't fret," he said. "Mrs. Ferrell and my brother have been on hand to play chaperone while you were ill."

For all that Mr. Vaughn was a clear-sighted man, that had not crossed her mind, though knowing that did give her a dash of peace.

"You ought to rest," he said, helping her settle into the bed once more.

And though her pulse quickened, Tessa felt the truth of his words as her eyes began to droop.

"We will be here when you wake," he whispered.

## Chapter 37

Dressing oneself was not a great feat. True, Tessa had rarely done so before she'd been forced to venture into the great world alone, but she had learned to manage what the vast majority of people did daily. She didn't purchase dresses or corsets that required a second set of hands, and thus, hadn't required assistance to dress in years.

Yet now, she required both Daphne and Mrs. Ferrell.

"Are you certain you should be up, madam?" asked the housekeeper, giving Tessa yet another thorough examination. "Mr. Vaughn wouldn't begrudge you a few more days abed."

"No, but I begrudge myself such idleness." Leveling an appreciative look at the lady, Tessa added, "And I will expire of boredom if I am forced to remain there another day."

Giving a crisp nod and a final brush of Tessa's skirts, Mrs. Ferrell ensured they were hanging perfectly before striding out the door, leaving her in Daphne's care. Silently, the young lady guided her mother to the dressing table and sat her before it, taking Tessa's locks in hand. With quick movements, Daphne brushed out the dark tresses and wound them up into a tidy coiffure.

"That is lovely," said Tessa, turning her head to the side to examine the style. "Simple yet elegant. I will have to copy it in the future."

Daphne's cheeks pinked, and she mumbled a quiet word of thanks before turning to leave once more.

Snagging her daughter by the hand, Tessa kept her by her side. "Are you still angry with me, love? About Mr. Spooner, I mean. I apologize if I embarrassed you."

Tessa was quite willing to acknowledge that much, though she didn't feel the slightest bit guilty about the end result of that scene. Just the memory of that blackguard pawing at her daughter set Tessa's pulse racing again, but she didn't wish to cause heartache of any sort.

"Yes," said Daphne, though her brow furrowed, and she added a quick, "And no."

Pausing, the young lady considered the question and her feelings before saying, "I truly admire Mr. Spooner, and you made him very angry. And I do not know what Mr. Gregory said to him, but he has kept his distance, and it is breaking my heart."

Rising to her feet—though unsteadily, as her legs were still weak—Tessa accepted Daphne's arm of assistance and led her to the bed so that they could sit side by side. Turning to her daughter, she reached tentatively for Daphne's hands.

And she allowed it!

Tessa tried to remain calm, but that little victory was enough to make her beam like a fool, though she had the good sense to school her features. Now was not the time for such displays.

Sorting through what she wished to say and what she ought to say, Tessa struggled to find the delicate balance between honesty and kindness. Daphne wouldn't listen if she simply told her Mr. Spooner was a blackguard who likely cared more about stealing her virtue or dowry than that beautiful heart beating in Daphne's chest.

And the connection they were forging was so fragile that even the slightest breeze might break it, yet Tessa couldn't remain silent. Could she ever build a proper relationship with her daughter if she must censor every word she spoke? Honesty was a cornerstone of strong connections, and being anything less than truthful would set a terrible precedent.

"I know that you care deeply for Mr. Spooner," she said. The words were bitter on her tongue, but whether or not Tessa believed it to be true love was immaterial: Daphne believed it. "But I worry about how he has treated you."

Straightening, Daphne shook her head. "But he is so kind. He will sit for hours and listen to my babbling without complaining." A slight smile graced her lips. "In fact, he seems to enjoy it. And he is forever bringing me presents. They might be little trinkets, but he will see a bit of ribbon in the shop and think of me."

Good gracious, the fellow was quite good at turning a young lady's head. Especially one so heartbroken.

"He has been nothing but a gentleman," added Daphne.

"I hate to disagree with you, but exchanging illicit embraces in public is hardly the action of a gentleman," said Tessa.

Daphne pulled her hands out of her mother's grasp. "He couldn't help himself. He said I am too beguiling to resist. And it was hardly public."

Tamping down the frustration that reared its head at the distance her daughter had placed between them, Tessa considered how to explain the situation without besmirching the sainted Mr. Spooner. Daphne continued to extol his virtues, and the more she spoke, the more it sounded as though she was an unappealing, awkward creature and he was beneficent enough to bestow his good opinion upon her.

Tessa's pulse quickened as she listened, scouring her thoughts for what she might say to this. Daphne was walking straight into a trap that far too many girls fell into, only realizing their mistake once it was too late.

"We have so much in common," added Daphne, her words coming quicker. "We like all the same things, and we laugh all the time. He is a burst of sunshine in my life."

"And how does he handle disappointment?" asked Tessa. "You've mentioned all the happy things, but have you seen him in a temper? Or when you disagree?"

Daphne smiled and shook her head. "We never disagree."

Oh, wasn't that the siren song of the young? It was as though she were sitting before young Tessa, and though Rodney was not unscrupulous like Mr. Spooner (nor would he have ever treated a young lady like a trollop), Tessa remembered just how appealing it was to find such an "effortless" love.

She doubted Mr. Spooner's aligned interests were genuine, making it doubly dangerous when Daphne was desperately searching for happiness from external sources.

A thoughtful smile graced Tessa's lips as her mind turned back to those younger years, when it had been impossible to imagine one's life being anything less than perfect. It wasn't as though she hadn't seen her fair share of heartaches and tribulations, but it was so easy to believe that the future held far grander things. That all one needed to do was find someone to love, and all would be set right in the world once more.

"I know how appealing that can seem," said Tessa. "When people describe the perfect mate, more often than not, they yearn for similar interests and hobbies, and they imagine their life during the good times, searching for someone who fits perfectly into that world. No alterations required."

Drawing in a deep breath, Tessa dismissed any words that strayed too close to describing Rodney. "But life is rarely that perfect thing you imagine, Daphne. Finding a husband isn't about securing the man who makes you laugh the most or makes the already lovely times lovelier. It is about finding someone who bolsters you through the difficulties of life. A partner. A confidant. A support."

Tessa sighed, her thoughts filling with all those hard-won lessons of the past. "You want someone who balances out your weaknesses. A pairing that improves and strengthens both parties. Someone who doesn't simply agree with everything you say but challenges you, pushing you to broaden your opinions and view of the world."

As she spoke, a face settled in her mind, and the more she described that perfect partner of a man, the more Tessa saw just how much Mr. Vaughn possessed those qualities. She hardly knew what she was saying as her heart fluttered, the erratic beat pulsing through her. Tessa blinked, hardly breathing, as the shape of the truth unfolded in her chest.

It wasn't a flash of thunder or a rush of wild passion. It was quiet. Gentle. A certainty that coalesced in her heart, taking shape as she spoke.

Gregory Vaughn was not perfect. He could be unbending, exacting, and positively infuriating. But he listened. Believed. Not blindly, not easily, but because he chose to see her as she truly was. And that meant more than any flirtation or compliment ever could.

"How will Mr. Spooner react when you lose a child? Or the economy falters, and your finances are strained? When those hard times arrive—and they will—what will he do?" she asked, finally daring to make a more pointed connection to Daphne. "Will he lash out? Blame you? Ignore the trouble and leave you to suffer alone?"

Daphne opened her mouth to respond, but Tessa held up a hand to silence her.

"Do not be hasty to respond. And I am not demanding an answer. I simply want you to consider that when any young man approaches you. Finding someone who enhances the happy times is easy. You want someone who brings light to the darkness, else those joyful moments will become more and more fleeting whilst the hardships grow ever heavier to bear."

Daphne sat there, her brows pulled together as she contemplated those words, and Tessa yearned to kiss her cheek. But her heart knew she'd reached the edge of what Daphne would accept, so Tessa squeezed the girl's hand, her gaze brimming with the words she wished to speak. How much she loved her. How important her happiness was. There were so many things Tessa yearned to say that Daphne was not ready to hear. Not yet.

Tessa couldn't say whether or not Daphne's heart accepted the advice, but she contented herself with believing that at the very least, it had not fallen on deaf ears.

Then, rising to her feet, Tessa left the bedchamber. Her footsteps were slower than usual, and her legs felt like jelly, but they carried her along as thoughts of Mr. Vaughn filled her mind. Tessa's palms grew damp. More so than they'd been of late. A rush of something coursed through her, not quite fear and not quite hope, and she didn't know what to do with the epiphany that had struck.

Her situation hadn't altered. Would she risk her children's affections?

But Mr. Vaughn's assurances rang in her thoughts. The family was warming to her, and it wasn't as though she was agreeing to marry the fellow. Simply testing the waters, so to speak. Given time, the children might accept the situation. Welcome it, even.

Was that too much to hope for?

# Chapter 38

Tessa arrived at the study doorway before she knew what she was about. She certainly didn't know what to say to the gentleman seated behind the desk.

Standing there, Tessa watched him working away, his pen scribbling across the page as he wrote out a letter, glancing between it and another. Mr. Vaughn was always occupied. Not that he rushed about willy-nilly or filled his days with meaningless work, but even when he was sitting still, he always had a book in hand.

Never a wasted moment.

Clearing her throat, she drew his attention, though he gave a start when he spied her there.

"I do hope your letter isn't ruined," she said with a wince as she entered the room. Mr. Vaughn motioned for her to sit, but Tessa waved it away, and when he rose to join her, she repeated the gesture. "Please, continue your work. I cannot bear to sit after so many days abed. Not yet, at any rate."

But though Mr. Vaughn kept his seat, he set the pen aside. "How are you feeling?"

The question was so benign, yet Tessa's pulse quickened at it. "Better. My strength is returning, and I thought it was time that I returned to the inn."

"You needn't leave until you are completely healed," he said with a frown.

"All in all, I am well enough. Another good night's rest, and I shall be set to rights."

Though Mr. Vaughn looked as though he was ready to argue with her, he paused and reconsidered. Setting aside his pen, he moved as if to rise. "Then allow me to escort you to town."

Tessa's heart melted just a touch more, but she waved him off. "I will manage."

But that was met with a raise of his brows, and she practically heard his voice in her head saying he knew she could manage and wasn't offering because she couldn't.

"What has you so occupied?" she asked, coming to the side of the desk and looking down on a mound of letters awaiting his perusal. "You have quite a stack of correspondence here."

"I fear it has gotten away from me," he said, sifting through the stack.

"Investments to review?" asked Tessa with her brows raised. But when Mr. Vaughn didn't answer, she stepped away from the desk. "You needn't tell me your business. I was merely curious."

A heavy pause followed that before Mr. Vaughn looked up at her with a considering expression. "How do you think the children would take to Leeds?"

Everything in Tessa stilled as she stared at him. "Leeds?"

Mr. Vaughn nodded.

"For a visit?" she asked.

"You know that I wanted to relocate my business there, but between my family demands and the children's situation, I didn't think I ought to," he said, glancing at the correspondence. "But I have been reconsidering matters. I hired a solicitor to explore some properties—both for my business and home—though I am in no rush to settle matters."

Tessa gaped as he rattled off the various details of his plan, seemingly unaware of the way the world was tilting beneath her feet. The children would be in Leeds? With her livelihood tied to that city, settling in Thornsby wasn't possible, but this would allow her to live and be near her children.

"My man assures me that I cannot transfer custody of the children," he added with a frown. "Legally, I am their guardian until I die, and though I could petition the courts to make you the testamentary guardian of the children, they are unlikely to overturn Rodney's will. As long as they are my responsibility, I feel I cannot abandon their care entirely to you. However, if we lived in the same city, that would allow you and the children time together whilst I fulfil my responsibility to them and their father."

Mr. Vaughn's head canted as he considered that. "And of course, the children are still warming to the idea, and it will take time before they will be comfortable with the arrangement."

"Of course," she said in a hollow voice, for it was entirely reasonable, though Tessa couldn't believe she was hearing this. Mr. Vaughn spoke in such a matter-of-fact tone, as though this was entirely ordinary and expected, yet she felt as though the ground had dropped away.

"And there is the added benefit of getting Daphne out of Mr. Spooner's clutches," said Mr. Vaughn with a sigh. "No doubt, there will be more of his ilk in Leeds, but with us working together to chaperone, perhaps we can protect her from making those acquaintances."

Another considering bob of his head, and Mr. Vaughn added, "There is no reason the boys shouldn't remain at Reed College. They like the school, and they require an education. They may not be able to visit home every Sunday as they have in the past, but the distance isn't so very great, and with the railway expanding, it will seem even closer in the near future."

Tessa watched him speak, hardly hearing the words. They came steadily, full of good sense and small kindnesses—concerns about the children's schooling, the question of where she might be most comfortable living, and what he might do to ease the way forward. But it wasn't the content of his speech that arrested her. It was the man himself. The gentle furrow between his brows as he thought aloud, the way his hands moved as he spoke, careful and deliberate.

And as he sat there, thinking only of how to help, Tessa realized the truth with a clarity that nearly buckled her knees. She may have been too afraid to trust herself—afraid that her heart would mislead her again—but there was no mistaking this. She would be a fool not to see it. He was a good man. Perhaps the best she'd ever known.

Mr. Vaughn wasn't Rodney. He never could be.

Something shifted in her. It wasn't a bolt of lightning or a dramatic jolt, but a slow, certain warmth that bloomed in her chest, building upon the epiphany her conversation with Daphne had granted her. It filled the hollow spaces that grief and guilt had carved out in her heart, spreading until she could scarcely breathe for the wonder of it. And in that moment, the fear of repeating the past fled, leaving her certain. Unshakeable.

Tessa knew what she needed to do.

"That all sounds brilliant," she said when he paused for her to comment. Leaning closer to the desk, Tessa held his gaze, her lips pulling into a gentle smile. "But there is a bit of business we need to discuss first."

Mr. Vaughn rose to his feet. "I do apologize if I am overstepping. I do not want you to think that I will make decisions for the children without your consent. The courts may hold my guardianship as more important than yours, but I do not—"

Tessa silenced him with a hand and a shake of the head. "Roughly a month ago, you proposed a joint venture between the two of us, and I wish to revisit that negotiation."

"Pardon?" Surely she couldn't mean the courtship, could she? Gregory couldn't think of any other matter she might be referring to, but hearing the lady speak the words he'd longed to hear made him question his sanity.

This wasn't a dream, was it? After exhausting himself with caring for Clark and Mrs. Stuart, Gregory couldn't be certain his faculties were intact, but the lady stood there, leaning toward him with a glint in her eye that he wanted to interpret as inviting.

"You expressed an interest in pursuing a partnership between us," she continued. "But the arrangement we negotiated is no longer ideal, and I wish to revisit that decision."

"You are in earnest?" Gregory had to ask the question. He still couldn't believe his eyes and ears weren't lying to him.

"Quite," she said, holding his gaze with a warmth that spread through him. "I have been giving it serious consideration and realize I am no longer amenable to the current arrangement."

"And you wish to renegotiate?" Gregory wanted to laugh, but the moment was far too serious for him to find much humor in it. "No need. Set whatever terms you wish. I agree, wholly and without caveat. I said before, I will accept whatever you are willing to give me."

The teasing smile faded from her face, and Mrs. Stuart straightened as she stared at him. Her eyes held her heart, brimming with far too much emotion for him to know what it meant. Gregory prayed it was good.

"Anything?" she whispered.

Stepping so close that her skirts wrapped around his legs, Gregory held her gaze, infusing his own with all the certainty of his heart. "I want anything you are willing to give."

Tears gathered in her eyes, and Mrs. Stuart lunged forward, wrapping her arms around his neck and yanking him into her embrace. Before Gregory knew what was happening, her lips were on his, and though instinct had him jerking back, his arms were wise enough to hold fast to her.

Joy surged up like a wave, bringing with it the impossible, unmistakable truth that he had never felt anything so beautiful as Tessa in his arms. Her fingers grazed the hair at the back of his neck, and it sent a shiver down his spine as his senses all sparked to life. The scent of her filled his nose, leaving him dizzy. Even a tad giddy.

Gregory knew it was too soon for such a display, but logic faded away as he reveled in the feel of her in his arms. Her lips against his.

Whatever fears she'd nurtured faded from view as his arms tightened around her, holding her flush to his chest as they sank into the embrace. Tessa had seen him at his worst. Experienced his anger and stubbornness. Had shown her own flaws and weaknesses. And yet, they both desired more.

The words she'd shared with Daphne echoed in her thoughts, shining like the bright beacons of truth they were. Gregory Vaughn was just the sort of man she had described. Imperfect, to be certain, but perfect *for her*.

Soon her thoughts faded into a tangled mess of feeling as she clung to Gregory, desperate for the love he poured upon her with every gentle touch. And when it finally slowed, he held her close, his eyes gazing at her as though Tessa Stuart—broken and flawed as she was—were a treasure.

"I may have gotten a little carried away," she whispered. Though Tessa wasn't about to mention it, the lecture she'd just given her daughter about not allowing men to take such liberties came to mind.

"I like it when you get carried away," he said with a smile. Gregory brushed a thumb across her cheek. "But we needn't rush things. It is enough to know where we stand."

"We are forty years old. I do not believe anyone could accuse us of rushing things," said Tessa with a wry smile as she rested a hand on his chest. Sobering, she met his gaze. "I am a grown woman. I have experienced so much in my life and made many mistakes, but I do not believe you are one of them."

Gregory chuckled, the sound reverberating through them both as he held her close. "I am quite happy to wait until you can say *you know* I am not one of those mistakes."

Leaning close, he feathered a kiss upon her lips that left Tessa feeling weak enough that it was a good thing he was holding her upright.

"A chance to woo you is more than I had hoped to have," he whispered. "For your sake and the children's, we can wait a little longer. I am quite content with this."

Wrapping his hand around hers, he lifted it to his lips. Gregory held her gaze as he sealed that promise with another kiss, and with the feel of him so close and the future unfolding before them, Tessa agreed.

She was content. Quite content, indeed.

# Epilogue

*Leeds, Yorkshire*
*Six Months Later*

The tightness gathered in Tessa's chest first, cinching her ribs until she could hardly draw breath. Her fingers twitched, restless with a need to move, to act, while her thoughts knotted themselves into loops she couldn't untangle. The air around her felt wrong, pressing in close and thick. A shiver rolled up her spine, sharp and unwelcome, as if her body were preparing for the worst even as logic and reason tried to calm her nerves.

Her mind conjured a dozen possibilities—none of which provided a happy conclusion—and though she spoke in a clear manner, her words meandered, dancing near the subject at hand without touching it. She was babbling. She knew it. But knowing a thing and stopping a thing were very different.

A hand brushed against her back, and Tessa could finally breathe properly. Gregory stood beside her, hardly touching her, yet his strength leached into her, allowing her to finally speak the words she'd needed to say.

"Mr. Gregory and I are engaged to be married," she concluded, her gaze darting over the children lounging on the parlor sofas and armchairs. Jackson glanced at the others, his brows pulled low, but the rest stared blankly back at the pair who stood before the fireplace, awaiting their reaction.

"I thought you were already engaged," said Eva with a frown, and Wesley shrugged as though agreeing.

"No," said Tessa, drawing out the word as though it were a question, though she knew the answer.

"But you live together," insisted Eva.

"Good gracious!" Tessa gasped, her hands covering her mouth.

Gregory moved to the child, crouching before her. "Dearest, please say you are not telling people that we live under the same roof."

Eva shook her head and ended with another confused shrug. Gregory chuckled, though it was more pained than amused, and he straightened and returned to Tessa's side. His hand rested at her back once more, and that (as much as Eva's answer) calmed her fraying nerves.

Drawing in a breath, Tessa forged ahead. "I understand it might be confusing, what with you splitting your time between this house and mine—"

"But you are always with him," interrupted Eva, looking to her siblings for confirmation of the truth she believed. "*Always.* Louisa's parents aren't together nearly as often as you and Mr. Gregory. And they are married."

At that, the man at her side stifled a chuckle and added in a dry tone, "I am very fond of spending time with your mother."

Wesley straightened, looking at the pair. "So you weren't married or engaged, but now you are?"

"They are engaged, not married," corrected Daphne.

"Oh," he murmured.

And with that, the children returned their gazes to Tessa and Gregory, and she didn't know whether to laugh or cry. Of all the reactions she'd imagined, confusion hadn't been one of them.

"We are engaged," said Tessa, and Gregory confirmed it with a nod. "We hope to marry as soon as we can secure a license."

"Will we stay here at Beechcroft?" asked Faith with a furrowed brow, which was echoed by the others with varying degrees of concern.

"Mama's home is nice, but I do not want to move away from Louisa," said Eva. "She is the best friend I've ever had!"

"And the library is so close," added Faith, a hint of horror in her tone at the thought of losing that paradise.

At that, the others lent their opinions, expressing far more concern about relocating to the far side of the city than they were about abandoning Thornsby itself. Granted, with as often as they visited the Vaughns and their country home, it wasn't as though they had lost Eden Place.

Holding up a staying hand, Gregory waited until they quieted to explain. "As Beechcroft is better suited for the family, we will be settling here."

Silence. A long, heavy moment in which the children simply watched the two of them with no hint of their feelings in their expressions.

Then, at once, the younger set erupted in cheers, hurrying over to embrace the pair, and though the elder were more circumspect in their reaction, they rose to their feet and drew near as well. Tessa didn't dare reach for Daphne, so she stood there, waiting to see what the young lady would do. And before she knew it, her daughter was embracing her.

"I am happy for you," she whispered into Tessa's ear whilst holding fast.

Tessa couldn't speak. She could hardly see through the tears gathering. So many little steps over the past months had led to this moment, and it felt as though all the tribulations she'd suffered melted away into this beautiful, glorious moment.

The two girls wrapped their arms around his and Tessa's waists, holding fast as they unleashed all the joy their little hearts held, and though Wesley was more circumspect in his display, he drew near enough to allow Gregory to throw an arm around his shoulders. He turned his gaze to his lovely bride-to-be, meeting her eyes with a waggle of his brows.

But for all his triumph at having been proven right, the feeling fled as he watched Daphne embrace her mother. All of Tessa's fretting had been for naught, just as his worries about relocating to Leeds had been, and he knew in his bones that this union would bless the children more than they would ever know.

Coming forward, Jackson shook Gregory's hand, giving his guardian a manly slap on the shoulder as though he were greeting a colleague. Gregory hid a smile at the overdone show of maturity in the lad.

Then his gaze met Clark's. The lad stood apart from the others, his hands in his pockets as he watched his guardian with a wary expression. Gregory stood there, meeting his gaze as he waited to see what the fellow would do.

Slowly, Clark crossed the distance, standing within reach as he watched Gregory. Pulling his hand out of his pocket, the young man extended it, and Gregory snatched it up, pulling the lad into his arms. Of course, Clark allowed only a quick embrace that was more of a thumping pat on the back than a proper hold, but he accepted it before releasing the lad.

A tug on his frock coat had Gregory looking down at Eva, who stared up at him with a puzzled frown.

"Does this mean I can call you Papa now?" she asked.

The others stilled, glancing at their sister, and Gregory wasn't certain what to say or do. Marrying their mother would make him their stepfather, which in the eyes of society was as good as the flesh and blood variety. Yet to usurp the title from his friend gave him pause as he considered his stance.

"Do you wish to?" Gregory asked.

Eva nodded, a smile stretching across her face, and he struggled to take breath into his lungs. Standing there, he looked at the others and saw them watching him with mixtures of hope and worry.

"Papa, Mr. Gregory, or anything you like," he said, bending down for a proper embrace. "As long as we are together."

"I love you, Papa," she whispered.

Gregory's arms tightened around her until he was afraid he might hurt the child, but he couldn't release her. The eight of them stood there, together. A family. An unconventional one, perhaps, but one he was proud to call his own.

...

The shadows of the night stretched across the house as the little ones finally nestled into their beds. The house was silent. Naught but the distant ticking of the clock and a few rattling dishes from the kitchen disturbed the quiet.

Sitting on the sofa, Tessa stared at the portrait in her hand. The face she knew so well. Though time had altered him some, Rodney hadn't aged much during their time as husband and wife, but she certainly felt far older than the young lady who had joyfully received this miniature and carried it with her.

The sofa sagged as Gregory came to sit beside her, his arm slung over the back for a moment before snaking around her shoulders and pulling her close. Curling into his chest, Tessa gave him a chastising grin.

"This is the reason our children believe we are already married, you rogue."

"The door is open, and the servants are about," he said with a waggle of his brows. "We aren't truly alone, after all. And I prefer it when you call me a 'lummox.'"

Leveling a narrowed look at him, Tessa elbowed his side before settling into the crook of his arm, the portrait still clutched in her hand.

"What is that?" asked Gregory, and she turned it to show him.

"Rodney had it commissioned as a wedding present. As much as I wanted to destroy it many times over the years, I couldn't quite bring myself to do so, and now, I thought one of the children might like it."

"Faith," said Gregory. "I think she would like it best. Or perhaps Wesley."

Tessa nodded, but her attention was fixed on the face staring up at her from her hand. And once more, a question rose to her thoughts.

"What would Rodney say about this?"

"Heaven knows I have struggled with that question, my love, and it isn't wise to fixate on it," he said, his hold tightening around her as he pressed a kiss to her temple. "I do not know if he is aware of what is happening, but even if he were angry, it wouldn't change my decision. You needn't feel guilty."

Tessa rested her head on his shoulder. "I don't. Not precisely. I suppose I find myself wondering because I hope he has found peace."

Silence followed that, though she felt Gregory's attention on her, and when she turned to meet his eyes, she found him watching her with warmth and admiration glowing in his gaze.

"You are incredible," he whispered, leaning in to seal that statement with a kiss.

Though Tessa still couldn't accept that assessment, she knew better than to argue with Gregory on the matter. The forgiveness in her heart had more to do with her own happiness than Rodney's, which meant it was far less self-sacrificing than Gregory liked to believe. Letting go of that anger and pain had been necessary. An effort of self-preservation. Nothing more.

When he released her lips, Gregory reached into his pocket and tugged out an envelope.

"I have a gift for you," he said as Tessa set the portrait aside and took hold of the offering.

"What is it?"

"You must open it," he insisted. "Consider it an early wedding present, as I couldn't bear to wait another moment to give it to you."

Leaning away just enough to free her arms, Tessa broke the seal and opened the page, unfolding it. "Your will?"

Brows furrowed, she glanced at Gregory, but he nodded for her to continue. As she'd read through her fair share of contracts, such legal wording was easy enough to decipher, though she couldn't say why Gregory would wish her to do so.

Then her eyes fell to a line a few paragraphs below:

"'I appoint my wife, Theresa Rush Stuart Vaughn, sole Guardian of our children...'"

Tessa straightened, her eyes scouring the paragraph again and again, studying the sentences that granted her full custody of the children and control over Rodney's estate. They were thorough (though she would expect nothing less of Gregory), tying the matter up so neatly that another couldn't usurp it.

When she turned to look at her husband-to-be, he gave her a sad smile.

"They are your children, and you ought to have legal guardianship over them, but even if I could convince the courts to recognize your claim, marrying would transfer it immediately to your new husband and revert the guardianship to me. So all I can do is ensure that you never have to be without your children again."

"*Our* children," she corrected, though he didn't seem to hear, babbling apologies as though the blame lay with him that the law denied a married lady custody.

"It is the best I can do—"

Setting the will beside the portrait, Tessa grabbed his lapels and tugged him close, silencing his lips the best way she knew how. The thought of him gone sent a shudder through her soul that drew her heart to the surface, filling the whole of her as she reveled in the feel of him. Winding her arms around his neck, she tried to show with every touch just how grateful she was for him.

This incredible man of hers.

Ten months ago, she had arrived in Thornsby, searching for the children she'd lost, and she'd found so much more. A treasure she hadn't known was awaiting her. Gregory wasn't the man she'd dreamt of as a young girl, but he was precisely the man she needed. The cold, frozen winter that was her marriage to Rodney had melted away, that pain and sorrow blossoming into this beautiful spring.

Her love. Her children. Their family.

And Tessa was going to revel in every moment of it.

How could one explain love? Gregory had tried so many times to tell Tessa his feelings, but no amount of words could describe the joy she brought to his life and the great gaping hole that she and the children had filled. It had been so large that Gregory hadn't recognized it for what it was. It had simply been him.

It felt as though he'd been stumbling through the moors on a cold winter's night, and Tessa was the warm hearth at the end of his journey. Gregory basked in the feel of her and wondered how he had almost allowed so many hurdles to turn him aside.

But now, with her in his arms and in his life, Gregory would never let her go.

This was his love. His life. And what a beautiful future they would build together.

Text

# Exclusive Offer

Join the M.A. Nichols VIP Reader Club to receive up-to-date information about upcoming books, freebies, and special behind the scenes content.

Visit www.ma-nichols.com to sign up today!

## More Books by M.A. Nichols

To find the rest of this family saga or other romances with your favorite tropes, visit:

www.ma-nichols.com/historical-romance

# About the Author

Born and raised in Anchorage, M.A. Nichols is a lifelong Alaskan, though she briefly ventured south to get a fancy bachelor's degree from Brigham Young University and a master's degree from Utah State University—neither of which had anything to do with why she became an author, but they kept her alive while launching her publishing career.

As a child she despised reading, but thanks to her mother's love and persistence, she saw the error of her ways and developed a deep and abiding obsession with books. Currently, she writes sweet historical romance and fantasy, but as a lover of many genres, she plans to explore more in the future.

For more information about M.A. Nichols, her books, and future projects, check out her on:

Website    Facebook    Instagram    BookBub

Printed in Dunstable, United Kingdom